NOTHING
SACRED

"I highly recommend this gathering of boldly original voices with a predominant tone of wild invention and fearlessness side by side with the intimacy of domestic life in our turbulent American times."

– Joyce Carol Oates
National Book Award winner and author of *Zero-Sum: Stories*

"Incandescent ... perhaps the finest, most courageous, most profoundly moving anthology I've read in a decade or two. Here gathered is genius, compassion, courage ... an exhilarating gift to readers everywhere."

– Junot Díaz
Pulitzer Prize Winner for *The Brief Wondrous Life of Oscar Wao*

"Pushing the boundaries at every turn, *Nothing Sacred* gathers twelve stories of virtuoso eclecticism and ingenuity. Its storytellers are wildly different in vision and formal approach, and the tales they tell form a literary crazy quilt that leaves the reader bewildered, dazzled, and wanting to read more. Often dark, sometimes hilarious, always distinctive, this collection is a revelation."

– Bradford Morrow
author of *The Prague Sonata* and *The Forger's Daughter*

"The brilliant diversity of visions and sensibilities represented in *Nothing Sacred* not only makes this collection entertainingly unpredictable but speaks to some of the deepest questions currently ripping our society apart, including the true meaning of diversity."

– Rebecca Newberger Goldstein
National Humanities Medal recipient and author of
36 Arguments for the Existence of God: A Work of Fiction

NOTHING
SACRED

Outspoken Voices in Contemporary Fiction

Edited by
Bernard Schweizer
&
James Morrow

UNBOUNDED CREATIVITY
HERESY
PRESS
FEARLESS EXPRESSION

Cover design by Elizabeth Cline
Bacchus by Michelangelo Merisi, known as Caravaggio, c. 1598

Library of Congress Control Number: 2023913275

Published by
HERESY PRESS LLC
P.O. Box 425201
Cambridge, MA 02142
heresy-press.com

ISBN 979-8-9887173-0-0

To

Liang Schweizer,
graceful visionary and prime mover

&

Nadine Strossen,
literary aficionado and champion of free expression

CONTENTS

FOREWORD
by
BERNARD SCHWEIZER

Who didn't write—or at least start—a novel during the Covid lockdowns? That seemed to be the preoccupation of those shut-in souls who weren't into baking sourdough loaves or brewing kombucha. I, too, joined that band of scribblers, and soon the novel that had been quietly gestating inside me began spilling out.

For nearly two years I fussed over every sentence, all the while soliciting frank critiques from fiction-loving friends, most of whom enjoyed my oddball, satiric narrative of a spiritual quest gone wrong. In the winter of 2022, I started sending query letters and writing samples to literary agents, first to a dozen, then several dozen, and, finally, nearly two hundred. When my brainchild failed to gain professional representation, I accepted this bitter pill—perhaps the book had no commercial potential after all—but the situation also piqued my curiosity. What sorts of novels and short stories, I wondered, were finding favor in the citadels of American letters?

I began collecting newspaper articles lamenting the narrow scope of what today's publishers were willing to acquire, and I quickly became familiar with the vocabulary—"sensitivity reader," "cultural appropriation," "trigger scene," "own-voice protagonist"—with which the industry was talking to itself: a lexicon that had nothing to do with aesthetics but instead seemed to mix a tacit condescension to readers with a chronic fear of offending them. It occurred to me that editors and agents had come to regard any unpublished literary effort not as a potential work of art but as a possible crime scene littered with evidence of violated decorum.

All this led to exasperation, which led to brooding, which led to tirades, which led to my dear wife losing patience with me. "Stop your whining and do something about the problem!" she insisted. "Start your own publishing house!" That struck me as an exceedingly ambitious and possibly quixotic endeavor, and I demurred… at first. But the seed had been planted, and I ultimately couldn't shake off the idea. A few months later, I had a name for the enterprise, a business plan, a partner, a small editorial team, and an advisory board who agreed that the time was ripe for a press that resolutely placed literary quality above ideological conformity.

After Heresy Press caught the attention in *The New York Times* and occasioned an interview in the *London Times*, the floodgates flew open. Clearly, there was much pent-up frustration among people whose lives revolved around crafting serious fiction—writers who sensed they were sitting on good material that was falling victim to a kind of undeclared censorship.

The inbox of Heresy Press swelled quickly and formidably. Only a few weeks after the first call for submissions, our editorial team had to announce it could entertain no more proposals at this time. We'd received seventy-five short-story manuscripts and roughly the same number of novel manuscripts, a mountain of texts that would take us months to scale.

What amazed me was the high quality of many submissions. Yes, we received a lot of dross, the sort of amateurish work you can dismiss after reading one page. But we'd also garnered a handful of excellent novels, which we shall be proud to publish in the near future, plus enough impressive shorter works to fill our projected twelve-story anthology twice over. While the dozen authors represented in *Nothing Sacred: Outspoken Voices in Contemporary Fiction* could scarcely be more diverse in their worldviews, cultural backgrounds, thematic obsessions, prose styles, and choice of subject matter, they all share two attributes: an abiding respect for their readers, and a ravenous appetite for audacity.

Michael R. Liska's "The Child Star" centers on an unnamed, washed-up Hollywood icon, a man whose worldview sometimes seems so puerile that one might conclude the title enjoys a dual meaning. And yet, for all the protagonist's narcissism, self-delusion, and eagerness to exercise the prerogatives of male entitlement, we would wager readers will neither regret nor quickly forget this hallucinatory journey into the besotted reaches of a wounded mind.

Set in contemporary Miami, Alex Perez's "Independence Day" tells of Cuban immigrant boys unhappily facing the impending arrival of a half-brother from the island, even as they indulge in macho fantasies and a paradoxical yearning for love uncoupled from obligation. The author merrily foils whatever moralistic expectations we might bring to such a state of affairs.

In "The Rise and Fall of Aleksandar Bundalo," Mikra Namani takes us to an unnamed Balkan country in the decades following World War II. The protagonist is a refugee from Hitler's Germany whose moral compass can no longer find true north. In the opening beats, this self-appointed "justice warrior" assassinates the notorious title character. But all is not as it seems, and as Namani's unreliable narrator continues to spin his tale, we find ourselves in a literary crucible where pathos, bathos, sorrow, loss, and acerbic satire fuse to become a meditation on the ways that war deforms the souls of innocents and executioners alike.

In "Night of the Living Baseheads," Tia Ja'nae gives us a mordant alternative history in which, upon his return from Mecca,

Malcolm X is spirited away to a secret underground chamber and menaced by narcotics-addled zombies who were once ordinary Black citizens—all so J. Edgar Hoover can enjoy the spectacle on closed-circuit television. Our naïve first-person narrator, a hick recently recruited by one of the American government's many "alphabet agencies," forms an unlikely bond with Malcolm, but not before witnessing him favor his living-dead brothers and sisters with his oratory.

"Thrust" is an unorthodox, occasionally rollicking, and ultimately poignant foray into the world of internet video porn. Lukas Tallent's first-person narrator relates his youthful adventures in a matter-of-fact and frequently droll voice that might seem at odds with a subject many regard as intrinsically depressing and automatically sordid. And yet it's difficult to think of a story that better evokes Terence's maxim, "Nothing human is alien to me."

Steven Fromm's "Gates" features characters of a species rarely found in contemporary fiction: elderly white males spending their retirement years in a gated community. In exploring the walled-off world of this quietly desperate circle, the author invites us to ponder a common question—when does the price of security become too high?—from an uncommon perspective.

In "Collateral Damage," T.N. Eyer challenges the social expectations that surround the fraught issue of sexual harassment. What sorts of tangled and politically irreducible thoughts might be visited upon the spouse of a person so accused? The author's multifarious answer provides food for thought and occasions for conversation.

In his cryptically titled "   ", Miguel Syjuco treats his readers to a virtuoso internal monologue. Braving accusations of appropriation, this male author offers his female protagonist both life and agency through his refusal to judge her. Meanwhile, Syjuco raises an urgent question: what is lost when we impose a censorious cultural consensus on people whose most vital intellectual and political tools are words?

Inviolable traditions and rigid protocols govern what people say and do at middle-class American funerals. In "Eulogy," Jonathan

Stone takes mischievous delight in deconstructing those rules, giving us a protagonist who begins his threnody with a remark no respectable grief-stricken husband should make about his late wife.

The narrator of "Paul's Ghost" is a young bibliophile secretly in love with his hockey-playing jock friend. As the plot unfolds, Lou Perez's protagonist keys his desperation to a haunting high-school encounter with a classic Willa Cather story, "Paul's Case." The result is a metafictional exploration of the tenuous boundary between life and fiction, and what happens when one bleeds into the other.

James Morrow's "The Optics of Infinity" is filtered through the mind of a fantastically sophisticated AI occupying a future iteration of the James Webb Space Telescope. As its mission unfolds, this digitalized intelligence finds itself competing with a stowaway AI bent on deceiving humankind with a fraudulent account of the birth of the universe. After considering other possible hoaxes, the cybernetic mutineer elects to legitimize one of the most heretical doctrines in the history of Christianity—which ipso facto makes this story a good fit for a Heresy Press anthology.

The final offering, Joshua Wilson's "Appalachian Gothic," gives readers an aging moonshiner, Shiloh "Homerun" Summy, famous for his strong whiskey and ornate rhetoric. He's so notorious, in fact, that he's gotten on the radar of a New York filmmaker who plans to incorporate him into her left-leaning documentary about the political culture of the Great Smoky Mountain region. From the instant he opens his mouth, Homerun achieves escape velocity from whatever ideological commitments we may hold dear to become one of the most gloriously repulsive-magnetic characters since Ignatius T. Reilly in *A Confederacy of Dunces*.

"Appalachian Gothic" is a quintessential Heresy Press story, privileging the potential of the fiction medium over the reader's presumed comfort level, and I shall keep you from Wilson's linguistic magic—and the efforts of his fellow contributors—no longer.

MICHAEL ROBERT LISKA

THE CHILD STAR

The child star is at his mother's house—which he purchased for his parents, in cash, at the height of his fame—to spray a wasp's nest she's noticed hanging beneath the eaves. He really shouldn't have to do this; he's reminded his mother several times that there are people you can pay to do work like this, and that this is exactly the kind of thing that's been distracting him from working on his COME-BACK. But no: his mother insisted she didn't like to bother people. As if hiring someone to do their job is bothering them. And when he took out his phone to call someone—someone more qualified to do this, who would probably be thrilled to meet the child star and get his autograph before removing the wasps efficiently, professionally from beneath the eaves—his mother had hissed at him to hang up and said that no, never mind, she would rather just live with the wasps.

So, he huffs across the yard, armored in some things from his late father's closet: a hooded sweatshirt with the hood up and the drawstring pulled, a stiff denim jacket, a wool scarf wrapped around his head. In the garage, he completes his protective suit with a scuba mask and a pair of gardening gloves, then jams a rusted, half-full can of wasp spray into the pocket of the jacket and pulls the ladder down from the wall.

The child star's mother is peering out the front window, urgently pointing up toward the nest as if he can't see it, as if he's an incompetent moron, and not in fact the person who'd lifted her from poverty, and bought her this house, and completely financially supported her since he was fucking *eleven*. Because his license was suspended, it had taken him almost three hours, on three city buses, to get there that morning. And in that entire time, not a single person recognized him.

The eaves of his mother's modest, suburban home are fifteen feet from the ground. The wasp's nest, which resembles a dried prehistoric turd, is tucked up in the corner where the stucco meets the soffit. A few wasps are lazily taking off to fly their maneuvers, heading out in search of whatever wasps desire. The ladder clacks against the stucco, then sags and rattles beneath his weight.

The child star balances with one hand on the highest rung, shakes the can, and sprays the white foam evenly across the nest, waving his arm back and forth to cover every inch. He catches a few wasps in midair, and they drop from sight like little downed fighter planes. Several more exit the nest, swirling their antennae and staggering as if they're drunk, and the child star feels a stab of empathy for these little creatures—what had they done to him, or to anyone, for that matter? They were just trying to live their tiny wasp lives. They were just like all of those people in the world who weren't talented enough to be child stars, going about their business, commuting to boring jobs, doing exactly what they'd been programmed to do. He pities them, really.

He watches with what he imagines is a tender, enlightened compassion as more of the wasps frantically erupt from the hive, clambering over one another in their panic. Then, noticing the child star looming in the immediate vicinity of their nest, they take flight all at once, directly at his face.

"Fuck you!" cries the child star, flailing at the top of the ladder.

The child star has twice been invited to host the *MTV Video Music Awards*. The child star has met Martin Scorsese enough times to feel comfortable referring to him, in conversation, as *Marty*. But the wasps don't care about any of this. To them, he is only a threat, another piece of soft, lumbering meat.

Nearly empty, the spray can sputters and hisses as he turns it on himself, coating the scuba mask in the noxious white foam. Immediately he can feel the wasps burrowing beneath his scarf, crawling up under his hood and into his thinning hair. The first stings are profoundly painful; he cannot believe that such tiny, fragile creatures can cause this sensation, like someone has set his face on fire.

There is a moment as he falls from the ladder that feels like flight, like a kind of victory, until he meets the unmerciful earth. His right leg snaps on impact with a sickening wet sound, and the child star crumples onto the artificial lawn and remains there, utterly defeated at last, at the end of a long, slow decline that has taken years, a decline that began so slowly he hadn't even known it was a decline until it was so far advanced that there was nothing he could do but flail as he slid, numbing himself with vodka and Percocets to quiet the disorienting feeling of his own downward momentum. If nothing else, he thinks, at least now he's finally hit the bottom, lying there in his mother's yard wrapped in his dead father's clothes, sightless and whimpering, his entire body a well of pain. And still the wasps keep plunging their stingers into him, again and again in what must be the same holes at this point, as if his face is getting fucked by the entire natural world.

Four hours later, the child star is picked up at the community medical center by Billy, who wheels him quickly along the corridors with a pair of crutches angled across his lap—though he can technically walk, the wheelchair will be faster and more discreet. This is a role Billy likes to play: the loyal, protective friend, helping the child star avoid the attention they both secretly cherish. They glide past a nurse's station, and Billy nods without stopping. The child star has been pumped full of drugs and has the visor of a baseball cap pulled low over his sunglasses, his lower right leg in a cast and his face so red and swollen it looks like he's been boiled.

At the front desk, a woman checks him out, gives him his prescriptions. The number on the bill staggers him—the cost of the ambulance alone is nearly four thousand dollars, before the doctors or any of the drugs. And unfortunately, the child star recently decided to stop paying for the private health insurance that had been costing him hundreds of dollars a month for *absolutely nothing*.

He hands her a debit card, knowing there is not enough in the account. Some part of him hopes the world will end before she speaks. The woman makes an uncomfortable face. "I'm sorry. It looks like it's not going through."

The child star hunches in his wheelchair and asks, in a quiet voice: "Is there a payment plan?"

Billy stares out the glass wall toward the parking lot as the child star completes the paperwork, and remains mercifully silent about both this embarrassment and the child star's recent wasp-related accident. As they cross the lobby, he leans down and whispers, "I'm fucking starving, bro."

Good old Billy! Billy is happy to drive the child star anywhere, to do anything with him, even just to hang around in the child star's home all day rewatching his old films, telling the child star that this or that moment, this one particular catchphrase or reaction shot, is *classic*, because, thanks to those few *classic* films, the child star's memory will remain in the public consciousness—albeit as a full-cheeked, awestruck boy, or a lean, perfectly-coiffed teen heartthrob—long after both he and Billy are gone from this world; and thus, his association with the child star provides Billy with the only small measure of immortality he might attain, as if his spirit, too, smaller than the child star's and doglike, will be allowed to accompany the child star into whatever paradise awaits those who escape from the cycle of life and death. And their appreciation is mutual, because Billy is the one person who constantly reminds the child star that he is, still, a star.

On the way home, they take a detour down Santa Monica for food in the battered Lincoln Town Car that Billy inherited from his grandmother, the child star so high on painkillers that it looks like the palm trees are waving at him. He has already decided that after his COMEBACK, Billy is definitely getting a new car.

The drive-thru line of the In-N-Out Burger stretches out of the parking lot, so he sends Billy inside with his debit card—there is at least enough in the account for this—and waits in the idling Lincoln while the line of cars creeps forward, listening to the squawking, disembodied voice of the teenaged attendant drifting over to him like distressed communications from another world.

Billy returns after what seems like only a few seconds with two greasy white bags and two young women.

"Do you have time for a meet and greet?"

He passes the bags through the window to the child star, who feels a dull, distant pain in his shin, a warm pressure where his face used to be. Billy gives him a thumbs-up, which is their agreed-upon, secret signal: he has checked, and they are over eighteen. The child star is aware he has to be careful these days, and he realizes that even this scene, in which he graciously gives of his time to meet two consenting adult females who happen to be fans of his work, might be seen as objectionable by some of the more puritanical moral scolds of the world; they might call this behavior *predatory*, and the child star would ask them: *What is an ecosystem, after all, without predators?* No, he is the wolf, the shark, the cheetah, the child star, a necessary purgative for the unfulfilled, perhaps even unconscious, sexual desires of those lovely young females just beginning to explore the world's erotic possibilities. One of the girls carries a cardboard drink caddy holding two milkshakes, which Billy reaches over and takes from her as he says, "Thank you so much for carrying that."

The child star evaluates their potential—the slightly prettier one is wearing tight jeans and an oversized white sweater which unfortunately obscures most of her relevant features; the other is overcompensating for being a little heavy with *fuck-me* boots and a short plaid skirt, hoop earrings dangling from her head like Christmas ornaments—and he cannot help but compare them to the heights he has previously reached: the doll-faced porcelain beauty, the dark-eyed Italian starlet, the chubby-cheeked serious-and-award-winning actress (that last, admittedly, whom he'd only dated for a few weeks).

Billy says, "We'll have to make this quick, ladies. He needs to rest."

"What happened to him?" the one in the sweater asks.

"He got burned doing a stunt for his new movie."

"Wow, sorry," she says.

"Hi," the child star says with a summoned, childlike innocence. He raises a hand to greet his adoring fans. His arm is covered in bruises and completely numb. He is in no shape or mood to flirt with these young women—all he wants, really, is to go home and obliterate his suffering, conscious mind with the bottle of Vicodins in his pocket. But still, it is a habit, and there is a glimmer, after having such a day, to the prospect of sitting by his pool with two lovely, curious young women to impress, whom he might conceivably convince to wear LINGERIE as they frolicked.

"I can't believe it's really you," the one in the sweater says. "I used to love your movies."

Used to, the child star hears. He says, "I'm always happy to hear that my work has touched someone's life in a positive way."

"Okay, that's probably enough, ladies. Do you want a photo before we head out?" Billy loves, in these situations, to pretend that he works for the child star, like a minder, a personal assistant, the bad cop who allows the child star to present himself, in opposition to this, as naïve and harmless, a delicate, sensitive creature requiring protection in this harsh world, as if he has been newly hatched from an egg.

"Hold up, Billy. I'm gonna be so *bored* today. I'm crippled!" The child star lifts his leg a bit, so they can all see the cast that rises to his knee. "What are you two doing? Do you want to come see my place?"

"Are you sure you're up for that?" Billy asks, his delivery flawless. Billy had, at one time, wanted to be an actor, and he would be one yet if the child star could ever finish his SCREENPLAY, and sell it to a studio, and add a clause into the contract requiring them to cast Billy in a minor role, maybe a barista the child star befriends while purchasing a coffee he could be holding in the next, more important scene.

"Have you seen my phone?" he asks Billy. "I need my phone. I had an idea for the screenplay."

"Does he want us to go?" the one in the boots asks. "We'll go."

"Goddamn it," the child star says, fumbling on the seat. There is something he needs to capture, some brilliant, fleeting inspiration, or he knows he's going to lose it. No, it's already gone. And the girls are sliding into the back seat, and they smell like fruit-scented body wash, and his limbs feel like they're a million miles away.

Los Angeles rolls past soundlessly as they ascend into the Hollywood Hills. The child star tries to keep his milkshake from spilling onto his lap as the two women blow all of the usual words past his head. Their names are Paula and Jessie. Paula in her *fuck-me* boots is going to school. Jessie wants to be an actress. She's looking for advice on breaking into the industry, and the child star quickly sniffs out the desperation in her voice.

He says, "I can make some calls for you. I've got a guy you should talk to. He won't take advantage of you like most of the people in this fucking town."

Everyone who visits the child star's home gets the tour, which begins as Billy gets out of the car to punch the access code into the front gate.

"This place used to belong to Tom Skerritt, for like a minute in the seventies," the child star explains.

"Who?" Paula asks.

Billy guides the Lincoln up the driveway and parks in front of the house. He walks around the car to help the child star to his feet and hand him his crutches.

The child star says "Welcome to *mi casa*" as the women shuffle out of the car and stand in awe before the stone-fronted mansion.

Inside, the child star walks them through the Italian-marble-floored entry hall, the gleaming kitchen, with its granite countertops and cookware which hasn't been used since he let his housekeeper go (his mother was happy to come over one day a week to clean for him, and treated her fifty-two-year-old son, in many other ways, like he was still a child star), the music room full of expensive guitars he almost never touched, the living room that is a museum of artifacts documenting his life's triumphs: movie tie-in merchandise and props from his films, including a molded resin vampire head in a glass case with fangs bared; his DVD, Blu-ray, and laserdisc collection, which contains every version of every film he's made, even the special editions from Japan, where he dimly believes he is still revered; theatrical posters framed along one wall, the last of which displays him standing in front of a gleaming black 1989 Lamborghini Countach, his arms crossed and a spit-curl dangling over his forehead, wearing a crisp denim jacket not unlike the one which, earlier that day, failed to protect him from the wasps. He tells them, "I still have that car, believe it or not. The director gave it to me after the shoot. I'll take you out to the garage later." He doesn't feel like navigating the stairs on crutches, so he waves at the basement door and tells the girls about the game room, with its pool table and beer signs and classic arcade games.

Then, as always, the tour ends in the palatial master bedroom he calls the *boudoir*, with its circular waterbed, leopard-print sheets, and walk-in closet full of LINGERIE.

"You've got to see this," he says, flipping on the light. "This stuff is classic. Most of it has never even been worn, I just collect it."

To the child star, there is nothing more important than surrounding himself with beauty, and there is nothing in the world more beautiful than women in LINGERIE. He loves it all: teddies and lacey bras and panties and nighties and satin kimonos, corsets and garters dripping from their hangers like harnesses for fragile, imaginary animals.

"Impressive," Jessie drawls.

"Try something on if you like. I have some bathing suits if you want to go in the pool. Or else, maybe something more comfortable. It's totally casual here, totally free. Just do whatever it is you would do at home …"

"I don't usually walk around the house dressed like this," Jessie comments, fingering a vintage girdle the child star has recently acquired, in an online auction he can't even remember bidding on.

"That's fine," he says. "Nobody's pressuring anybody. Go ahead, keep those tight, uncomfortable jeans on if you want."

But Paula shrugs and says "I'll try something on. Why not?" and begins to pull some items from the rack.

The child star waits in the *boudoir* as Jessie and Paula whisper in the closet. Paula emerges in a black lace bra and panties, with fishnet stockings attached to a garter belt. Jessie follows her out and hands her a silky black half-length kimono with an embroidered dragon on the back, which Paula drapes over her shoulders but thankfully doesn't cinch. She says "Look, I'm a porn star!" as she twirls in front of the bedroom mirror, and they both crack up.

This is the power that remains even in the meager, faded vestige of celebrity that the child star still possesses: it could convince two otherwise-sensible young women to get into a car with a complete stranger and go to his house, where one of them feels comfortable enough to flaunt her body before him in these deliciously objectifying undergarments. Because he isn't a stranger, not really. He has already been with them for their entire lives; they could never believe he was anything other than that boy they remembered from movie-night sleepovers, from the covers of teen magazines, whom they'd always imagined would love them, in a fairy-tale way, if they ever happened to meet. And he does, he does!

"Stunning, amazing," he says, making a rectangle with his fingers to view her through, as if he's already planning to put her in his next film.

In the backyard they expect a view of the valley, but there is an eight-foot wooden fence designed to prevent the paparazzi from harassing the child star, which they still do from time to time, if only to follow the details of his various meltdowns and public embarrassments.

"Maybe if we stand on a barstool," Paula suggests.

Billy is behind the outdoor bar, with its thatched awning, preparing margaritas and rolling a blunt simultaneously. The child star pours himself a glass of vodka with lime, despite the ER doctor's admonition that he shouldn't be drinking with all the painkillers and antihistamines in his blood. The sun is shining, the pool is pooling, and the child star, for the first time today, can remember the good feeling, the promising feeling, like his career has only stalled out and is ready to launch him again into the stratosphere, possibly like John Travolta in *Pulp Fiction* or that other guy, the pretty one who was at one time a child star himself, who later became a renowned character actor and eventually landed a gig on a popular, long-running sitcom. Things like that happened all the time.

Jessie, still dressed for winter, is sitting cross-legged beside the pool on a bamboo lounger. She took some acting classes, she tells him, in the Suzuki style, which she considers vastly superior to the Method school. "Suzuki is all about the body," she explains, "the way you move. It's like Greek drama, or Noh theater … the audience perceives the physicality first. Method acting is just an excuse for male actors to behave like infants on set. You don't have to *feel like* the character, internally. You just have to *act* like the character. I mean, it's called *acting*, right?"

"That's so true," he says. "I've always thought that."

"I'd love to hear your thoughts on the craft," she says. "Did you train anywhere? I mean, you started so young ..."

The truth is, the child star has never really considered acting a *craft* per se, at least not one requiring any skill. He'd stood at his mark, made faces for the camera as his agent-slash-manager argued with some PA about the catering. None of it seemed very difficult, and this, his agent assured him, was because he had *talent*, the same gift from the heavens his mother must have seen in him when she started sending out those tapes from their home in Missouri, which for a time had seemed inseparable from his being, though obviously it must have dribbled away somewhere, leaked out of his pores over the years as he waited for the phone to start ringing again.

"Do you want some advice?" he asks Jessie. "Forget technique. It's just like, they roll the camera, you *go*. You're *on*. You make it happen."

She seems disappointed with this answer, so he asks her what her favorite film is (before he even thinks about how he'll feel if it isn't one of his).

She says, "But what was that other one called? The one where robbers are chasing you around the marina? Hilarious! And why are there always robbers in these films? Were there a lot of burglaries in the eighties?"

Jessie laughs at her own joke as the child star struggles to untangle the threads of what has just happened. If she doesn't even know the name of the movie, he's thinking, then it couldn't be her favorite. Did he miss something? He's only just finished his first beverage of the day, but already he feels inordinately drunk.

Paula, stretched out in her finery and sipping one of the margaritas Billy has prepared, says that she doesn't really like movies, not even those time-tested classics which defined their generation. The child star has noticed that she has only about a ten-second window of attention before she needs to change her activity—tapping her phone, refreshing her makeup, unwrapping a stick of gum, shifting her position on the lounger. She says, "By the way, your place is really nice."

The child star's backyard oasis boasts not only the pool and the bar but also a tiled hot tub and a gas-powered fire feature built into the cabana table, all of it shaded by banana trees in massive planters. He thought, once, that with his residuals he might conceivably remain lounging in this paradise for the rest of his life, sipping vodka, inviting women into his hot tub, without having to accomplish anything else. But now, if he doesn't get more money coming in soon—and he *will not* go on the nostalgia-convention circuit, no way, so not his style—he's going to have to downsize. He might have to go live with his mother. Her house, the house he bought for her, is in Lakeview Terrace, way out in the desert, where at least his trickle of income can handle the taxes. He shudders at the thought—the two of them stumbling over one another in close quarters, the smell of her oniony, cheap cooking, him shut up in a child-sized bedroom to hide from the sound of her watching TV judge programs with the volume turned up deafeningly loud.

He says, "I like to sit here in the afternoon and get ideas for my screenplay. It's like my little Zen garden."

"What's it about?" Jessie asks. "The script?"

"I'll tell you all about it," the child star says, "but first, where the fuck is that blunt? Jesus Christ, Billy. Are you growing it?" Paula snorts, and the child star continues, hoping to milk the joke for more feminine attention. "Like, is he planting seeds? Does he have a little greenhouse over there? Hey! Farmer Billy!"

Billy submits to this ribbing in a noble silence. He uses a cigarette lighter to dry the misshapen blunt and passes it to Jessie, who declines to light it.

"I don't like pot," she says. "It gives me anxiety." The child star is beginning to like her less and less. When, he thinks, did young people become so *boring*? And entitled? Because hadn't he opened his home to her, and provided her with margaritas and free drugs, and asked for nothing in return except for her to maybe consider putting on something a little nicer, something that made him feel more calm and comfortable, in his *own space*?

Paula will smoke though! Paula has abandoned herself to life and all it will teach her. She accepts a shotgun from Billy, and then from the child star, and then gives them shotguns in turn, the hot smoke that has been inside of her passing over the child star's lips. There is something so intimate about this—being penetrated by her warm breath—that the child star asks if she wants to come sit on his lap. But Paula says no, she's fine where she is.

"I would do some coke, if you have any," Jessie says. "And do you have seltzer?"

There is coke! There is seltzer!

Thankfully, Billy is willing to go retrieve these things, because, ahem, the child star is a bit injured, confined to his lounger with his broken limb propped up and his crutches leaning against the faux-Roman patio column.

Jessie leans back on her lounger, revealing the shape of her pert breasts beneath her sweater, and the child star wonders if he was wrong about her. Maybe she just needed a little time to warm up. Maybe he isn't really perceiving things correctly, he thinks—in a rare moment of self-awareness—because of the pain, the shame, the antihistamines, the painkillers, the vodka, the weed. She is beautiful, he realizes, as if seeing her for the first time: her eyes wide and dark with scorn, her hair straight and untreated, the angles of her face so sharply defined that she looks like she might have a small amount of alien DNA.

"So how are you two even friends?" the child star asks her, perhaps too loudly, nodding toward Paula. "I mean … you're so different."

He thinks he hears her say *Actually, we just met*, but before he can ask what she means—Aren't they best friends? Hadn't somebody said something about childhood sleepovers?—Billy is back! With the coke! He plops the baggie on the cabana table and asks the child star to *do the honors*, and the child star shimmies over to dump it out and separate it into neat lines with the edge of his debit card.

Jessie leans over the table and snorts the first through a rolled twenty dollar bill. As she wipes her nose, she says, "It's weird, I have like a reverse polarity. Weed makes me super anxious, but coke actually mellows me out. I think it's something in my biology."

He isn't really listening, because after doing two lines in rapid succession the child star is thinking about his COMEBACK, and the exact combination of elements he would need to create in his SCREENPLAY to make that happen, a perfect balance of romance and action and callbacks to his most popular movies, because people love that sort of thing, and soon he is furiously speaking into his phone—it had been with him the whole time, right there in his pocket!—recording all of these notes, this gold. In fact, he thinks, he needs to record this very moment: the sun, the rippling pool, the girls arranged on the loungers like a Greek chorus, like his own private angels, with his steadfast companion nearby, mashing cold French fries into his mouth, a moment of such pure and complete beauty that he senses it should be the final scene in the movie, an epilogue of sorts, the hero's rest after all his weary struggles.

"You could do that thing again," Billy says, a moist clump of cocaine spilling out of one nostril, "the thing you did in the car, when the vampire was trying to get in. But don't make it a vampire this time. Vampires have been done too many times. You know this, you already did vampires, right? But here's the big question: if it's not a vampire, who's the guy hanging on the trunk? Why is he there? If you figure that out, you've got the whole movie."

Jessie rubs her finger on her gums and asks, "What's the movie even about?"

This is a question the child star cannot answer with any degree of precision, because he has not, to date, written an actual word of the

SCREENPLAY, though his phone is full of sometimes-cryptic voice notes outlining the broad strokes: *it opens in a lighthearted way, with a familiar, comic figure, maybe like what he did in that one movie, the star-crossed romance between the nerd and the beauty, where he started in dorky glasses and then later became cool with nothing more than a change of clothes and a new hairstyle; at some point, nail-biting tension would be introduced, a villain, or villains, why stop with one, maybe his agent, who had obviously been using him for years, or the film director, the one who befriended him and took him on vacations to "establish a relationship" with his star, and who once tried to give him a blowjob at his lake house when the child star was fourteen, an attempt that was aborted when the child star flipped out, calling his agent, calling his father, who by that time wasn't even treating him like a human being anymore but some kind of investment property—always hiding behind a tight smile and saying things like* Hey buddy, let's not get overexcited, are you sure that's what happened?—*until eventually a car was sent to retrieve him in upstate NY and take him back to the airport, after which neither he nor his agent nor his parents nor the director ever mentioned the incident again.*

"It's my life story," he tells Jessie, "but there's a universal aspect to it. The main guy is like an everyman. It's about Hollywood. But in the movie, Hollywood is just a thing. It could be anything. All that matters is that the guy is alone, fighting against dark forces, and there are people who do not want him to succeed, for whatever reason."

He explains that his SCREENPLAY is going to blow the lid off of the whole entertainment industry. It will show how things really work, behind the scenes, in a no-holds-barred way, all the abuse that goes on, which no, he can't go into detail about, because these revelations are the only cards he has to play, so to speak, and he has to save them for the SCREENPLAY. He won't use anybody's real name, of course, so he can't get sued. But the world will know what was done to him: how he was plucked—*plucked*, the word feels right, because he hadn't asked for any of this—from his home and brought to this city to have his once-cherubic face flashed on giant screens for people to ogle and laugh at and worship, without any thought for how it all made him feel, how lonely it was, never going to school or having sleepovers or trick-or-treating, speaking at night to his mother and father on the phone, telling them, yes, he was fine, no, it wasn't hard, he was fine, everybody was very nice, his father trying to rational-ize away any discontent as the checks kept coming, and every day the child star feeling further away, more isolated, signing autographs without knowing whose name he signed, throwing tantrums in the hotels where he was kept like a rare animal, until finally the vul-tures had picked his bones clean and he was left behind, a piece of Hollywood jetsam without any sense of who he was if he wasn't be-ing filmed, abandoned to be slowly consumed by the weight of his own bitterness in this admittedly fabulous mansion.

Jessie says, "Wait, I thought you were already filming your come-back movie?" She looks at Billy. "Didn't you say he got hurt doing a stunt?"

Billy is shirtless, his tribal tattoos undulating as he jerks his head in time to a music only he can hear. He says, "Can I refill your 'ritas, ladies?" He turns to the child star and asks, "Are they called 'ritas? Or Margies?"

Jessie says, "Can somebody please answer me?"

The different substances in the child star's bloodstream are mingling in hitherto unknown ways so that it feels as if he's poised at the head of a pin, as if with one more push toward the sky he might become an angel himself, a being of pure, radiant light. "Someone will …," he assures them both. "Someone will answer all of your questions."

He tips a bottle of Grey Goose toward his tumbler. He's used up all the lime wedges in the outdoor bar, but lime wedges are no longer necessary. He realizes, with only mild surprise, that he is no longer bound by time, which jumps around like someone changing channels. Billy gets into the pool and then he's out and dry, as if he hasn't been swimming at all. The child star wonders, idly: Is this *after* ... *or before?* Paula has been engrossed in her phone for so long that it looks like she's been paused.

He believes that Jessie will understand him, at a soul-deep level, when he leans over and whispers, "All of this"—he points at his broken leg, his swollen face, which feels like it has been peeled off and placed on someone else's body—"this is not from a movie. This is *real life*."

She considers this, staring at the fence as if she actually can see out over the valley, and says, "Everybody feels like their life is a movie. It's basically a cliché."

Of course! the child star thinks. Her words are so profound, so obviously true, that he wonders if she's not just acting as a mouthpiece for some cosmic force trying to tell him the things he needs to hear. And what he's hearing is: *Life* is the movie. The world wrote itself! He didn't have to write anything, actually! What a relief! All he had to do was get out of his own way, and record everything that happened to him, exactly as it happened, and *voilà!*: there was his award-winning, crowd-pleasing, career-reestablishing SCREENPLAY.

Billy and Paula have entered into some sort of impassioned dialogue about a social issue, and from the blunt generality and obvious untruth of the things they are saying, it is clear that neither really knows what they're talking about. But still, they have taken positions and keep repeating the same things to one another in a loop, neither of them understanding or responding to the other in any intelligible way.

Politics in America! the child star thinks. A perfect metaphor, or symbol, whichever word you would use! This is definitely going in the SCREENPLAY!

Then, a heavier thought: if everything, literally everything he did, was going into the SCREENPLAY, he would have to start acting as if the cameras were on all the time. He would have to start doing more heroic things in his daily life, to *be* the kind of protagonist audiences would fall in love with. He shifts his broken leg on the lounger, leans left and right. He drinks his drink. Where were the opportunities for heroism? The water in the pool is totally flat, heated to seventy-eight degrees and glowing from the lights that kick on automatically at eight p.m., so that it resembles a glowing disc, a UFO, a portal to another world. No one was drowning in it. If there *was* someone drowning, the child star thinks, he would definitely jump in and save that person, perhaps one of the two women, it didn't really matter which one, though maybe it could be Jessie, because he's really starting to feel attracted to her, possibly because she's a little bitchy and intimidating and he desperately wants to win her approval. It would certainly help things along, though, if she slipped and hit her head and fell into the pool so he could leap in, drag her back onto the patio, figure out how to do CPR, and then bask in her adoring gaze as she opened her eyes, blue water rolling from her face like tears.

No, he has to think bigger. Moviegoers want spectacle, higher stakes. He briefly wishes there could be another terrible event, a natural disaster, or something like the Holocaust—not because he wants anybody to get hurt! Of course not!—but only so there would be people for him to save. He imagines them as an oppressed minority of some type: good, struggling people, families with children, whom he could protect by hiding them from the authorities, maybe downstairs in his game room. But there is an unexpected pang of regret as he realizes that his father wouldn't be alive to witness all of this, to appreciate what a good, heroic man he's grown into, which would leave their relationship forever frozen in the state it was in when his father had the heart attack, reduced to bitter conversations about the child star's weight, his general puffiness, his lack of ambition, all of which were things, his father had insisted, that maybe the child star might try considering for a change.

He is attempting to explain this complex puzzle of emotions to Jessie—about the refugees in his game room, and how they relate to his feelings about his father, which honestly he's still figuring out, and about how literally all of this and even what they're saying right now is going into the SCREENPLAY—but she seems to be misunderstanding him, because her face isn't making the right shapes, so he tries to calm her by saying, "Don't worry … there hasn't been an actual holocaust. Yet."

She says, "Wait, are we being filmed? We didn't sign any kind of release."

Paula says, "Oh my God, are you saying we're in the movie? Is that why you wanted me to dress like this?"

"You are," the child star assures Paula. "Both of you are definitely in the movie." To Jessie, he says, "Don't worry, nobody's making a movie."

Jessie frantically looks around the patio, searching for the hidden cameras.

Billy, who is doing his katas by the edge of the pool, hisses out a lungful of air and says, "Well, somebody is. Just not us."

"Not true! Nobody's filming anybody! Shut the fuck up for one second, Billy!"

Fucking Billy!

Jessie says, "I think we should go."

"What?" Billy says, wounded. "I mean, there's lots of movies in production right now, including ours. We're in preproduction."

Paula is sliding around in the background, looking for her clothes.

"Wait, I thought you two just met? You don't both have to go at the same time, do you? Come on, it's early. I'll be so lonely if you both leave."

"What are you talking about?" Paula says. "I've known her since we were like five. Sorry, I have class tomorrow."

Is it night? It's night. Night has fallen, descended, whatever, at some point. More and more, things are slipping past him like this. Days, nights, weeks. The sky over Los Angeles is neon purple, filled with smog and city light. Jessie and Paula's names have already been penned on his cast with a Sharpie, surrounded by hearts.

Jessie is on her phone, no doubt looking for an Uber. Paula emerges from the house in her original clothing and discards her LINGERIE on a wet patio chair. Wadded up there, the stockings look like nothing more than tangles of black string.

There might have been a time when the child star would have raged at this sudden departure, harangued Billy for hours about how they were stuck-up cunts just trying to take advantage of him, like everybody else. But not today. Because today is the day he realized that THIS IS ALL GOING IN THE MOVIE.

He is not the person he was yesterday. He is not the person he was a few hours ago. He is a better man now, he has been transformed. *It's possible!* he wants to say to a crowd of eager schoolchildren. *Look at what happened to me! All that it took was a wasp attack, a broken leg, a novel combination of pharmaceuticals, and this very wise young woman to show me the error of my ways.* All that he wants in this moment is to be a friend and a mentor to her. He wants to help her on her journey and to make sure that nobody ever does to her what was done to him. He wants to be a guide, a good shepherd, for all of the hopeful, wide-eyed girls pouring out of buses, disembarking from planes, spilling into Los Angeles with the mistaken notion that anybody there might give a fuck about them. *Go back home!* he wants to tell them. *Embrace the oblivion of your own dumb lives!* He would buy them all bus tickets. If they didn't have a place to go, if they were running away from broken homes, from abusive fathers or whatnot, he would let them stay downstairs in the game room with the others, and he imagines his mansion becoming a shelter for all of the world's rejected and oppressed peoples, and him like Mother Teresa, like Florence Nightingale, like Angelina Jolie, only the man version.

He says, "Can we at least give you a ride home? Billy? Are you good to drive these ladies? Did I show you guys my cars?"

He is up on the crutches, swinging along the edge of the pool. Despite his broken leg, he cannot remember ever feeling so agile, and so capable. He opens the side door of the garage and flicks on the lights and there they are: the Beemer that he used to get around town before his license was suspended, and next to it, glimmering like a rocket ship beneath the fluorescent lights, the black LAMBO the blowjob director had given him after the shoot, the LAMBO he'd driven along the coastal highway during a wild, passionate weekend with the dark-eyed starlet, the classic LAMBO worth, at this point, nearly a million dollars, which he hadn't been able to bring himself to sell, though he hardly ever drove it these days, and which, technically, he is not even legally allowed to drive anymore, thanks to the dickhead cop who pulled him over and decided to breathalyze him for no fucking reason while he was obeying every single traffic law and going well below the speed limit. In the SCREENPLAY, the child star is certain, something bad will happen to that cop, because this is what all movies affirm: that there is a secret moral code, a power in the world higher than ourselves, which distributes gifts and punishments among people in accordance with their deeds.

This is why the child star will do only GOOD DEEDS from this moment forth. He will surprise the world with his generosity. And the audience, learning about all of this from the movie, will be amazed at what a kindhearted person he'd secretly been, all that time they were ghoulishly studying his decline, and, with the way public sentiment worked, maybe the academy would pick that year to finally give him his Oscar nod.

He takes the keys off a peg on the wall and tosses them to Billy.

"Oh my God," Billy says. "We can take the Lambo?"

The child star has never, in all of the years he has known Billy, allowed him to drive the LAMBO.

He says, "You're not just going to take it, my friend. You're going to *keep* it. It's yours." He wants to give Billy a hug but doesn't know how to accomplish this on the crutches, so he just raises one crutch a little in salute.

Paula and Jessie are crushed in the doorway, as if afraid to enter. Paula says, "You're really giving him the car? Like, right now?"

Billy laughs. "You're just fucked up. I'll bring it back tomorrow? Is that okay? I wanna hop over to my crib."

"No! I'm serious. Come back tomorrow and we'll do all the paperwork," the child star promises. "You totally deserve this. You're my *best friend*, man. I just want to show you how much I appreciate … I appreciate …" He has forgotten just what he appreciates about Billy, but whatever it is, he appreciates it with a full heart, an overabundant love that is ready to spill like water over the world.

Jessie says, "This is a lot."

"Are you fucking serious?" Joy blooms on Billy's face, a joy which the child star is responsible for. He wants to make everyone around him this happy, all the time. And he does, doesn't he? Didn't he buy that house for his mother, and break his fucking leg that very morning while getting his face devoured by wasps, all to take care of her? Hadn't he opened his home, his life, to these two hopeful fans Billy found at an In-N-Out Burger?

Billy barely touches the door of the LAMBO and it slides up like a dream. One time-jump later, the garage door is open and he's rocketing down the driveway with Paula and Jessie smooshed into the passenger seat, and the child star is left there in the garage, in a cloud of exhaust, alone.

He wanders back out to the pool, where the bamboo loungers slide across his field of vision like animals on the move. He can feel his blood sloshing against the inside of his skull as he gathers up the stockings, the bra and panties, the kimono. He wads them against the arm of the crutch and shuffles through the French doors, back into his dusty museum, his *casa*. There he is, on the poster. There he is, on the DVD. All that he's ever wanted is for someone, a woman preferably, maybe one like Jessie, or Paula, or perhaps a combination of the two, ideally, to point at these images and say to him: *that's not the one that I love. I love you, you, you.* And then to poke him reassuringly in the chest with her finger each time she says *you*, to remind him that he's there, that he's real, that he's not like the character he played in his disastrous final flop of a film, the one who drank a formula which caused him to shrink, to grow smaller and smaller until he was suspended at the center of the screen, flailing his arms and legs in the infinite space between atoms.

He passes through the empty parlor to the bedroom, and then the walk-in closet, where he unfurls the garments and hangs them back up. He stands there for a long time, among all those beautiful things, running his fingers along the delicate fabrics and wondering if this, in fact, is the end of the SCREENPLAY. Not the epilogue, or dénouement, or whatever, but the very end, the end end, the moment where the screen goes dark and the audience breathes and feels whatever there is to feel.

And a cosmic voice whispers: *Become the thing that you desire. Become the beauty that only you can perceive in the world.*

Surprisingly, as enamored as he is of his LINGERIE collection, this has never occurred to him before. But it makes perfect sense. He removes his shirt, leans against the wall to free the cast from his pant leg, then shifts items on the rack until he finds his favorite, a purple satin baby-doll nightie, and wriggles his swollen, middle-aged shape into it like sausage into a casing, thinking: the audience is going to love this.

He wedges the crutches under his arms and hobbles into the *boudoir* to regard himself in the mirror. Was he beautiful enough yet? The nightie hangs crooked on him; one of the straps is tangled on the arm of his crutch. From the neck up, he is a mass of red welts, his face so swollen that he resembles a movie monster from the fifties, some hapless soul scorched by nuclear fallout and transformed into a moaning, disfigured beast. And the drugs must be wearing off, because his face is burning.

He throws the crutches down, finding that he no longer needs them, and clomps into the kitchen to retrieve his painkillers from beside the sink, and takes two more, four more, he doesn't know how many he takes. He's holding the bottle, trying to figure out if he took them already, or if he still planned to take them. Two more, why not, just to be sure. His face is screaming.

He can hear whispering coming from beneath the basement door, drifting up from the game room, where all of those refugees, the wide-eyed Hollywood hopefuls, the holocaust people, or whatever, are starting to complain: *Why won't you help us? What kind of man are you?*

Wait a minute, he tells them. *I'm going to do everything I promised … I just have to cool off my face.*

He also needs to find his phone again, because he's having a kind of holy vision, a transmission from the same cosmic voice that's been whispering to him all day, and he knows exactly how to end the SCREENPLAY. It's so simple, he can't believe he's never put it together before: every screenplay is a circle. Every film has to end exactly where it began. After he puts on the purple satin nightie, after he takes the painkillers, after he goes out to the patio to pour a glass of Grey Goose that he will never drink, the camera will retreat into the sky, his backyard oasis growing smaller and smaller, until it soars out over L.A. and the surrounding communities, flying along the bus route he took that morning to finally arrive at his mother's house (the house he bought for her, let's remind the audience of that), and then it will swoop down through an open window, like a tiny camera mounted on a wasp, to show his dear mother, the person who made him, and the first one to recognize his talent, whom he's having very tender feelings for at this moment, which is appropriate, because this is gold, this is good material. And then, hard cut, back to the moment of his conception, within her body. He's thinking about sperm, actually, and their noble struggle upriver, life's first salmon—if he could only find his phone and record one word, at this moment, to remind him of all of this, it would be SALMON. And he is overcome with emotion, and knows intuitively that this is the right image to end on, because what is more beautiful, and sorrowful, than this epic inner pageant happening every day, with each little sperm racing and fighting to be the only one of these colossally insignificant, doomed tadpoles that might one day, against all the odds, rise to become a child star?

His face! His face!

Just remember SALMON, he thinks. Don't let go of that fish. That fish is your COMEBACK.

There is the pool, a shimmering blue light, cool and inviting. He isn't supposed to get the cast wet, but fuck it. What good is it to be a child star if you can't go for a little night swim in your own fucking pool? If he's not going to get laid tonight, can he at least have that? Please??? He hurls himself toward the radiant portal, expecting a slap in the face, a shock of cold, but no. The water rises to meet him, accepts him so gently that he barely feels the impact. It is the exact temperature as the night, and he feels like he is only slipping through a thin membrane into another universe, one with a thicker kind of air which suspends him, so that his body is suddenly rendered graceful again, angelic even. He floats across a startlingly bright white vista, the thin fabric of the nightie billowing and rippling against him in slow motion, acting as a kind of armor that will protect him in this new landscape, where things work differently, and what is required to protect him is not talent, or love, but only this thin, shimmering film of beauty, that is enough, and he knows that he is prepared. Life is glorious, and he's ready to do it all again.

ALEX PEREZ

INDEPENDENCE DAY

I couldn't sleep. A few hours earlier, over an uncharacteristically quiet family dinner, my mother told my brother and me that our half-brother was coming from Cuba on the Fourth of July. I didn't know him, had barely heard anything about him over the years, but now he was apparently joining a family that had never felt like much of a family to begin with. My brother must've been as shocked as I was, because he didn't say anything after the announcement, which was rare for him.

"Are you awake?" I said.

"The rule is that we don't talk once we're in the room," my brother said. "Follow the rule."

"Why is he coming?"

"Eventually every person in Cuba will come to Miami," he said. "I'm surprised his skinny Cuban ass didn't arrive three or four years ago."

I'd never thought of it that way, probably because I'd never really wanted to believe that my pain-in-the-ass older brother wasn't my only older brother. Whom else didn't I know about? What else?

"What are we going to do?"

"We're going to get us the loudest, most dangerous fireworks and welcome this brother of ours with a bang."

That wasn't the answer I was looking for, but my brother, sixteen at the time, certainly didn't know what was expected of us any more than I did.

"Maybe we can get some Roman candles," I said.

"Fuck those Romans and their candles. This is America. We need shit that explodes. Explosives."

"We don't know anyone who has explosives."

My brother laughed and sat up in bed.

"Ruben," he said.

"Not Ruben," I said. "No way."

Ruben was the psycho who, two years earlier, had shown us how to make an acid bomb before his parents sent him away. It was Noche Buena, and Ruben, always a devious little motherfucker, waited until the adults were good and lubricated and then brought us into the garage and said, "Acid bomb time."

At previous parties, Ruben had broken into and pissed in cars, jerked off onto a mailbox, and stabbed an iguana with a fork, but now that he was fifteen, apparently it was time for him to blow shit the fuck up. We feared that Ruben would blow our heads off if we didn't grant him an audience, so we watched him take off his fake gold chain, put it in his pocket, and walk to the other end of the garage, where the pool supplies were.

All night, Ruben had been chugging from a liter of Coke, and just as he bent down and found the hydrochloric acid, he finished the bottle. "I've been planning this since last year," he said. Then he pulled a couple of sheets of aluminum foil from his pockets and began to rip pieces from the foil and fold them into little balls, which he passed out to us.

He picked up the jug and led us outside. I was convinced that the little foil balls were going to blow up in my hands, so I kept dropping them, until my brother grabbed my hand and dragged me toward the patch of dead grass in the middle of the street where Ruben had just finished uncapping the bottle of acid. Like a demented Little League coach, he said, "Get in here, boys."

We surrounded him and, following Ruben's lead, dropped our aluminum-foil balls into the empty liter bottle of Coke. When the bottle was filled a quarter of the way, Ruben waved it at us so we could get a whiff. I was sure it had singed my nose off, and in unison we stepped back and kept retreating, as Ruben filled the bottle to the brim with pool acid. He capped the bottle, placed it gently in the middle of the patch of grass, and bolted in our direction, which is when the rest of us started screaming, because if Ruben ran from something, the end of the world was at hand.

We ended up half a block away and hid behind cars, poking our heads over hoods, where we saw that the bottle had now expanded to three or four times its normal size. Holy shit, we all said, to which Ruben, who was now shirtless for some reason, said, "I am greater than Alexander."

The bottle kept growing until it reached the size of a tire. It was then, convinced that the explosion was going to blow a crater in the ground and suck us in, that I closed my eyes and got in the fetal behind my brother. When the explosion finally happened, my brother rolled over me, and what I thought were blood and guts showered our trembling bodies. My ears, even though I'd covered them, still rung, and when my brother dragged me up and forced me to open my eyes, I saw that it was sod and dirt that had landed on us. The patch of grass was no more, and in its place stood Ruben, beating his chest and yelling something or other about being a conquistador and the one true bad ass. Dirt in my hair, piss in my pants, I never wanted to see him again.

"Anyone but Ruben," I told my brother.

"If anyone has what we need," my brother said, "it's Ruben."

That's exactly what I feared.

"Isn't he locked up?"

"No place can hold Ruben," he said.

Two days later, we biked the three miles to Ruben's parents' house, my brother hoping that one of the most notorious juvenile delinquents in Miami history was back from the place he'd surely burnt to the ground. We huddled behind a tree across the street and watched as Ruben's father pulled weeds from the lawn.

"He's not here," I said. "Let's go."

"Ruben is everywhere."

Ruben's father had lost thirty pounds since we'd last seen him. He was either in the last stages of cancer, or Ruben was indeed back and had sapped all remaining life force out of him. The front door opened. A jacked and tatted Ruben appeared, and as he approached his father, a man so weakened that he was unable to pull out a weed, I had to fight every urge not to take to the fetal and piss myself again.

"This isn't a good idea," I whispered.

"Look at him," my brother said. "He's got what we need in his room."

I didn't want to think of Ruben's room, or what he had in there, and didn't have to, because Ruben lifted his leg and kicked his father in the back. His father rolled three or four times, finally coming to a stop when he slammed into a bush. He stood up, head down, weed in hand, and walked through the front door, trailing dirt inside the house. Ruben stood there, surveying his kingdom, waiting.

"He's crazier than ever," I said.

"He probably has dynamite, maybe even nukes."

I went for my brother's arm, but it was too late. He stepped out from behind the tree and made his way toward Ruben, who cocked his head like a lion appraising its prey.

"Is that the little pussy I think it is?" Ruben said.

"It's me," my brother said. "It's the little pussy."

"Come here, little pussy."

My brother jogged into Ruben's arms, and like two ex-cons who hadn't seen each other since their last spree, they embraced. When they separated, Ruben started looking around, until he said what I feared he would say: "Where's the other little pussy?" I hoped my brother would say that I hadn't made the trip, but instead he pointed at the tree I was trembling behind.

"Don't make me come and get you, little pussy," Ruben said.

I had a fleeting thought that I could escape on my bike, but fearing that my brother would pay for my intransigence, I stepped out from behind the tree, the little pussy that I was. I somehow made it to Ruben without pissing or shitting myself and hugged him. When he put me down, I was sure he would follow up his act of kindness with a physical attack of some kind, but he merely smiled and said, "To what do I owe this surprise visit, little pussies?"

"We need cherry bombs," my brother said. "M-80s. Maybe some Black Cats. Explosives."

"I knew you'd get the taste for it," Ruben said. "Two weeks after Noche Buena, I blew up three acid bombs at once and took a bridge down. That's when they sent me away."

I'd heard that Ruben had been shipped off after knocking out a homeless man, but the thought of him blowing up a bridge was altogether more terrifying.

"What you need," he continued, "isn't some pussy-ass M-80s or a few Black Cats. You might as well get in line with little kids and buy some fucking poppers. You pussies need the real shit my boy gets from Montana."

"Montana?" my brother said.

"Those crazy fuckers blow up mountains over there," Ruben said. "The cowboy's bringing in a shipment next week. You want the Montana shit?"

"Yeah," my brother said. "That Montana shit is what we need."

"Meet me here on the third," Ruben said. "I'll be loading up for my next demolition."

When we got home, we found our mother moving around the dozens of pictures she'd placed on the refrigerator over the years. It had been ages since I'd noticed them, but now that she was rearranging my childhood, I wanted her to stop. There I was learning how to swim. My failed third-birthday party, when one of my cousins blew out the candles and stole my wish. Me and my brother on the first day of school, with our matching red book bags. Whatever happened to those book bags? My mother grabbed the picture, and, just like that, a memory was tossed atop the fridge, where it landed next to a stack of dusty magazines.

"You hated those book bags," my mother said.

She placed a new picture on the spot that had belonged to me for over ten years and stepped aside. It was a yellowing picture of a baby who had the hairiest head I had ever seen.

"So he feels part of the family," she said.

She went into her room and left us to look at him, this baby who had been around before we had. It hadn't felt real when she'd first told us, but now that I saw him, this hairy Cuban bastard, the invasion felt imminent.

"He has your nose," my brother said.

"No he doesn't."

"That flat nose you and Mami have," he said. "You and Mami and your new older brother."

"He's your older brother too."

"Fuck off."

For the next week, in preparation of our half-brother's arrival, our mother worked and made calls and ordered the requisite Cuban pastries for the guest list of over a hundred that would be joining our family in celebration. The hoopla was more than enough justification for my brother, who was convinced that such a bash needed fireworks from Montana.

"What's more American than explosives from Montana?" he said. "That's some Wild West shit." He was spending his days cleaning the yard in the guise of helping our mother, searching for the spot where the fireworks would be exploding from.

A few days before we met up with Ruben, I walked the two blocks to one of the firework tents that pop up around Miami in the days leading up to the Fourth. Every year, my brother and I, after begging our mother for twenty bucks, would head to the tents, and from dirty Cubans buy as many fireworks as possible, which usually amounted to ten minutes' worth of tepid explosions. He'd been in the yard when I asked our mother for the money, and when she realized that my brother had apparently moved on from fireworks, she slipped me an extra ten. I was convinced that with thirty bucks we'd be able to find something worthy of our half-brother, but when I found my brother hammering a hole into a tree at the edge of the yard, he ignored me.

"Mami gave me thirty," I said. "We can get some good shit with thirty."

"You can stick a thousand dollars' worth of tent fireworks in this hole, and not even a branch would fly off this tree."

"What about tradition?" I said. "We go every year."

"It'll be a new tradition when I pack the Montanas in here and this tree explodes and that flat-nosed brother of ours finds out what America is all about."

I walked into the tent and immediately encountered the same stuff of years past. Little kids were filling up their baskets with fireworks I didn't want, but since I was alone and had thirty dollars, I searched for something big and powerful, the pseudo-explosive that would win my brother back. I had passed the Roman candles, some bottle rockets, and dozens and dozens of sparklers, when a skinny kid stepped in front of me and crossed his arms.

"I know what you're looking for," he said.

I shrugged, afraid the kid was a young undercover cop.

"You want the real deal," he said. "I see you looking."

I finally met his eyes, and he glanced at the tent's owner, who was probably his father.

"Follow me," he said.

The guy came out from behind the mountain of sparklers, and I followed him toward a white van parked alongside the street. He opened the side door, exposing what looked like more of the same kiddy shit I'd seen under the tent.

"My dad doesn't know I'm selling on the side," he said, "so act cool when we're done with the deal."

I nodded.

"How much you got?"

"Thirty."

"And what kind do you want?"

"Something that explodes," I said. "That can maybe rip a branch off a tree."

"Right, right, of course," he said, disappearing into the van.

I looked back at the tent, at the little kids smiling at their bounty, and felt like a big man. If only my brother could see me now, buying white-van fireworks from a shady dude. The guy jumped out of the van and handed me a plastic bag weighing a couple of pounds.

"This is thirty bucks worth of what you want," he said.

I opened the bag and saw what looked like M-80s.

"M-80s?"

The guy grinned and leaned in.

"Nah," he said. "M-100s. Straight from South Carolina. Perfect for blowing up mailboxes."

This was dangerous enough, exactly what I needed, so I handed over the thirty bucks. As we walked back to the tent, the guy told me that if I needed anything else, I knew where to find him.

"Do you have anything from Montana?" I said.

The guy froze. "I've been looking for a Montana hookup for a few years. You know anyone?"

I told him no, and now, more than ever, I feared what went down in Montana.

After dinner, I opened our closet, where I'd hidden the M-100s, and pulled out the plastic bag, holding it out to my brother.

"We don't have to see Ruben again," I said.

My brother reached into the bag and removed a single M-100, holding it up to the light.

"This," he said, "is what little kids play with in the great state of Montana."

"But it's from South Carolina," I said. "The guy said it would blow up a mailbox."

"South Carolina is full of pussies."

My brother tossed the M-100 in the bag and threw it in the closet.

"Your ass got conned," he said. "You paid thirty bucks for glorified birthday candles. M-100s my balls."

"They're the real deal," I said.

"Next you're going to tell me you bought them out of a white van."

"Real deal," I repeated.

"You'll see the real deal tomorrow when Ruben takes us to see the man from Montana."

"I'm not going," I said.

"Of course you're not. Pussy."

I woke up in the middle of the night, sweating and fearing the man from Montana. Any friend of Ruben had to be a tried-and-true sociopath, especially one from the great American West. I just knew that he was going to bring enough explosives to blow up half of Miami, and I didn't want me or my brother to go down as accomplices. I went to the closet, grabbed the bag of M-100s, and woke my brother up.

"What the fuck do you want?"

"Let's blow up a mailbox," I said.

My brother turned over.

"Go on," he said, "put one in my ass and light it. I bet you I won't even feel it."

"Shut up."

"Be a good little brother and slide it in."

"If it doesn't blow up, I'll go with you tomorrow."

My brother got out of bed and led us into the kitchen, where he found our mother's lighter. He opened the sliding glass door, and we stepped into the backyard, a single M-100 in my hand. I was rolling it between my palms, trying to warm it up or something, praying that it would do the trick. I was never one for vandalism, but as we hopped the fence and began our search for the proper mailbox, I was sure that the M-100 would cause an earthquake and take down not one but two or three mailboxes. We walked two blocks, far enough that we wouldn't be implicated, and then my brother pointed at one of those concrete mailboxes resembling the house it was stationed in front of.

"That's a bomb shelter for mail," I said.

"Pick one then."

The house next door had an old-school wooden mailbox, and as it looked halfway decimated already, I picked it.

My brother laughed and said, "Your firecracker won't even take that piece of shit down."

"Yes it will."

My brother pushed past me and opened the mailbox.

"Do you want to do the honors?" he said.

I really didn't, so I handed the M-100 to my brother, who, without even looking around, lit it and placed it in the mailbox. As he started to shut the mailbox, I took off, finding refuge behind a car, but my brother stayed put.

"Shrapnel," I whispered.

He tapped the top of the mailbox, as if challenging the M-100.

"Get over here," I said.

After thirty seconds and still no explosion, my brother said, "It must've been so loud that we didn't hear it. Let's take a look."

"No," I yelled.

My brother opened the mailbox and stuck his whole damn head inside it.

"Boom," he said.

Then he stepped back, laughing his ass off, and gave the mailbox a single swift kick, toppling it.

The door to Ruben's house was open when we arrived. I'd begged my brother to let me stay home, declaring that I wanted nothing to do with Ruben and the man from Montana, but he'd dragged me outside and pushed me against my bike. I'd thought about turning around when we were halfway there, but out of some stupid brotherly loyalty, I kept pedaling and ended up in front of a terrifying open door. Who the hell left his door open, afraid of nothing and no one? This is how it must be in the Wild West, I thought, doors flung open and a man in a cowboy hat stepping out and greeting you.

The man from Montana looked exactly how I expected a man from Montana to look. Cowboy hat obscuring his stubbly face. Cowboy boots on what looked like size fifteens. A belt with a silver buckle that said *Go West*. My brother, who'd been feigning courage up until that point, grabbed hold of his bike's handlebars and tried to steady himself.

"He's from Montana," I said. "Let's go."

My brother mumbled something, perhaps even agreed with me, but then Ruben, wearing a Cowboy hat, too, appeared. He's a demon without a cowboy hat, I thought, so imagine what he's capable of as a Cuban Cowboy. I saw Ruben taking down dozens of bridges and raping damsels and tossing babies into corrals and making me go along with him, strapped underneath a horse.

"I don't want to go," I said.

My brother didn't say anything.

"Are these the boys?" Montana said.

"Me and these pussies go way back," Ruben said.

Then Montana yelled something in Montanian, and my brother, obeying his new master, dropped his bike. He walked over like a man heading for the gallows. I couldn't move, not until Montana meowed and called out, "Here, kitty kitty. Here, kitty kitty."

I followed my brother, trembling and holding it in. Montana greeted my brother with a slap to the back, propelling him into the house. When I reached Montana, he faked a slap and, like a gentleman, stepped aside. Only then did I realize that Montana, who was no older than eighteen, had an eye patch over his left eye.

Inside, Ruben's father lay catatonic on the couch, until Ruben said, "Break over. More weeds, Donny."

His father, barefoot and shirtless, ran outside, diving onto the lawn.

"I thought he was Ruben, too," my brother said.

"There's only room for one Ruben in this city," Ruben said. "He's Donny now."

There were at least another twenty thousand Rubens in Miami, so I feared that Ruben, with the help of Montana, would beat and rename them equally ridiculous names, sentencing them to decades of lawn care.

We followed them into Ruben's room, where, on the bed, lay dozens and dozens of the smallest cherry bombs I had ever seen. They looked like tiny red thimbles with fuses, but I feared them like nothing else I had ever feared.

"My great-granddaddy," Montana said, "killed him hundreds of Indians with these little bastards."

"They also got us kicked out of that fucking prison," Ruben said. They laughed, and I imagined Ruben and Montana, wearing cowboy hats, blowing to smithereens their school for at-risk monsters.

"How many?" Montana said.

My brother, who'd stashed away a couple hundred bucks of birthday money, said, "Twenty."

"That'll set you back a little over a thousand," Montana said. "And anyway, ten Indian Killers is more than enough to take down an entire tribe."

"How much you got?" Ruben said.

"Two-fifty," my brother said, handing over the cash.

Montana took a knee in front of the bed and picked out five "Indian Killers" and placed them in what looked like a Ziploc bag that was painted black. He handed the bag over to my brother, whose hands were shaking.

"Treat them with care," Montana said, "as they've been known to explode without even being lit. And when you do light them, you have less than 1.2 seconds to get away. And then ..."

Montana went silent and pointed at his eye-patched eye.

"Be quick," he said, "or else."

After hearing all the warnings, I looked at the hundreds of Indian Killers on the bed, fearing that, at any moment, one, or twenty, would go off.

"It's going down," Ruben said. "Like a thousand acid bombs."

Montana tipped his hat at us, and Ruben pointed at the door. Outside, as Donny pulled weeds, Ruben, flipping an Indian Killer in the air, said, "Pull, Donny. I don't want to see a single weed."

Montana, whom I'd hoped to never see again, appeared and slapped his right thigh, saying, "Come here, little pussy. I have something for you."

I didn't want anything else from the state of Montana, but he must've been in a giving mood, because when I didn't go to him, the man from Montana took two long strides and stood in front of me. He reached into his pocket, and, fearing that he was going to pull out a six-shooter, I peed myself a little. He pulled out an eye patch and stuck it in my hand.

"Wear it with pride," he said.

Did this mean that I was the one who would light the Indian Killer? Was I going to lose an eye? Which eye?

Before I could ask, Ruben said, "Whatever you do, don't go to South Beach tomorrow. Now get the fuck out of here."

We got the fuck out of there.

My brother wanted to hide them under my bed, but when I threatened to tell our mother, he placed the Indian Killers under the sink in our bathroom. I couldn't sleep, waiting for the five Indian Killers to go off and send the faucet through the bathroom wall, braining me. In the middle of the night, I threw my pillow at my brother. He jumped up and covered his face.

"Did they go off?" he said.

"Do you want to meet him?" I said.

"He's our brother."

"Do you think he's manlier than us?"

"There's no way he's manlier than me," he said.

"He had a lot of hair."

"What are you talking about?"

"In his baby picture."

"Shut the fuck up."

We sat there in silence, waiting for the Indian Killers to go off.

It was too dark to see him, but I stood in front of the fridge and wished him into existence. If only that little baby were in front of me right now and I could kick and further flatten his nose, I thought. If only I could tell him that he wasn't wanted here, and that he'd never been wanted at all. You are not my damn brother. She left you when you were a baby and forgot about you. She was ashamed of you. She probably even fucking hated you, which is why she left that island in the first place. You made someone leave an island. How does that make you feel? It was you, don't you dare think otherwise. I'm her son. My brother, my real brother, is her son. You, you're a damn bastard, and if I'm being honest, I refuse to share a room with a bastard. And fuck you for dragging Ruben back into our lives. You're not even here, and you've already started ruining things.

The kitchen light turned on. My mother, in her nightgown, sat down on a stool in front of the kitchen counter.

"I was thirsty," I said.

I opened the fridge and grabbed the water as my mother reached into the cabinet and removed two glasses. I filled them and stood across from her.

"I'm too excited for sleep," she said.

Not once had my brother and I ever excited her. On the contrary, we were always stressing her out and making her tired. All she'd do was complain and yawn, but now, in the middle of the night, she was excited and full of energy over the arrival of her firstborn.

"We need to buy him a new bed," she said.

My brother and I had slept on glorified cots our entire lives. Fuck him.

"Are there others?" I said.

"What do you mean?"

"Do I have a sister I don't know about?" I said. "Is she coming too? Or is your old dog next?"

"No."

"Are you sure?"

"You look like him," my mother said.

You haven't even seen him in years, I thought. How the hell would you even know? Or have you seen him and we just don't know about it? And if we do look alike, it's him that looks like me. I wanted the Indian Killers to go off and kill this conversation, blow up the house like the acid bomb.

"Goodnight," I said.

I was ready to explode.

The Cubans, cousins and uncles and grandparents, had taken over the house. It was all Spanglish and pastelitos and excitement over the impending arrival of a new Cuban. My brother was hanging out with our neighbors, anxious about the moment when he'd have to enter the bathroom and retrieve the Indian Killers. As for me, I was in a haze after having slept no more than an hour and just wanted the whole thing to be over. I'd give this new brother of mine the hug I was expected to give him, the Indian Killers would go off, and I'd retreat to my room, far, far away from these Cubans I only saw once a year.

He was slated to arrive at five, so at four, my mother, along with her sister, left for the airport. The Cubans went outside, the booze flowing, the lechon nearly finished. My brother, who'd said maybe ten words to me all day, joined me at one of the tables overflowing with croquetas. He grabbed two and stuffed them in his mouth.

"I hate these fucking people," he said. "And they just keep coming."

He was right. Every couple of years, a new Cuban, some fourth or fifth cousin, an uncle twice removed, arrived. But this, this was something else.

"We should just move to Cuba," my brother said. "Let them have this shithole if they want it so bad."

"When are you going to do it?" I said.

"As soon as they arrive."

"How many?"

"All of them."

At four forty-five, the Cubans started looking toward the sky, as if they'd be able to point out the plane he was arriving in. They were passing around booze and cigars, slapping my brother and me on the back. "A new brother," they kept saying. We nodded, staring at the tree that would soon be going down, the tree that would hopefully crush all these people and finally send them away for good, maybe even back to Cuba. For the first time, I understood the rage that must've driven Ruben, why he blew shit up and renamed people and wanted to remake the world in his image. With every slap on the back and every sloppy kiss on the cheek, I wanted Ruben and Montana to materialize and lay waste to this party—my family.

At five, a cousin put down his rum and Coke and yelled, "It's five. He's here. America!"

The Cubans took to the street, swarming every car that headed in our direction, chanting, "Braulio, Braulio, Braulio!"

Whenever my mother had said his name, I'd always thought: What the fuck kind of name is *Braulio*? You can't make it here with a name like that. Now I thought: Fuck that name, and fuck you, Braulio.

"Are you going to hug him?" my brother said.

"We have to," I said, pointing at the end of our block.

Our mother's beige Camry had turned the corner.

"Braulio is here," my brother said.

My mother honked, and the Cubans, led by a great-grandfather with a cigar in his mouth, ran toward the car. They reached it and, like a band of looters, slapped the windows, opened the doors, fishing Braulio out and, as if he'd accomplished some spectacular feat, raising him in the air.

"It's not like he came on a raft like a real Cuban," my brother said.

I hadn't been able to accept that he looked like me, but now, as he approached on the shoulders of one of my traitorous cousins, there was no denying that we were nearly identical. As he got closer, I waited for his nose to go pointy, his eyes to change color, for him to all of a sudden turn black, but when my cousin finally put him down, there was no doubt that Braulio and I were brothers. The hugging and kissing and grabbing of the balls began, and all the while, Braulio was looking around, trying to find us. We hadn't moved yet, but then he spotted us and smiled. He pointed at my brother.

"Ricky," Braulio said.

How did he know my brother's name? Ricky broke away from me, but instead of going inside and grabbing the Indian Killers, he went to Braulio, who embraced him. I couldn't believe he'd joined them. When he was finished with my brother, who looked like a dazed boxer out on his feet, Braulio pointed at me. It was my turn now. Everyone, all the Cubans, wanted to see the two identical half-brothers embrace. This would be the great American moment they'd all been waiting for.

"Brian," Braulio said.

He knew my name. Who had told him my name? He said it again. Stop saying my name.

"Brian."

I looked at my mother, who was crying, at my grandmother, also crying, and at Ricky, piece of shit, weeping. Every Cuban in Miami, except for Braulio and me, was crying. Then he reached behind his back and took off a red book bag. It was mine. He came at me, arms open, and it was then that the tears came. I turned around and ran inside, and when I could still hear them, I locked myself in the bathroom. You're a crying Cuban, I said to myself. You're a pussy-ass bitch and a crying Cuban and he took your book bag and your brother and now he's here to take everything else. I slapped myself in the face. Stop crying. I punched myself. I stopped. There was a knock at the door.

"Come and meet your brother," my mother said.

I stood up and went to the drawer under the sink, opened it. It was all there. I selected the biggest Indian Killer, grabbed the eye patch, and shoved everything in my pocket.

"Your brother is waiting," my mother said. "Everyone is."

Braulio.

I opened the door and walked past my mother, who started clapping as she tried to catch up with me. And then I was outside, and they were all clapping. Braulio opened his arms, and like Ricky, who was still crying, I went in for the hug. I embraced Braulio and, giving them what they wanted, lifted him in the air, spinning him around. I put him down and kissed his cheeks, his forehead, the top of his stupid Cuban head. They yelled, "Brothers!" Yes, I nodded, we are brothers, and like brothers we will misbehave and nothing bad will ever happen—keep thinking that, fuckers.

When I reached into my pocket and produced the Indian Killer, the Cubans laughed at what they thought was a harmless firecracker. No one, not even my mother, told me to be careful. Braulio was here with his brother, and now Braulio's bro was handing him a firecracker. Here was Braulio, miraculously having made it to America on Independence Day, holding the firecracker over his head. I reached into my pocket again and realized I didn't have the lighter, so I went over to Ricky.

"Give me the lighter," I said.

"What are you doing?"

"What you don't have the balls to do."

I patted his cheeks, dried the tears.

"I'm not giving it to you."

"Pussy," I said.

Ricky shoved the lighter into my chest. I raised it in the air and walked over to Braulio as the Cubans cheered. As soon as I handed it to him, I stepped back and smiled, giving Braulio the brotherly go-ahead.

Braulio, finally free, finally with us, flicked the lighter and brought the flame to the fuse. Braulio lit the Indian Killer.

America!

I'd stayed close enough that, when his left middle finger flew off and bounced against my chest, I picked it up and handed it to him like a good brother. Welcome to the land of the free, Braulio.

That night, with all the Cubans at the hospital, the house was the quietest it had ever been. I was sitting on the porch, looking up at the sky, when Ricky joined me. He didn't speak, and I didn't speak, and for the first time in our lives, we understood each other completely. Perhaps I should've hugged my brother, but I was too busy thinking about what I'd done and why I'd done it. I was four-teen, and at fourteen, one isn't prepared to deal with the past and its consequences. I didn't know then that no matter what you do, you can't erase or alter or blow up the past. There is no clean break, and there is no blank slate, and if you come from the island, the island will always be where you came from. The past is with you, and if you don't think so, one day it will show up on a sunny Miami day and remind you. "I'm here," it'll say. "I've always been here."

"What happened to your eye?" Ricky said.

I looked at him. "What are you talking about?"

"You have a black eye."

I remembered punching myself, and touched my right eye, which was swollen. We went silent again, waiting for Ruben and Montana to blow up Miami, but apparently they'd gone silent too. I reached into my pocket and pulled out the eye patch. I put it on.

MIKRA NAMANI

The Rise and Fall of Aleksandar Bundalo

I used to think my life's biggest accomplishment came one day in the murky year 1976, when I invaded Aleksandar Bundalo's home and killed him. For thirty years, he had lived under the false name of Zoran Kovaći in Vukojebina, a town that after World War II became home to a colony of retired mass murderers with fake identities. In the many years I lived there, I investigated, tracked down, and executed quite a few of these homicidal monsters, but regrettably many others will go to their graves without so much as a scolding. After eliminating Bundalo, whom I considered to have been one the worst offenders and whose story is worth recounting here, I retired from being a justice warrior and left Vukojebina for good.

Tonight, lying in my shack at the edge of these scraggly hills, within earshot of ancient Mostar, where I've spent eighteen hermitic years, I can hear yet again that old music of guns and shelling in the distance. Another war is underway. Why not? Let us irrigate these scarred Balkan lands with more young blood. After all, doesn't the world remember that not far from here a starving peasant with a little pistol and a big dream launched the so-called Great War? Let this region do what it perhaps does best: nurse the next generation of assassins, murderers, and psychopaths.

The old ones are on their way out and being missed already. How they once played, laughed, dreamed, and killed, before transforming themselves into uncles, husbands, memoirists, and honorable retirees. Aleksandar Bundalo was no different. Once a prolific murderer with a seductive smile and an odd habit of pouring large amounts of salt over his victims' naked bodies in their mass graves ("Worms appreciate well-seasoned food," he'd say), Bundalo eventually transformed himself into a quiet neighbor, becoming a docile citizen of this schizophrenic country that emerged out of the carnage of war in which Bundalo had dutifully played his part. Though his name was all but forgotten in the great brouhaha after the war, he had initially risen to be a prodigious killer from a humble and sad household where he'd been taught that his race had come from a special part of heaven. His ancestors, the story went, had been frozen in ice, and when heaven thawed, they descended to earth to exterminate other lowly races. Every morning, his father would force Bundalo and his brothers to chew on chunks of ice to remind them of their ancestral home. On the coldest of days, the old man would force the kids to jump into the frozen Danube and order them to stay under the ice until images of their forefathers appeared and beckoned the boys into the darker depths. Two of Bundalo's brothers yielded to the temptation and never returned to the surface.

Although he survived those wintry excursions to the Danube, little Bundalo was a weakling. He often sought the solitude of the family garden, digging out worms and weeping if he accidentally mutilated one. To harden the boy's soft heart, der Führer (as Bundalo called his father later in life) would regularly beat Bundalo's unclothed body with a wet rope and then force him to eat live small chicks. It worked. His heart became sturdy, his eyes dried. He shed his timidity and grew into a thug. He'd barely had his first shave when his name debuted on public record for theft and attempted rape. Later, when the time came for him to maim, torture, and execute people, he'd often turn to a subordinate, form a fist, and, through clenched teeth, declare: I want to feel and hear their hearts, brains, and bones as they burst, split, and crackle, as one feels the brittle ribs of a live chick crushed in the mouth.

Whether or not he killed my parents is almost an irrelevant question. To take an innocent life is akin to killing multitudes. Whether or not a murderer believes that nonsense about descending from some frozen heaven, he will always take satisfaction in righting some presumed cosmic wrong.

Identifying and investigating murderers like Bundalo utterly consumed me. Mine has been a life of endless waiting, skulking, probing, judging, sitting until constipation ensues or the innards turn against you. During those trying times, I learned to dissect the subtlest behaviors of disguised criminals: how they walk, exchange pleasantries with strangers, the way they scratch their groins in public and spit at the same time. Or the way they sweep the frenum with their tongue in a semicircular clockwise and counterclockwise fashion, collecting some stranded sesame seed; or how they excavate shit from their mouths with used toothpicks from broom bristles; or the way they use water from a fountain as mouthwash, gurgling with upturned faces and then spraying out a cascade of homicidal germs that can yellow and wilt the grass.

Yes, it takes these kinds of shrewd observations to detect revealing behavior patterns among retired and bored murderers. Gradually, though, I noticed how the bodies of former criminals grew bent under the weight of their secrets and sins, bodies that are eventually betrayed by the eyes, those evil, darting eyes, full of criminal alertness, scanning the space for half-forgotten war ghosts that are sure to show up and seek retribution.

In their final years, these criminals become timid and carry themselves with that typical docility and resignation of the elderly, their mouths oscillating because toxic anger is brewing inside them, or maybe they enjoy grating their toothless gums. The retired killers go for walks to the park on summer afternoons and watch kids play, return a stray ball with a cripple's kick and a smile, pick up trash dropped by degenerate teenagers, clasp hands behind their backs and nod in fake contemplation while looking at the sky, making small talk with random strangers, *Beautiful day, isn't it?*

Eventually they lose their keen sense of vigilance.

In the dusty little plaza at the center of Vukojebina, a band of dying oldsters would, in warm weather, crawl beneath the centenarian oak and sit there gawking at a world long grown hostile to them. You could see their arthritic hands vibrating on their cane handles, their mouths perpetually masticating something, like cows in the shade. Sometimes these dotards played chess, and when they laughed, it was hard to tell if they were gasping for breath or trying to imitate a pack of cackling hyenas. It was to this plaza that Bundalo came daily to flee from his dismal abode and kill a few hours.

"Here comes Zoran," one of the octogenarians would bark, his eyes bereft of any light. Zoran Kovaći. Just another man with a sad past who'd not only failed to make something of his career as "a man of letters" but had also lost most of his family in the war. I'd sit a few feet away from this crowd of scarecrows and observe him approach the plaza. He watched his step with the carefulness and dread of someone walking through a minefield, clutching a newspaper under his arm, then dropped a few coins in my bucket before greeting the other seniles by touching the front of his beret and bowing slightly. Day after day, he observed this ritual, feeding my bucket, walking away with a pitiful smile, touching his beret, bowing.

I thought he found my appearance repulsive, but one day he came over, and we began to chat. Who knows what mysterious impulse made him deviate from his routine, but there he was, the infernal Bundalo posing as Zoran Kovaći, having a conversation with me! And who was I? A homeless wretch with a bronze, lice-infested beard who sometimes imagined himself a reincarnated Diogenes waiting for Alexander the Great to show up and beg for a scrap of wisdom, whereupon I'd ask the general to move aside because he was blocking the sun.

What is this life but an accumulation of tiny mysteries amounting to nothing more than a series of profound banalities: the wrong place, the misjudged time, a squint, a turned corner, a bloated cloud. For many silence-haunted nights in my lowly shack, I thought about that encounter and wondered why the great criminal had spoken so casually, so freely with me: what demon had propelled him to make that fateful stop, open himself up and reveal things that would convince me to seal his fate a mere forty-eight hours later in a spasm of violence I'd been nursing inside me for many agonizing years. I don't know the answer, but perhaps he was intrigued by the quotation I'd scribbled on a piece of cardboard: "His name alone is sufficient to hang him." I laughed and—while feeling a bit self-conscious that my body odor might offend him—slurred, lied, oh, hah, ho, heh, no, dear sir, the saying is not mine, someone smarter than me said this.

He talked and talked, speedily descending into the labyrinth of his manufactured past, his kingdom of lies—and as I observed him with awe, I swear I saw a halo suspended above his head that I took to be the dregs of his soul abandoning him forever. Even today I cringe when I think of that moment. Souls abandoning the bodies of criminals.

He recalled how in his youth he'd loved a book on Diogenes where he learned how the destitute philosopher wanted to be treated as a dog, an animal he had respect for and regarded as more honest than men of his times. Anyway, Bundalo said, laughing nervously while looking at the sign. He sat next to me on a plastic crate and launched into a rambling tale by turns boring and sentimental that I half listened to as my mind filed it under Inconsequential Criminal Palaver.

He had a poignant way of talking, adorning his reminiscences with brief lost-in-thought pauses, followed by that wistful middle-distance gaze I detest so much. Naturally, he had been forced to leave his hometown when war destroyed everything—yes, yes, his family perished, his ancestors' village was burned, refugees, hunger, fear, etcetera. Too many awful memories. He found Vukojebina friendly and inviting, he said, especially after his wife committed suicide, the woman who had been a dutiful spouse, the love of his life. She'd been depressed about their childless marriage, Bundalo rambled on, even though, of course, he never blamed her for her "damaged womb," as he delicately put it. What can a man do in this predicament (and here again the pause, the angled gaze with the subtle headshake), he asked, and reflected: return his wife to her place of origin or throw her out just because she malfunctioned through no fault of her own? Of course not. He understood and said so many times. No big deal, he told her. Love is love, even when spent on damaged goods. Alas, the guilt was too much for her; the guilt of wasting a good man's life, standing in his way to family happiness. And so, in her suicide note, she begged Bundalo (aka Kovaći) to get on with his life, find another woman, and have the family that she could never give him.

Oh, such a sad, moving story, no doubt about it, but one that I now remember not because it was fictitious but because it took him so long to finish while I struggled with an intense need to piss, and I knew that if I excused myself, I might miss a clue that would become an important piece of evidence against him. But besides this fabricated tale of his depressed wife, what offended me most was his driveling lies about being deported, his family perishing in the hell of some furnace or shoved alive into mass graves in the gray fields of this or that awful country. As my impounded bladder neared the bursting point—incontinence being a curse of my paternal line— the great murderer kept speaking about how, after all these years, he still struggled with nightmares, and the memory of his "exterminated parents" was unbearable. He seldom talked about it, he added, and didn't understand what got into him during that chat with me.

Ah, such audacity to purloin a story like this from one too many of his victims! That was an unforgivable insult. As if that scum of a killer knew what it means to be chased out of your home on a spring day, leaving behind warm food on the table, the chicken soup, the bread that your mother had baked that morning, the mother who would never bake again.

Simmering with anger and convinced that this soft-speaking swindler was none other than Aleksandar Bundalo, I followed him two days later along a trash-strewn street. I stayed a safe distance away and was annoyed each time he stopped, clasping his hands behind his back, like those boring men of a certain age in this country who scoff at teenagers and pollute the road with their inexhaustible stocks of phlegm, just as they pollute the wombs of their fine women with their venal seed, churning out little thugs who become big thugs and start wars. He would walk a few more steps, then stop again to watch a group of skinny children chase a football up and down a trampled field. To my dismay, he took his time, looking at those dirty children, shaking his head—whether with amusement or sadness, I couldn't tell. Soon, he left the kids and got distracted by a magpie pecking at something on the road. And then in a typical behavior of an enervated and retired murderer, he picked up a rock and threw it at the bird.

Zoran Kovaći. I still wonder why he picked that name as he scrambled for an exit from his past. How does a criminal choose a new identity? Did someone start a specialized trade after the war, offering a catalogue of fake names to retired criminals who wanted to make a fresh start amid the traumatized rabble? How did Bundalo decide on "Zoran Kovaći," that rustic-sounding Slavic name that suggests blacksmith ancestry, an heir to a great line of nobodies. Did Bundalo wish to finally be just another nobody? I don't know, but these great butchers are much like those old predatory beasts that, when their day of reckoning comes, having wreaked havoc on their habitats, slip into their dens and hide away to die. Death finally appears at the door and, like an ancient man of the steppes guiding his last lamb into the slaughterhouse, shows these murderers how the life of a giant can shrink to the size of a field mouse that ceased breathing in the humiliating loneliness of a summer afternoon.

At some point, cloaked in their fake identities, their best criminal days behind, the mass murderers sit in swampy silence and take stock of their murky histories. The forgotten genocidal cutthroats begin to shrink in their dens, disgusted that they must hide but dreaming of parades and throngs of mourners. That is how they depart, unless someone like me steps in and prevents so romantic a passing.

The man of mystery finally gave up trying to kill the magpie and continued up the road toward his home. He lived in a neighborhood called the Slope, a chaotic and dangerous slum teeming with destitute squatters, illegals, hooligans, mud-caked peasants and whatnot. The narrow alleys stank to heaven. Farther up, the Slope became steep, and houses and huts yielded to a wilderness of stunted pines and scree where nature seemed bewildered by the tenacity of squatters determined to clear the mountain with their picks and saws. One did not need an active imagination, just a little patience, to wait for a day when a beautiful landslide of crumbling rock would joyfully glide down and devour those human goats and roll back the boundaries of the neighborhood to where the streets were named after martyred thugs and so-called war veterans.

I had visited the Slope a dozen times, walked up and down its violent roads, horrified by the squalor and filth; yet I was moved by the delicate light of the evening and the sounds from the town below. But never was I more struck with an intense feeling of both sadness and anticipation than on the day I followed Bundalo and waited for him to settle inside his lonely home. After years of self-doubt and despair, here I was on the cusp of delivering one of the century's greatest acts of justice. And yet there was no one to witness it, a simple fact that saddened me, even though deep down I've always believed in justice delivered without fanfare and pomp. The monsters must be put away in the shadow and silence of our own egos.

I found a secluded spot in which to pass my vigil, lit a cigarette, and stroked my bronze beard. Carefully, out of its murky depths I pulled a huge louse and set it in my palm; it was a parasite of enormous proportions, scrambling madly in the dim light of the evening. I placed the tiny beast on the surface of a rock and watched it try to get its bearings in that alien landscape.

It's strange how I've always rejoiced in such simple pleasures as lying on my back, a blade of grass or cigarette in my mouth, delousing myself, lifting these parasites out of my body and tossing them into an unforgiving world. Talk about refugees. Here's a case of pathetic creatures deprived of their homeland, with its lush blood and filth, and deported to the surface of a barren rock, lost in mindless panic. It's a heartrending story.

I felt good, too, when I saw Vukojebina sink into the night, its lights illuminating the smog—an image that returned me to the Salonika of my childhood and those dreamy evenings on the veranda when I'd stand and gaze out, picking my nose, just before mother would slap my hand, shouting Stop that disgusting habit!

The lights in the Slope started going out, but the neighborhood was still stirring, as though its disoriented residents were struggling to find their sleeping quarters in their huts—dwellings so ramshackle and ridiculous they looked from a distance more like children's drawings than physical objects.

From where I stood on that crooked rocky spot, miraculously spared from the scourge of that squatting architecture, I could see Bundalo's home a few streets below. A dim light burned in his window. I imagined him with an adventure novel in his hands, reading himself to sleep, or maybe he was adding more words to a memoir already buckling under the weight of calamitous history. I waited for another hour, as the clamor of Bundalo's invisible neighbors died down, then walked toward his house. The closer I got, the more determined I grew; bloodlust rose to my throat.

After the many houses I'd broken into to attack murderers in their dens, the business had become routine and even boring, especially when I had to deal with a criminal who cravenly begged for his life. The dim light I'd seen earlier in Bundalo's window was still burning, but I couldn't see much inside through the tightly closed blinds. I heard a faint melody, which sounded like a classical tune or something of the sort. I grew impatient standing by the window and knocked on the front door. A few seconds later, the light in the hallway came on. Then, after a protracted moment, a fumbling Bundalo rattled his keys; even that little gesture of clumsiness offended me. Then the door opened, and the man froze like he'd seen his Führer brandishing a wet rope. I shoved him inside, grabbed his keys, and locked the door behind me with a few quick moves. He said something like, I'll give you food, as much as you want, please don't hurt me. Then, with the same iron bar that had become my choice of weapon on these missions, I struck him a few times, until the bones of his hands and arms cracked, and blood spurted from his mouth. I usually did this part with lightning speed so I wouldn't have to endure pathetic pleas. As usually happened, my assault took away his voice, and he crumpled to the floor.

He dragged himself into the living room with book-lined walls. I stood there for a second and marveled at the library of this great scholar who was now leaning against an armchair and howling with pain, horrified at the sight of his detached fingers clinging to his hand by the skin. I pulled up a chair and sat before the great criminal. I laid my iron bar down, pulled out my old knife, and stabbed the parquet floor, leaving the blade upright and quivering, then busied myself lighting a cigarette.

In such moments, the victim remains remarkably present with his senses, despite the trauma, shock, and pain inflicted on him. The victim says *please* and *thank you* as he tries to figure out what is happening to him, why he's alone on this night in front of a stinking, deranged attacker. So many whys and hows must go through his head in those final moments. In a few cases, the victim tries in desperation to reach for a weapon or my knife to counterattack, only to spoil the long-awaited moment for a little dialogue between two men on the opposite ends of justice.

With Bundalo, though, it was different. Before I could ask him any questions, the man fainted and slumped to the floor. At first I thought this was going to be another sad attempt to counterattack, so I politely ordered him to sit up, but he didn't move even after I kicked him. More bewildered than vexed by this temporary setback, I sat and watched his unmoving body. The melody that I'd heard from outside had now stopped, and the stillness unsettled me. My ears rang with the sound of the cracked bones, which is difficult to unhear. Like an impatient halfwit, I didn't quite know what to do with him, so I poured some cold water over his body, returning him to a miserable consciousness.

Owing to his senility, he appeared befuddled and disoriented, asking me what had happened and who I was. Then he remembered his terrible pain. He groaned, wobbled, and threw up. I realized the great murderer was in no position to retaliate; his killer instinct had deserted him. I told him I knew his real name was Aleksandar Bundalo and his murderous past had finally caught up with him, and so on and so forth.

He shook his head vigorously as tears rolled down and blended with the blood oozing from his nose; his words came out garbled and incoherent. For the love of God, he said, I am not that person, I am Zoran Kovaći, please see my ID and my passport and my bills, and my photos with my long-dead wife, and call anybody to verify my identity.

Yes, I know, I said. You told me about your—how did you put it, "malfunctioning wife," or did I misremember that? Anyway, I went on, I already heard all of that. You thought I was just a homeless wretch shedding a tear for your poor woman—yes, yes, everybody thinks you're that man with the boring name, mild-mannered, a beret-wearing nobody who still clings to the false hope that posterity will one day recognize his great artistic talent. I must admit that you've been quite good at fooling people.

I said that I'd spent years investigating him because the machinery of justice always fails to catch scum like him. Scum, who threw me on that train that smelled of cow shit, filled to the brim with screaming people, that drafty car where, by a miracle, I found my parents, who had been dragged out from our home earlier.

Why didn't you stay hidden in the attic, my poor baby?

I did, Mother, I did, but someone alerted the soldiers, and they found me. They sat me down at our dinner table, Mother, seemed at ease, like it was their home. They made me taste your leek—or was it chicken soup? —which was still warm. Delicious, they said, delicious!

Who told them? My father demanded, squeezing my head in his hands like he wanted to crush my skull.

I don't know, Father, I don't know.

It didn't matter, my dear criminal, it hardly mattered what my old man said. He was no longer the father who once carried me on his shoulders on the cobbled streets of Salonika. He had gone mad. God, what agony it is to witness your father go mad with fear! You will never be able to unsee that face, you'll never grasp—but wait, maybe you can relate, I said to Bundalo. Recall when your own mad Führer made you chew ice, or whipped your naked body with a wet rope when he discovered you crying over some massacred worms.

Bundalo shook his head, his gray stubble smeared in blood and vomit. He managed to say, I am so sorry for what happened to you. I too lost.

Stop it, I snapped at him.

It was then that he must have realized he had no chance against a wounded animal like me, no chance whatsoever, even if, by some remote possibility, he was not Aleksandar Bundalo, as he desperately tried to convince me. The most dangerous man in the world is one who's been humiliated.

Please, please, he begged, shaking his head. Aleksandar Bundalo is not, was never a real person. If I am guilty of anything, he went on, it's to have created that character in a story I wrote for a magazine many years ago. You must have read that fiction and confused Bundalo with a real person. I have evidence, he continued. The original manuscript is in that top drawer. Please go see …

At this point I gave him a swift blow that forced him to stop talking. His eyes rolled, and he fell to the floor again, unconscious. The loud silence returned. The ringing in my ears got louder; the train memory always brought out the worst in me. While he was unconscious, I fetched the manuscript in which he claimed to have "created" Aleksandar Bundalo, about whom I'd supposedly been mistaken all these years.

Once again, I must admit that the great impostor was more creative than I had imagined. He went around fooling people, telling them Aleksandar Bundalo was just a figment of his imagination. I began to think that in addition to his day job as a mass murderer, Bundalo had always been a great storyteller. Except he didn't imagine that a justice warrior like me would read between the lines of his "fiction" and discover the true identity of this giant fraud with his long trail of lies. That's what a good reader does: he reads between the lines of fiction and discovers truth hiding in plain sight.

At least that's what I thought that evening when Bundalo's broken body lay motionless on the floor in a pool of blood. He regained consciousness and fainted again, woke, fainted, woke, threw up. This ping-pong between oblivion and consciousness lasted until I ended it all with my signature finish: two deadly blows on each side of the head, listening for that crack in his skull, the same way he had savored imagining his victims' hearts exploding.

Mission accomplished, the justice warrior in me celebrated with a glass of *rakia*, or maybe half a dozen, gathered my things—my iron bar, my knife, the food, the manuscript—then stuffed them into my bag and stepped outside, leaving the rest of the house as

I'd found it. Almost immediately, I felt hungry. Maybe the brandy had aroused my appetite, or maybe it was the two hours I'd spent playing cat-and-mouse with him. I stepped back inside and fetched some bread—why let it go to waste? —took another look at Bundalo, who was soundly dead, snuck that half a bottle of *rakia* under my arm, and headed out. It was a lovely night, with crisp air, stars and all, and I could not bring myself to dwell any longer on the events of that evening.

The next morning, I woke up with a sour stomach and found myself on the steps of a church. A shoe was prodding my side. Had I been caught? Then I saw and heard the cadaverous physiognomy and dry voice of a black-robed priest who smelled of burned butter saying something about how God doesn't like to see his house desecrated by filthy drunkards. I propped myself on my elbows and shook my head, saying something about Jesus being homeless too. The priest looked at me like I was an insect. I could not tell whether it was my blasphemy or my cheese-and-*rakia* breath that made him twist his face into disgusting folds. I rose and skulked away, leaving behind the empty bottle of *rakia*, which he kicked down the steps.

In the days that followed, I scanned the newspapers, hoping to spot a headline announcing Bundalo's deserved end, but I couldn't find anybody who had heard anything about the passing of the great criminal. I checked the papers every day. Nothing but page after page of vulgar journalism. I read articles about flying cars of the future, a successful campaign to impound stray dogs, a distant war that had turned into a cataclysmic event, and on and on, bored reporters amassing huge amounts of garbage, spilling all that ink. No major paper bothered to mention that justice had finally been visited upon the great murderer. I was about to give up, when, flipping halfheartedly through *Goontimes*, an offensive tabloid specializing in news about all kinds of human scum, I came across a squib about Bundalo sandwiched between stories about a politician fornicating with a goat, the rape of a ninety-year-old woman by two teenagers, and the plight of a transsexual. The headline read, "Little-Known Writer Found Dead at Home in Slope." Such a pedantic headline. Accompanying the report was a photo of two white-robed men carrying a putrescent black something. The reporter noted, "Not much is known about Zoran Kovaći, a writer of sorts who apparently never found much success with his craft." The reporter had heard, but could not confirm, that Kovaći once headed up an association appropriately called "The Obscurists: Architects of Mystery," a small group of writers snubbed and ignored by society. I laughed out loud reading this nonsense. Police said that Kovaći must have died many weeks ago, as his body had "collapsed on itself." What writing! One officer stated, "There was not much left of him except a pile of squirming maggots we had to shovel into a bucket." It appears to have been "a lonely death," the reporter surmised before spending two paragraphs citing some ridiculous statistics about the increase of "lonely deaths."

As for the cause of death, the article said it was imponderable. *Imponderable?* I shouted, scaring off a frail woman waiting for the bus. What the fuck does imponderable mean? On the same page, next to the bungled Kovaći announcement, was a piece headed "Phallic News," about a new penis-enhancement device. In the photo, the machine looked like a medieval torture tube used to crush human fingers, and yet apparently men afflicted with tiny penises were sticking their things into the tube, including the president of the country, a man long tormented by his critics not for his political failures but for his stunted dick. The article said the president was rumored to be using the device in a desperate effort to prove to the nation that, contrary to widespread belief, nature had generously endowed him. His rivals were circulating posters that purported to show the president searching fruitlessly for his miniscule organ between his legs. One copy made it to Parliament and was briefly displayed on a large easel while politicians debated what to do about a drought in the south, which had brought large swathes of peasantry to near-famine conditions. The resolution under consideration would have sent the national army to quell what some politicians called "starving rebels," though in the newspaper photos the "rebels" could barely raise their half-clenched fists. When the humiliating image of the president was put on view, the chamber roared with laughter—seconds before an imbecilic presidential underling stepped up and removed the poster and gave a brief unctuous speech shaming the opposition for wasting time on such slander at a moment of national crisis.

I must admit that, furious as I was at not finding any serious news about Bundalo, this amusing article dampened my rage. I'd known before that the president, a parvenu whose biggest achievement was to have been born rich, was the butt of many jokes, but I'd been unaware that his small dick had consumed the nation to this degree. I'd given up on newspapers, but at some point I had read a notorious book by a woman who'd been romantically involved with the president. I don't recall much about the exposé, but certain details remain etched in the memory of everyone in this country. The woman had written in brutal detail about how the president was depressed and even suicidal because of his small penis, which "when erect," she wrote memorably, "looked like a feisty teat on a heifer's udder" (she had grown up on a farm) but when flaccid "was no more than a pointy, pink wart."

During her multination book tour, the president's ex-lover was asked to describe an actual sexual act with the president. With characteristic flair and a mischievous smile, she'd replied, "I had an adequate experience with the president's fingers, OK?" Those present in the room laughed until tears rolled down their faces. The tour turned tragic, however, when the woman died in a car crash on the Amalfi Coast. No one believed her death was an accident. The Italians launched an investigation that concluded the death was an accident. But Italian justice is much like the existence of a benevolent god: people desperately want to see proof of it, but it remains elusive. No one believed in the findings of the first investigation, so an investigation into that investigation was launched, but then global scandals intervened. Richard Nixon in America resigned, oil prices and unemployment skyrocketed, and peasants brought their pitchforks and their smells to the capital. Everyone forgot the flamboyant woman who met her end along that storied coastline. Indifferent though I was to the national political twaddle or the gyrations of the world economy, our president's genital crisis had fascinated me, but after his paramour died I lost interest in any news that didn't help me find retired criminals.

And so I stayed away from things that passed for news in this nation of losers. Deep down I believe I've always been an unsung hero who went about quietly working on behalf of forgotten victims of war in a society that had long ago abdicated its moral responsibility. But though it might be too late for me to get the recognition I deserve while alive, one day this ungrateful country will learn about my sacred mission and work. And when these losers discover the truth, they will honor my legacy the only way the know: erecting a cenotaph to me in a trash-strewn city park beneath a large tree where garbage-eating crows or hideous starlings will congregate and shit on my head and shoulders.

For abuse I have known since the day I escaped from the train that carried my parents to an unknown end. Three days in that miserable boxcar, crammed with the sick and dying, including the man inside who succumbed to madness and started laughing as the train stopped near a ghost village. To cut the lunatic's laughter short, the soldiers shot him and threw him down the embankment, inside a fenced stubble field where three cows lunged for the corpse. Such fantastic lies we're fed about these meek and haunted bovines grazing their innocent lives away in peaceful pastures. Lies. Lies. Lies. Nothing can erase from my memory the sight of those herbivorous monsters tearing the flesh of that laughing man.

Small as I was, though, I learned that day it wasn't just cows that will eat human flesh. I learned that men will soon eat one another.

That sudden realization propelled my legs when, two days later, the train stopped, so the soldiers could once again "dump the dead." It was early afternoon, bright sun outside the boxcar, stultifying heat inside. The adults had stopped moaning but lethargically bobbed their heads; the children were too stunned to whine, the babies too weak to cry. Occasionally the corpse-dropping ritual provided an opportunity for brave souls who still had some strength to jump off and run for the hills.

Go, son, go, my father whispered in my ear.

Yes, for the love of God, Mother rasped. Run, my baby, hide yourself—no wait, let me kiss those eyes one more time.

I jumped off. Dear God, I did. A few others behind me also took the chance and followed. Almost immediately the soldiers fired. I heard howling and screaming. I ran like a cheetah. I didn't want to be eaten. Bullets flew past me, but I kept running over the fields and hedges my father had seen through the slit in the boxcar door, until bullets no longer whistled through the air—God, how fast I ran, away from the eaters of men, whether cows or maggots or other men. I ran all the way to the hills, then stopped and turned to see the train in the distance, which was now crawling again, like a gigantic worm, and I knew I had been faster than a bullet. I also knew with unequivocal certainty that I would never slurp mother's soup again.

As weeks passed without any serious journalist reporting on the death of Bundalo, I took matters into my own hands. I wrote an anonymous letter to the editors of all the leading newspapers in Vukojebina, chiding and shaming them for not knowing anything about the "writer of sorts."

Shame on you for betraying your duty to inform the public. Shame on your Latin mottos inscribed in gothic on your mastheads, your calligraphic bullshit, your pompous headlines, shame on your typewriters, shame on your printing presses. One of the greatest criminals of the century, an impostor who for thirty years assumed the cloak of a humble writer with a blacksmith name, lived and thrived among your children and collected his pension like a sweet old grandpa. What kind of news organization can't dispatch a half-decent reporter with a conscience to investigate who Zoran Kovaći really was?

I signed the letter, Champion for the Voiceless Victims of War.

Whether out of curiosity or because I reminded them of their gross incompetence and dereliction of duty, someone took my letter seriously and investigated the matter. Two weeks later, on the kind of morning that is neither cold nor warm, neither bright nor dark, a morning with an oppressive air and heavy, sagging skies, the clouds so low and dismal you imagine the gods up there want to suck your balls, I picked up the *Zema*, the country's most respected daily news-paper, which everyone called the gold standard for impartial report-ing. One glance and it looked like finally my victim had received the coverage he deserved. Two full pages of material about his life, his hometown, his family, his friends, his drinking habits, his career, and finally his demise. It was all there, meticulously researched and gracefully woven into a vivid portrait of his life, in as much as a man's life can fit onto the pages of a daily newspaper. An impressive investigation, I thought.

The reporter had even found a few of those corny fading-along-the-edges black-and-white photographs of the man's family and his school days. Picture the little up-and-coming criminal as no more than six or seven; he is neatly dressed and standing erect as an ad-olescent cock beside a stiff-looking, stern father with a gaze already turned to the fast-approaching irrelevant stage of his life. To their left materializes a weathered-faced woman with her daughter and younger son. They all look like they'd put on their best rags and fixed their hair for the family picture. In another such memento, our mysterious protagonist stands in a row of schoolboys wearing uniforms. The picture had been poorly preserved, and little can be discerned beyond a strip of black sky above their dirty heads. The final photograph shows the man in his prime with a pencil behind his ear, a cigarette in his hand, looking casually at the camera. The photographer has caught our man in a moment of repose or self-doubt. How poignant, I thought. Our pictured hero wears a rugged handsomeness on his creased face, a slightly receding hairline and a roughness about him that attracts certain women and repels others. He looks a bit like that Monsieur Camus, whose book I came across once, read but didn't quite like, as it reminded me of my mother in her worst moods.

The text of the article, infused with an elegiac tone, traced the life of a man who made a little stirring, a man who'd tried to leave a small mark on the road he'd traveled, but in the end, "his was a largely unremarkable existence," the author concluded, as if existences must be remarkable to mean something. An unknown writer among an ignorant mob. Nothing new here. Still, the narrative was moving and impressive in scope. Except that not one line of this lovely prose was about Aleksandar Bundalo. The life and the person whose remains were found as—to use that memorable phrase from the officer—"a pile of squirming maggots" and buried in a bucket was Zoran Kovaći and only Zoran Kovaći. The damned journalist had obviously set out to discredit the person who had written that angry letter.

For the rest of the *Zema's* readers, the story might have sounded like a puzzle, an annoying distraction from the trashier news and gossip they had come to expect from journalism in this country. Maybe some readers found the article poignant, but seriously, why go to these lengths and tell such a remarkable story about a completely unremarkable man. I imagined that most of the reactions the editor received sounded something like this:

Salutations, Editor! I just read the longest story about some dead writer who pretended that his hobby was his job, and guess where I found it: IN YOUR NEWSPAPER. Outrageous! What the hell happened to the honest business of reporting news that affects our lives? Stories about that terrible famine? Those people with pitchforks. (By the way, aren't those agricultural tools supposed to be considered deadly weapons when displayed like that in public?) Anyway! Those dirty dungarees, those

*gaping mouths with no teeth? God save us. Is that all over yet? How
about some news about that new device? OK, I know some aggressive
prudes are disgusted with it, but not me. And believe me, I speak for,
I don't know, most people. Did it work for our president's thing? And
finally, dear editor, who the fuck is/was Zoran Kovaći?*

Sincerely, Confused Citizen.

And here's a letter that actually got printed:

Dearest Editor,

*I was moved to tears reading about Zoran Kovaći. Not for the ac-
tual person though. As you already know, this country is tired of hearing
about sad, pitiful, and traumatized lives. No one is impressed anymore
with war stories or tales of people growing mad with poverty or dying
alone. No. That aspect of the article hardly impressed me. What made
me weep was the portrayal of the miserable fate of writers in this country.
For those who pick up the pen and delude themselves into believing they
are doing something worthy of respect.*

*Tell me, dear editor, what do you feel—deep in your soul—when
you walk into a library and see row upon row of dead books bursting not
just with stories but also with wasted fortunes, canceled weekends, lost
years, soiled existences? What do you think, dear editor, when you con-
template the utter desolation of such souls? Do you ever go to the library,
my dear editor? Do you? For—if? —you do, you might stumble upon my
own soul trapped in the ten books I wrote over fifty years. Ten books, fifty
years, a vulgar profusion of 1.5 million words that probed for … what?*

*When I was a boy, my dear editor, I thought that writers could cheat
death. I really thought they were immortal. They were a unique species
whose mortality I could never conceive. How could I? How could such
people with all that volcanic life in them, with their infinite imagina-
tions multiplying, with the universe crashing inside their hearts—how
could they one day simply vanish, like a squirrel or the memories of
a snowfall in a yesteryear? Imagine my agony, deary, imagine how I
felt when I finally learned the truth that these fuckers are exactly like*

squirrels or ferrets or raccoons that drop lifeless by the road on a mean winter's day. Ah, Lord! The magic of literature died within me right there and then. Novelists, poets, playwrights, they were no saints. Mere ferrets, curs, roadkill. No revelation has been more devastating for me than the notion of writing as a delusion under whose spell we fall in a pathetic quest for immortality, only to discover at the eleventh hour that we, too, meet the dust.

Yes, dear editor, I am that writer with a fatally wounded ego who, even after his awful revelation, continues bleeding onto his pages, which he huddles over during endless nights and interminable days. What is this disease, dear editor, for which we still haven't found a cure? How many Zoran Kovaćis are out there who will likewise end up in a bucket?

But let me stop before I drown in an acid sea of self-pity and start telling you that ha ha ha all I really want for my 80th birthday next week is to have an epic orgasm that will catapult me back to those blissful days and nights of youth filled with rivers of cum, sweat, cascades of madness—all those brief eternities before I began licking my wounds with words. How can I, my dear deary, how can I return to those intoxicating nights when my erections forced me awake as despair does now, return to those moments and drool at the sight of a young and unruly nipple pushing against a threadbare blouse, salivate like a Pavlovian dog, use my hand to guide a young and trembling waist through an evening dance or squeeze a lithe breast under the sheets—this hand, this bony paw, which now measures the dwindling circumference of my dying cock, limp as a wet rag, unable to summon a last drop of life but only a gasp of air like a dry spigot—here in this room with my cock and my clock, tick-tock, tick-tock, beside a window with half-drawn blinds, where a crow stares at me from a tree branch, waiting to pounce on this diseased, fallen phallus, worn out by an insistent hand and disgraced by a lifetime of cruel devotion to books. FUCKING BOOKS!
Sincerely, Someone Who Gave up Living for Writing

This last letter, inconsequential and irrelevant (though funny, I must admit), was published in its entirety. The editors didn't even bother to edit out any of the vulgarities.

I passed two days in a state of disbelief. I kept reading and re-reading the article about Kovaći for any evidence that the reporter, who, I discovered, enjoyed the respect of her colleagues, had acquitted herself incompetently. I found nothing. Yet I still felt that she was wrong. I racked my brains for ways to discredit her research and disprove her assertions. The more I pondered how to undercut the integrity of her story, the more I found myself trying to remember how I had deduced that Zoran Kovaći was an impostor.

Until then, it had never occurred to me to question my investigative methodology. What had I seen in Zoran Kovaći that convinced me he was Aleksandar Bundalo? The voices inside my head became more hostile. I rummaged through my cart, searching in vain for the manuscript I'd taken from Kovaći's house. I went to the library, where I learned that, because the *Zema* article had ignited interest in Zoran Kovaći, the head librarian had exhumed their copy of Kovaći's short-story collection. Alas, it was checked out. Repelled by my appearance but obligated to help me, the head librarian promised to reserve the book for me, then asked for my phone number. After an awkward pause, uncomfortable coughing and nose puckering, the librarian suggested I check back again in two weeks.

In the days while I waited for the book, I thought about my mission over the years. How many war criminals had I uncovered? Two? Three? No, the exact number was nine. Nine monsters who'd changed their identities had eventually succumbed to my justice. I'd assumed no one would ever miss these despicables, but for the last fifteen years, the government had been searching for "a notorious serial killer." After a two-year hiatus in which no murders occurred, the *Zema* piece on Kovaći got everyone talking about the cold case again. In a follow-up article, the *Zema* reporter speculated about the "elusive monster" who evidently took "sadistic pleasure" in exterminating old people. All kinds of phrases and epithets like these were flying around in newspapers. Some of them I found amusing. Like "compassionate murderer," which at first I took to mean that I was a compassionate person, but then the reporter elaborated on his theory, asserting that the killer was "liberating old people from their decrepit physiques and humiliated egos."

This interpretation annoyed me because I couldn't care less about the elderly or their decrepit physiques and humiliated egos. I've never been fond of old people, and if anything terrifies me, it is that I might last as long as my grandfather, whom I loathed for always poking me with the tip of his cane. I shall never forget what happened one afternoon while I was pushing my toy freight train along its circle of track, making train noises, choo, choo, chugga, chugga, choo, never imagining a train would eventually figure so horribly in my life. Just as the locomotive was pulling its cars near my grandfather's armchair, he roused himself from his stupor and pressed his cane against my neck.

I'd forgotten that he was still alive—he always looked like those ancient pines that stop living but still stand.

"Lemme tell you something, boy," he drooled. "In the other life, when we appear before God's tribunal, we won't be able to tell lies like we do on earth. Our body parts will turn against us and betray our souls. Your hand will confess to the times you stole something, your leg will speak of sinful journeys, your eye will denounce your lustful stares, your ear will recount those times when you eaves-dropped. Even your"—and here he pointed with his cane to my genitals—"weeny peeny will tell of sticking its head in the wrong or-ifices. Lead a clean life, boy, or you will never enter God's kingdom."

Because that centenarian zombie with his drivel had filled me with dread, I've always harbored a grudge against the elderly. I could hardly bring myself to help when I happened to see an old lady strug-gle to stand up after having slipped on the ice or needing an arm to lean on to navigate a flight of stairs. At worst, I had a persistent urge to verbally humiliate or harm them. Once I pulled my grandfather's chair out from behind him as he was about to sit down, then hid be-hind a curtain. I hoped he'd fall and break his neck. Even as a child I felt the throb of justice pulsating inside me against that ancient menace. He fell hard on his ass but to my disappointment broke nothing.

I fantasized about other ways I might get rid of him, but because his existence was confined to three rooms on the ground floor, my means were limited. And then, one day, Salonika was finally relieved when he failed to wake up from his stupor. At first, we all thought that he'd broken the record for not moving while sitting in his armchair, but he'd simply stopped breathing. We left him there all day and all night long, and when in the morning my father checked on him, his body was stiff as a rock. The zombie had finally gone cold. Naturally, his death was a joyful event for me, and the rest of my family likewise shed no tears. My father and my uncle carried him outside and buried him hastily. But I still thought that he might be alive somewhere and would return one day to poke me with his cane.

Seeing that Bundalo's death, almost a year later, wasn't seen for what it was, I got tired of the journalistic blather about the elusive serial killer and made plans to leave Vukojebina. But before I abandoned the town, a place that had never truly adopted me, I spent a few days walking around, reflecting, second-guessing every major decision I'd made in my life. Perhaps. Perhaps. Perhaps. A squandered youth had turned into a series of perhapses and lapses.

One day I passed by the boarding school where I'd been taken in 1943, shortly after I was collected from the streets as "yet another Jewish foundling." The mere sight of the building still tormented me after so many years.

Here they made me put aside my mother's tongue and instructed me in a new language. The teacher, a certain Miss Bubka, was a woman of gigantic proportions and small doses of patience. At the tiniest classroom disruption, she'd smack kids or throw stuff at them with the same zeal I throw my shoes at promenading rats in my shack. But to me she was mysteriously nice. I was her "little Jewish puppy." Often she would retrieve a half-melted bonbon from her bosom and hand it to me, which I furtively sniffed a long while before putting in my mouth. The sugar coating of those memorable sweets nurtured all kinds of debauchery and illicit musings about Miss Bubka and her breasts. She was a perceptive woman, read my mind and detected my secret desires. One day when I was in third grade, she told me we needed to have a "quick chat," then led me into her "office," a large, smelly custodian's closet at the end of a corridor. At first, I was terrified. Was I in trouble? Would Miss Bubka strike me with her ruler? But her voice was soothing, echoing through a moist darkness tempered by the soft glow of a corner lamp. I got ready to receive another bonbon, but she had other things in mind. She invited me to sit on her copious lap and immediately proceeded to whisper with a melodic voice that I still hear in my torturing dreams. This is the mother I never had, I thought, as she cocooned me in her warm embrace, easing my head against her enchanted breasts, the wonders that produced all those bonbons.

Oh, my little *jevrejski* puppy, she half-sang to me, taking my hand and guiding it under her blouse. Her soft, slippery hand meanwhile slid under my pants, like a magic snake, and I quaked and burst into flames, an eruption that was to last for weeks, months, supplanted only by another session in the closet, where my crotch received a lengthy tongue treatment. She squealed, My little *jevrejski* love, and then she suckled me, filling my mouth with an auburn nipple as big as a plum. My dirty *jevrejski* magician, who taught you these tricks? My mouth, my jaws, my mother, my maws, my legs, darkness, light, night. Sickness arrested my senses. Mysterious, otherworldly. I couldn't tell what was happening to me. Only later did it dawn on me that I had been struck hard by hallucinatory love, a fever of such passion that it almost killed me. For weeks I was confined in my room in the orphanage, looked after by a mean nurse with bad breath. For weeks I went without my heavy-breasted love, who in the meantime gave bonbons to another student, a blue-eyed turd whom I saw, through the haze of my convalescence, walking out of the closet with bowed legs, and I was gratified to know that I was not the only boy who wetted himself in her embrace. I ambushed that pest behind the school building and left him gasping for breath. This is what you get when you take someone's girlfriend, I told him.

Ah, Miss Bubka, Miss Bubka. My muse, my tormentor, my true and only love. Try as I might, I've never found another pair of woman's breasts that made me tremble, a pair of nipples that filled my mouth as I contemplated giving in to the temptation of sweet suffocation. After all, if one is to take leave of this piss of a life, what better way to slam the door on it than with a mouth full of those bonbon-producing wonders, which sometimes took me into territory so dangerous I tasted blood instead of milk. Dear God, had I gnawed at her nipples? Had I hurt her? Was I so clumsy a lover?

In the years that followed, my recurring dream found me resting my head on her soft, warm breasts, listening to the deep throbbing inside her chest. When I wake up, I realize I am crying. The dream tells me I will never be as close to another woman's heart as I was in those interludes with Miss Bubka. Could I have stolen that heart forever? Had I missed my chance to wrap it in a lifetime of joy, protect its beating rhythm, steady and unhurried, shelter it from sneaky attacks, polluted blood, pimps and politicians?

Alas, my Miss Bubka, a woman of insatiable generosity, had other mouths to fill and lent her heart to a string of Jewish puppies. And yet, for all her promiscuity and philandering, my love for her never dimmed, despite the hundreds of unanswered letters I sent her over many years. I admit that writing letters might not have been a good idea, as I knew she hated writing and writers. Her father had been some sort of a scribbler. An irresponsible and irrational man, he deserted his family when his daughter was only nine, leaving them destitute, to chase after some whore who stole his heart, his money, his clothes, and then ditched him. Fuck him, Miss Bubka remembered her mother saying through tears. But the father returned one day, begging his family to take him back. I wanted to, Miss Bubka told me, her voice stained by remorse. I wanted him even though I hated him. Maybe a daughter's hate for her father is not disappointment but longing and love. I wanted him back, but my mother turned him away.

After the father vanished, Miss Bubka's mother found a practical man who paid the family bills and visited her nightly. Not long after, though, the caretaker's attention began to shift from the mother to Miss Bubka and her budding breasts that had yet to be suckled by a greedy mouth or cupped by a stranger's hands.

Over the years, Miss Bubka grew more mysterious in my memory, but that story she told me about her family helped me make sense of her restlessness and her lecherous habit of frequently changing lovers. By the time I'd been expelled from her school, she'd broadened the horizons of at least two dozen boys. Orphans have strong hearts, she once told me. It's not so easy to break them. But mine was shattered when I learned that one wintery day in 1969, Miss Bubka had died after enduring two years of intimidation by a ruthless justice system determined to destroy her with dubious charges of child molestation. Her heart, her magnanimous heart, had finally ceased beating.

Ah, such agony it is to surrender to memory, shake the treacherous hand of history, behold an eye brimming with the pus of life, scold a meek soul, listen to the humming void of unuttered promises, relive the disappointment of an unplayed game, or lay the head upon a broken heart. The longer I live in solitude, the more I am emptied of the present. Memory consumes my waking hours. My nights are filled with ragged shards of my former self. I dream of congealed blood, scuffles, snubs, pitiful smiles, rebukes, breakdowns, moments of grace, dizzying heights, tempting abysses, swallowed nails, succulent holes, exhumed photographs, rattling bones, pollarded trees, impaled moles, sterile sunsets, psychotic owls, rotten teeth, fallow fields, angry prayers, broken glass, folded flags, rotting penises, wistful breezes, blocked carotids, startled stars, joyful funerals, dispersed toys, strangled pigeons, blood-rusted bayonets, electrocuted dwarves, lost hats, writhing tumors, disembodied fingers, flying rabbits, crooked saints, averted eclipses, cooked cats, scorched riverbeds, withered onions, lynched dogs, dancing centipedes, fugitive bees, blue worms, abandoned eggs, cold chimneys, betrayed friends, velvet nights, punched faces, acidic vaginas, moldy tongues, injured ants, boiled refugees, undented pillows, green blood, groaning rats, blind chickens, unlit fires.

Dreams, my faithful companions to the end.

Tia Ja'nae

NIGHT OF THE LIVING BASEHEADS

I

America, 1964. The cold, bitter spring formed the backdrop for an epidemic of civil disobedience. Alphabet agencies were waging war against any unsanctioned political, religious, or racial organizations foreign or domestic. I didn't know anything about that. In those days I was just a punk kid living in the middle of the sticks. Hadn't seen too much of nothing and hadn't been nowhere to know anything but what I was told. I was cherry enough for Uncle Sam to spring a one-way ticket to Vietnam on me as soon as I graduated high school. Would have gone, too, had these flat feet not flopped the physical.

Unfit for service and having no plans to go to college, I got a gas-station gig pumping octane for a thirty cents an hour plus tips. Nothing spectacular. But I did make small talk with a guy passing through who worked for the government and gave me his card. Can't tell you his name, as that's classified, so I'll call him Mr. Unknown.

He offered me a job on salary fighting for my country in a different way. I figured it beat being in the hot sun working full service all day, so I took him up on his offer. That's how I wound up working for a government alphabet agency that no longer exists officially.

Having a government job after being a reject soldier fulfilled my private hero fantasy. I was a proud American serving my country, helping to maintain its freedoms. After eight weeks of basic training that would make the hardest sociopath weep, I graduated in a small class of recruits. We were then parceled out like chattel and assigned targets for field work. I was sent to the House of the Lord, which was code for the division that monitored religious subversives. Threats from such dissidents were on the rise in the United States. I was ordered to research a religious spook unknown to me at the time called Malcolm X.

He was something else!

Before Malcolm, I'd never heard about spooks traveling the world talking politics, followed like movie stars, speaking better English than any white man, or changing their names to fancy-sand spook gibberish. Back then it was against the societal norm for spooks to use political rhetoric to stir up good coloreds that knew their place. Racism is America's bread and butter. Keeps oil in the machine. Mr. Unknown wanted a lid put on him. After reading his dossier I had no problems trying. Keep in mind I hadn't seen a spook in person, but he was such a thorn in the country's side, he would surely be worth catching.

The initial issue was that the spook was abroad at the time, touring after his pilgrimage to Mecca. Most European countries were giving safe haven to spooks like him on the lam. Intel reports said Malcolm X had support and safe harbor in any country he stepped foot in. None of our pinko friends in low places would help us because they liked his anti-government rhetoric. Mr. Unknown turned to J. Edgar Hoover to reel him in, a decision my boss regretted later. At first Ol' Hoover did prove useful; he strong-armed France and other countries into barring Malcolm from re-entry when he attempted to visit their respective shores. That move cut the spook's speaking tour short. How my agency forced Malcolm X to return stateside was for many years a well-guarded secret.

The day of his arrival back in the United States, I was waiting for him. It was my idea to stage a press conference at JFK airport and snatch him in broad daylight. According to his file, the spook had yet to miss any publicity opportunity, and I figured he'd never see an ambush coming while answering questions from planted journalists. It was a masterful manipulation of the spook's vulnerability! Our people bombarded him from the tarmac with questions about debt, disgrace, unemployment, and poor relations with his old pal Elijah. His old muzzie pals were waiting for him, too, and we let them get close enough to distract Malcolm from our stealthy moves.

Once the spook started yapping out the new collection of names he wanted people to call him and jabbering about the future plans he would never live to execute, I made my move with backup and snatched him into custody under the 1930s subversion acts. It was my first bust. He went peacefully. I was proud to have collared the enemy without a hitch. This was also my big break, a chance to show all the higher ups what I could do as an agent. All of my ambitions were short-lived though. Ol' Hoover sent two of his agents to intercept Malcolm X as we led him away. There was nothing I could do about the change in plan. I was just a pawn, same as the spook, thrust into a game of chess while playing checkers.

Operation Sunny Red, named for the spook's religious conversion and reddish hair, took place the last week of May. Ol' Hoover had his agents transfer the subversive to a secret underground facility the FBI used for people like him. Mr. Unknown raised holy hell about it, so to add insult to injury Ol' Hoover relegated the task of interrogating the spook to Mr. Unknown like he was a second-rate lackey. Refusing to lower his status in his own agency, Mr. Unknown assigned me to play inquisitor on his behalf. Those are the breaks.

Fifty some odd years later I still wake up in cold sweats over what happened in the underground facility, a story that has never been told until now.

II

A random suit led me into the interrogation room where they were holding Malcolm. I figured they were preparing to kill him. Ol' Hoover, for all his bullshit, declined to go down in the trenches with me. An agent pointed to a TV camera and told me Ol' Hoover would be in a nearby suite called Mission Control, enjoying the show on closed-circuit television, getting his rocks off and schmoozing with heads of state. Ol' Hoover had a weak stomach and didn't want to risk getting blood on himself from the snuff film he planned on directing remotely. Everybody knew he wanted Malcolm tortured.

My part in all of this—you might call it the opening act—was to play head games with the prisoner. I did my best Elliot Ness impression and, sucking in my gut, entered with authority. Malcolm didn't notice. He was too busy checking his pockets like he'd been robbed. Imagine that, a spook felon with robbery on his rap sheet, having the nerve to think a government agent would steal from him!

The man had plenty of nerve.

"Nothing on your person has been taken. Your glasses are on the table over there," I said, pointing to a rusted stand with bent legs. "We had to make sure you would not resort to using them as a weapon."

I could not keep up with the spook's mouth, which was running a mile a minute. He chattered about seeing warrants, reviewing lists of charges, making phone calls, and requesting rights to an attorney like he was ordering room service. The suits watching were hanging on every word. I went into my tough guy talk to let it be known his constitutional rights were the least of his worries.

That's when the spook went into his jive.

"My name is El-Hajj Malik El-Shabazz, and I am being held against my will."

"I know who you are, spook. None of that civil rights bullshit works here. You are being detained due to subversive activities against the American government. You'll leave when we decide. Shouldn't be that much of a stretch for your smart ass, seeing as you've been in the joint before," I said proudly like Cody Jarett from *White Heat* would. I was on top of the world, ma!

"Before we go any further, you will call me by my appropriate title and speak to me in a respectful, formal manner, as I do you, Mr. Chalky," the spook sternly warned.

"Chalky?" I laughed. "What in hell makes a spook like you think that's my name?"

With a sinister straight face Malcolm retorted, "Your pale skin is the whitest of white of chalk on a blackboard, is it not?"

"I ask the questions here, spook!" I snarled. "If you know what's good for you, you'll answer 'em."

"Once you change your thought pattern you can change your philosophy," said Malcolm, chuckling.

Spook had brazen balls, let me tell you!

"That's funny," I retorted like a wise guy. "But I got jokes too in this little party we're having for you. Not smiling now, are you, spook?" I said, like I controlled the situation.

"Brotherhood is a two-way street," he said, unmoved. "I believe in the brotherhood of all men, but no, I'm not a brother to those who don't want to practice brotherhood toward me. Respect must be mutual and equal, like one hand washing the other. Both must come together to be clean no matter which side has the most dirt, Mr. Chalky."

I leaned toward him like a discount Perry Mason and said, "Have it your way, Mr. Shybass." The spook had me pegged, but I was still going out fighting the good fight.

Pronouncing his mumbo jumbo name correctly, especially with Ol' Hoover watching, was a good way to mock him. No self-respecting white man working in government would let a spook of all people get the better of him. But in fact my correct pronunciation was a happy accident; to this day my tongue mixes up the consonants of "El-Hajj Malik El-Shabazz" with the vowels. Malcolm didn't care, regardless. Nothing could cause that spook to lose his nerve.

He smirked at me and said, "Once you change your thought pattern you can change your attitude."

"I'm so fucking thrilled this meets with your approval," I sarcastically flexed. "Now if you don't mind and can keep that fat mouth shut and off the soapbox, I can get on with this."

I followed the agency script and questioned him about things we already knew—and he knew we knew, since he had nonstop tails. Most of it came off at best like a bad Cool Hand Luke impersonation in an all-drag-queen musical of *Death of a Salesman*. For brownie points I threw in some cracks about his intelligence. Ol' Hoover loved seeing spooks put in their place like that. None of my theatrics were moving the loudmouth in the cheap seat playing it cool. Malcolm could smell bullshit a mile away, so I knew he could smell mine standing right in front of him.

"Death does not scare me, Mr. Chalky. Let us not shatter our fragile truce with threats. I can abide death but not betrayal," he said with the shine of hellfire and rage in his eyes.

"Jesus Christ! That mouth of yours never stops running, does it?" I chuckled. "Maybe you should enter it in the Olympic games instead of letting it undermine the stability of this great country."

"That is a matter of questionable opinion. I think with my own mind. You remind me of my past," he said with calculated composure. "Asleep at the wheel, letting others I looked up to control me. Freedom starts in the mind and not in this corroded room with you whitewashing the enemy's atrocities."

"Is that so, Mr. Shybass?"

"Yes, Mr. Chalky." he said calmly. "Any time you have to rely on the government for work, you're in bad shape."

"Spare me the sermon," I yelled, getting in his face. "People like you are tearing down this country with your hatred, poisoning well-behaved spooks on your mission from your sand-nigger God. But let me tell you, the people of this government are none too appreciative of your efforts."

"Sitting at someone's table doesn't make you a dinner guest unless they fix you a plate," the spook smirked. "Patriotism doesn't make you patriotic. Being the enemy's flunky doesn't make you their friend."

Four of Ol' Hoover's agents entered as I said, "Throwing fancy words together doesn't excuse you from being a spook out of his place." They were holding shackles and chains.

My time was up. One of the agents wheeled in the kind of hospital gurney that years later would be used to administer lethal injections to death-row inmates. Neither the shackles nor the gurney seemed to shake the spook. He likewise remained cool during the rough handling he received when they strapped him to the gurney. Malcolm remained silent but didn't take his eyes off me. He watched me like a hawk scoping out its prey, until they slid a black hood over his head. After that he was wheeled out of the interrogation room, and then he started praying in that spook language. Guess he had that feeling he was going to need all the help from his sand-nigger God to survive whatever Ol' Hoover was going to do to him. I followed behind. I didn't know where we were going, and they didn't make it a point to share, but I figured I'd find out when we got there.

Thirty minutes of hard walking along underground corridors featuring Malcolm's nonstop praying ended in a place one of the agents called the Chamber. The insides were like an immense iron shoebox. Lights were dim; there were no windows. An agent told me this was Ol' Hoover's "playground," and he could operate it remotely from the Mission Control suite. And the smell, forget it! The stench of intestinal pig cancer left out to rot hit our nostrils as soon as we propped the main door open. It was so bad, everybody other than Malcolm choked on the stench.

The agents rolled him into the center of the Chamber, transferred him from the gurney to an elevated wooden chair facing the rear wall, and secured him with wrist and leg restraints.

Malcolm did not resist. He was cool as a cucumber.

"Comfortable, Mr. Shybass?" I said, snatching off his hood.

"If I were not ready to die for freedom, it would have been uncomfortable indeed," he retorted.

"You saving souls types just love to play the martyr to the end, don't you?" I said, struggling not to toss my cookies from the smell.

Colored lights over the main door blinked and buzzed; not a one of us could ignore the weird noises rising up from the Chamber floor. The sounds mixed agony, ecstasy, and gurgling. The combination of that racket and the aromatic essences that emulated a decade's worth of unrefrigerated hog maws and raw eggs made the Chamber absolutely unbearable.

"How long have you lived in this country?" Malcolm asked.

"Long enough to serve my country and put my life on the line for it," I croaked.

"Or long enough to forget you're in a state of voluntary incarceration?" the spook said with his trademark smile. "The enemy never does anyone a favor unless they get something out of it. Blood on their hands doesn't come clean on yours."

"Now you're a mind reader—that's rich," I said, retching from the pit of my stomach. "Every spook I've seen is a fucking comedian."

"If you don't stand for something you will fall for anything," he said as the last of the restraints were secured. "The future belongs to those who prepare for it today. Know that the truth will come out in the wash no matter how many times you hide the stains."

Ol' Hoover got on the loudspeaker microphone and told us to haul ass out of the Chamber, or we would be locked in with Malcolm. A robotic voice started counting down from one hundred and twenty seconds.

"Looks like that's my cue. What's that thing you spooks say, Mr. Shybass? Oh, yeah. Peace be with you. You're going to need it," I arrogantly joked.

"And also with you, Mr. Chalky," Malcolm said calmly as we left him inside his tin-can tomb. "And also with you."

III

The hall leading to the Mission Control suite featured cracked plaster and piles of junk, but inside it was so plush it rivaled the high-rollers suites in Atlantic City. We're talking cigarette girls, cocktail waitresses, and a bartender keeping the ice cubes cold. Television monitors were implanted in the marble walls. In the middle of all the decadence was Ol' Hoover, claiming credit for bagging and tagging the spook. All the people at his pay grade ignored me to blow smoke up his ass between highballs. I didn't care since I was the new kid in town and knew nobody. This was Ol' Hoover's show. I was merely an uncredited actor hoping for more screen time in the next production.

Ol' Hoover grandly directed everyone's attention to the closed-circuit monitors, which were just then displaying pure blackness. A few of his lackeys were behind a console clicking buttons as he praised himself for subduing the spook, then took a five-minute standing ovation for his fealty to the nation. After he settled down, the wall Malcolm was facing rose like a metal curtain, and the closed-circuit monitors came alive as the camera zoomed in on the spook. He was ready for prime time, sitting on his elevated chair with a bright floodlight beamed at his face. The same creepy gurgling sounds rising from the Chamber floor were coming in loud, clear, and much more agitated. Ol' Hoover grinned like the devil as Malcolm's restraints were released by remote control. A look of elation and wonderment overcame the faces of his associates around the room.

"Gentlemen!" Ol' Hoover proudly proclaimed, flipping a switch on the control console. "An enemy of this country has been captured thanks to years of hard work from the people in this room. Behold the punishment we shall inflict on all such future dissidents, especially red-headed niggers. Without further ado, Project Necro!"

The floor in front of Malcolm slid away to reveal a gaping pit. Everybody in the control room gasped as a rusted cage rose from the pit to floor level, filling half the Chamber. The cage, big enough for a few full-grown elephants, held a couple hundred or so bodies piled on top of each other. They looked like spooks at first glance, but their complexions reminded me of stiffs in the morgue after rigor mortis kicks in. It was hard to make out their faces on the black-and-white monitor, but all the things in the cage looked like they'd taken an acid bath in a junkie wash.

The sounds coming from the speakers were guttural, like noises predatory animals make before they rip the flesh off their prey's bones. As they got to their feet, the creatures looked like they were salivating to tear Malcolm limb from limb. I fought back waves of nausea as every agent in the control room smiled with eyes wide open in delight. Some of the caged things had bullet holes in their faces, lynch marks around their necks, and organs hanging from holes in their backs and guts. I had seen all kinds of corpses in basic training, and even sat in on a full autopsy of a partially rotted cadaver, so I knew these were dead people with gangrenous complexions, looking lifeless. Let Ol' Hoover tell it, they were troublemaking niggers, perfect specimens for practicing his psychological warfare against all such people. I might just be some kid from the sticks, but even I was smart enough to know that was a bad idea. Let the dead rest. You can't kill what has stopped living.

"Those things down there look a bit putrid, don't you think?" one of the agents said.

"Don't you worry about that none," said Ol' Hoover, laughing. "The brains of these malevolent niggerish creatures still function while the body naturally decays. Some of them are fresher than others, thanks to a serum we give them made from a pure cocaine heated to a high temperature in a base of ether mixed with flour."

"Ether? Flour?" an agent just below Ol' Hoover's pay grade guffawed. "What is this, *The Julia Child Show?*"

Ol' Hoover chuckled and said, "Yeah, it's a nigger cake. Our boys in conjunction with assholes over at the CIA cooked this up to handle our subversive jigaboo problem."

"Ain't nothing a nigger likes more than chicken and watermelon except a good cake," another agent giggled.

"This is a special kind of nigger cake. It's so special that when we get the time machine built we're going back to the Antebellum South and turning the slave masters on to it!" Ol' Hoover grinned as he gleefully passed around a cellophane bag full of lumpy white rocks. "It's better than religion for your average nigger—for a hit of this candy, coons will do whatever we tell them."

I kid you not, that son of a bitch hit a switch and a huge transparent globe filled with white rocks descended on a chain into the Chamber. The stuff looked like a million sugar cubes sitting in a piñata for a giant. The globe came to rest midway between the cage and Malcolm, hovering a couple of feet above his head. At the sight of the globe the creatures lost their shit. They acted like wild possessed animals, clawing, biting, and crawling over each other as they tried to bust out of their prison. Applause filled the control room. I couldn't believe it. I wasn't clapping for no shit like that. Besides, it only served to egg Ol' Hoover on further. He hit a button, releasing the latch on the cage. I'm pretty sure his dick was hard as soon as those things got free.

Creature after creature piled out and headed for the globe. All they cared about was getting their fix. Ol' Hoover was as giddy as a Geechee as he yelled into the loudspeaker microphone, telling them the cocaine was theirs for the taking as long as they did his bidding and ripped Malcolm from stem to sternum. Boy, did they do what they were told! Their attention went from the globe above them to

Malcolm at their eye level. They clawed, slashed, and scratched, clos-ing ranks on him. That religious spook didn't even flinch! Instead of running for his life to whatever corner he could find, he seized the high ground, climbing straight atop the empty elephant cage and addressing them like he'd known them their entire lives! He acted as if it was just another speaking engagement with a rowdier crowd than usual.

"Brothers and sisters," Malcolm said with authority. "Here you are, in a dark cave, barely able to see, worrying about an invisible somebody with a microphone in another cave. Before you attack me and do the dirty work of the American government, just remember that those white men have cast you off as unfit to exist in their world. Who taught you to hate the color of your decaying skin? Who taught you to hate the texture of your disintegrating hair? Who taught you to hate your rotting appendages before and after they fall off? Who taught you nothing matters except the narcotics flooding your veins from the top of your head to the soles of your feet? Who poisoned you this way? Who taught you to hate your own people when you were alive and made sure you'd still hate them after they transformed you? Before you come and kill me in your new incarnations as toxic agents of death, ask yourself, who taught you to hate being what God originally made you?"

And those *things* actually bought it!

Nobody thought it possible a preaching spook could run circles around Ol' Hoover's junkie crawling and clawing science project. Everybody in the room including Ol' Hoover could have dropped a crab cake in their shorts from watching that spook play circus master, let me tell you! I had shadowed the guy; saving souls was his great talent and Ol' Hoover sorely underestimated it. His show-stopper was quickly spiraling into the worst failure in government history. Malcolm, despite the adversity, kept his pace smooth and his stride on target.

"By allowing the United States government to warp your sensibilities," Malcolm preached, "you are condoning the falsehood that the enemy are your God Almighty, holding life and death in their hands! You are allowing them to pervert the truth that there's a higher power no matter who you pray to! You can't become a citizen unless the enemy gives you their government seal. You can't get declared dead unless the enemy gives you their government seal. You can't climb into your own casket without breaking the enemy's government seal on the lid. Here in America the government creates your identity, throws you into their system of slavery, and gives you accommodations in their jails. Here the government puts poison in your veins and makes you their baseheads, controlling your minds and your bodies through addiction to their substances. And while you serve your prison sentences without possibility of parole, those same government men impose a death tax and a dissection tax on your grieving loved ones while they make you their experimental lab rats today and their junkies for kicks tomorrow."

Those things in the Chamber stopped moaning and lauded Malcolm's speech with cheers!

Fifteen minutes running his mouth was all Malcolm needed to turn Ol' Hoover's best laid plans into the spook's personal militia, making everybody in Mission Control an enemy to hunt. Everything happened fast after that. Ol' Hoover pressed some buttons on the console, thereby locking the main door and dropping the rear wall back into place, so that the monitors went black again. Without any further cajoling from Malcolm, the creatures must have clawed the walls apart or tore down the door, because the next thing we knew, they had breached the Chamber and were scrambling around outside the Mission Control suite. Ol' Hoover had thought his cake concoctions would slow them down, but it was too little too late. He was plenty pissed, let me tell you! He hit the panic button—a detonation countdown commenced, just like some James Bond last-ditch villain shit.

It was every man for himself now. Ol' Hoover got his select people safely out of the underground facility and left the rest of us behind to slow his creatures down. Mostly, and it's just my opinion, that bastard did that shit out of spite and to keep anybody from talking about how Project Necro blew up in his face. It was chaotic, but I got lucky; I managed to climb out through the elevator shaft, right before Ol' Hoover shut it down to make sure no one could use it after him. I barely got a safe distance away before the whole complex exploded. The stench of roasting bodies was in the wind for miles. Lots of agents, scientists, and cigarette girls lost their lives over Ol' Hoover being such a sore loser after the enemy got the best of him, and millions of dollars of research and development went up in smoke on his watch.

Days later, when things calmed down and Ol' Hoover took an inventory of the survivors, he wasn't happy to see I'd made it out. He lectured me about secrecy and oaths, as if anybody would believe me if I told them about the baseheads. Mr. Unknown thought Ol' Hoover was going to put out a contract on me and ordered me to a safe house, but that's another story.

In the hours immediately following the explosion, I was stuck out in the middle of nowhere in the backwoods with no landmarks and miles away from the closest major city. I hoofed it in case those things had escaped and were chasing after me.

Three klicks in, I came to a parked car camouflaged by leaves. That delighted me since I could hotwire a car. Scary thing was, I wasn't the only breathing entity out there. Footsteps were closing in behind me before I could get the old girl started. I immediately hid and got my gun out; them things already had me jumpy and I wasn't taking no chances. After a minute or so had gone by, Malcolm came out from behind the trees.

The spook was still alive and holding on!

Seeing him with his hands raised didn't make me lower my piece right off. The thought of getting a promotion by icing him was in the back of my mind; my finger was one trigger pull away from making me an American hero with a pay raise and a promotion. Killing a troublesome spook like him would move me up the ranks, too. Something was eating me, though; my heart wasn't in sending him to meet his maker like that. Don't get me wrong, I didn't have an aversion to taking out an enemy of my country. My agency had given me a real-life license to kill. I just felt like a hypocrite icing a guy for exercising his constitutional rights. The First Amendment is supposed to cover everybody, even the spooks. And what just happened to Malcolm, throwing him in with those things trying to tear him a new one, was taking his rights as a citizen away. We were wrong. Speaking his mind shouldn't have made him an enemy of the state.

I cut the guy a break.

"Need a lift, Mr. Shybass?" I asked, putting my gun back in its holster.

"Depends on where you're headed, Mr. Chalky," Malcolm stated firmly. "I've had enough of a night of the living baseheads to last me a lifetime."

I pointed toward the smoldering remnants of the secret underground facility and said, "Well, I'm definitely not going back there. Or to anywhere with alphabet agents crawling around. I'm going back to civilization."

"Seems like the enemy of my enemy has become my temporary associate," he said, coming over to the car.

"A simple 'Sure, I'd love a lift' would have sufficed," I said sourly as we both got in the vehicle.

That was that. I hotwired the car, and Malcolm gave me the benefits of his previous life with a few pointers on a better way to connect the ignition system. Normally, I'd be cross about a spook showing me up, but that wasn't the time to get my undies in a bunch, hightailing it back to safety. Soon as she turned over, we were out of there and down the road like cowboys. He wasn't bad company on the ride and a pretty funny guy. Not uptight at all despite what we'd just put him through. If the situation were different, he'd be the type of spook I'd want as a friend. In reality, we were enemies enjoying a truce.

New York City's skyline never looked prettier to me.

Malcolm's people were definitely looking for him, as he'd been gone almost three days. To turn the heat down and keep any agency from learning he was still alive, he wanted us to part ways near Staten Island. Let him tell it, people in the city barely even knew the other boroughs existed. I took his word for it and dropped him off at the Verrazano Bridge.

"Well," Malcolm said as I parked the car. "I never mind shaking hands with human beings. Are you one?"

"Yeah, I think I am," I smiled.

Shaking my hand, he quipped, "It takes heart to be a guerilla warrior. They're on their own from day one, fighting until they win or die."

I took a long pause and said, "Yeah, they are. Rest easy, Mr. Shybass. Get home safe."

Malcolm exited with, "There's never any rest for the weary. No one can be at peace until they have freedom. But I'm safe with my people. Take care, Mr. Chalky."

He went on his way into the dawn, and I went on mine.

The very next morning he was right back in the saddle preaching and teaching. I was waiting for word about my safe house. Things would never be the same for me; Malcolm got me questioning my country's right to persecute private citizens. What good did it do bugging toilets to make dossiers on how many times a target wiped and flushed? Ol' Hoover was fit to be tied. He hated the idea of Malcolm going around blabbing about that freak show he put on. Nothing was official on paper, but Ol' Hoover promised all types of bonuses to whoever went beyond the call of duty and put the bite on that spook who'd survived Project Necro with its obscene funhouse. Ol' Hoover set his sights on me, too, and got me blacklisted from any future assignments involving Malcolm.

First Malcolm's passport was taken away. Then Ol' Hoover sabotaged his speaking circuit. This business is a lot of things, but going after a father trying to feed and clothe four children with twins on the way seemed low and cruel to me. Family is what America is supposed to be about. Agencies trying to take Malcolm's livelihood away for hoots and giggles made a mockery of that heritage. It wasn't right then and still ain't now. I drew the line when I found out they wanted all agents in the field to start going after Malcolm's family. That was not in my job description; my old man taught me better than to mess with a pregnant woman and her babies.

Unfortunately there were too many cooks in one kitchen stepping on each other's toes as they tried, without official authorization, to neutralize him. Agents were tripping up agents trying to beat each other into being the one that finally iced him. I watched from the sidelines. Mr. Unknown shipped me down to the jungles of South America to chase some spic ex-doctor turned revolutionary named Che Guevara. I didn't know him, his language, or the terrain, and it was hotter than hell warmed over, but they wanted to get me as far away from Malcolm as possible. Three weeks later, after wading in malarial waters tailing that pompous spic leading his lambs to slaughter, I found out why.

The assassin clipped Malcolm in front of his wife and kids at the Audubon Ballroom in the city.

I'd like to have curled up and died when the news came through channels. All I could imagine was Ol' Hoover dancing a jig over his victory. If I'd been there at the Audubon, it wouldn't have happened. No man should be shot down like a rabid dog with his family watching. The spook deserved a better exit from this world than what his government gave him. Even Che was in a fit about it! Just wasn't right! Unfortunately, what is right and what Washington sends its henchmen to do are two different things. The devil's chicken scratches were all over the setup for sure, but my people swore up and down that the assassination caught them by surprise.

For the record, I don't believe them.

All the agencies knew the hit was going down. Why else would so many moles have attended his Audubon speech? Every last one of those spineless bastards got their kicks destroying that man and devastating his family, who they knew would be in the ballroom that night. The cocksuckers!

Malcolm got the last laugh. He was smart enough to see the end coming. I hope he thought better of me than to think I was a part of it. I've thought a lot about that spook since he passed. I miss what could have been, you know? Malcolm pegged me from the start as somebody who wasn't cut out for the business, somebody better than the dupe they were creating. He was right on the money.

I'm just sorry it took his death for me to realize that.

LUKAS TALLENT

THRUST

There came a point during my freshman year of college when I discovered I had a previously unacknowledged aptitude for nudity. Not that there was a specific day or some epiphanic moment when I consciously decided I liked being naked. But there were tells. With a group from the dorm, I went regularly to the Fort Dickerson quarry, drank Fireball, and skinny-dipped, shimmying out of my jeans and leisurely slipping into the water while my cohort watched. This we laughed off as mere drunken revelry. When not at the quarry or in class, I would return to my dorm and strip completely, where I made an art of flinging my underwear onto the corner of the book-shelf. I could spend hours taking selfies, splayed across my bed or in front of the bathroom mirror, and I would later print them in the library on that creamy photo paper (which was technically reserved for visual-arts majors). Studying these photos, I could easily imagine doing what some would consider "terrible things" to myself. Days withered, neglected homework and assigned readings piling up, as

I stared at these pics, tracing the contours of my muscles and bones with a felt-tipped marker.

My roommate, Darryl, tolerated this behavior surprisingly well at first, but the third time he came back to our dorm and found me full-frontal, he suggested that I put on some clothes and go with him for a cup of coffee. His treat.

"You have to stop," he said, gesturing with his hand at my entire body. I wore a pink bro-tank, baby-blue basketball shorts, and Chacos—the idea being to allow as much air on my skin as possible, to display my bangability. When I politely inquired as to why I had to stop, Darryl admitted that my continual overexposure in the dorm was making him uncomfortably hard.

Pre-med student that I was, I reassured him it was perfectly normal to be uncomfortably hard. We were growing boys.

"I don't want to be hard for you," he said. "I mean, you're cute and all, but I don't want to feel the need to come on your chest."

"What a *shame*," I said, stretching the middle vowel of that last word the way we Southerners do to show affection. Darryl and I were close. We had gone to the same high school, been forced to endure the same pep rallies and prom nights and cafeteria lunches, which was why we'd thought it pertinent to room together. I mean, I didn't particularly want his cum on my chest either, but the thought made me a little giddy.

Alas, I agreed to wear a minimum of boxers and a T-shirt when he was in the room.

Forbidden to titillate Darryl with my own body and too busy with myself or schoolwork to seek some freshman romance, I watched a lot of porn, mainly free videos on Pornhub and xHamster, where I gravitated toward clips from a studio named Thrust, which worked exclusively with college students playing at your typical fantasies—coupling in locker rooms, reveling at frat parties, having liaisons with professors. Thrust had an amateur-esque, all-natural aesthetic. As if what you were seeing wasn't porn but simply incredibly private moments you weren't supposed to see. The camera would move, in what seemed a continuous take around the room, with often dizzying closeness. At the top of their homepage, a thick black font spelled out: The secret to life is *thrust, thrust, thrust.*

And sometime during those weeks, or maybe winter break, I noticed their ads for models. Never before had I realized you *auditioned* for porn. I'd always figured it was something you were chosen for. Like jury duty, but naked.

In the aforementioned coffee shop (this time, my treat), I said to Darryl, "There's nothing wrong with masturbation, right?"

Spring semester was about to commence, and after spending the holidays apart, we were reconnecting, discussing the advantages and disadvantages of doing porn. Specifically, whether or not I could do it. Darryl studied accounting and embodied for me the words *practical* and *safe.* Naturally, he was not very supportive. He sipped his espresso, slowly mulled over the masturbation question, then said, "Depends on whom you ask."

"I'm asking you, dickwad."

"No," he said. "There's nothing wrong with jerking off, but that's not the same as jerking off in front of a camera, as wanting people to *watch* you jerk off."

Darryl then set his cup down, too hard, causing espresso to spill over the rim and create a tiny caramel circle on our table's surface. I had the urge to bend over and lick it up, thought that might make an excellent lead-in to a video. Starbucks Sluts, or whatever. He said, "How do you go from 'I like to be naked' to 'I want to do porns'? There's a missing link here."

"It seems like fun," I said. Barista Babes?

Maybe it had to do with being eighteen, away from home, overladen with schoolwork, and—for the first time in a long while—not having a girlfriend. But I *did* think it sounded fun. I mean, what eighteen-year-old doesn't want to have a ton of sex with other hot people? Wasn't that the *real* unspoken purpose of college anyway? Thrust could provide a more efficient, even safer, way to accomplish that. I wouldn't have to go to a bunch of parties, get wasted, and pretend to be really into someone. Or speak to the random strangers in my classes. Or download a dating app.

Darryl said, "But what happens when you want another job? These videos don't disappear from the internet."

I sighed. Darryl wasn't unattractive, but he hadn't had a whole lot of sex. Eight months out of high school, and he was already a little thicker, his beard perpetually in progress, which, combined with his tendency toward flannel shirts and ball caps, made him look like a redneck. People who don't have a lot of sex tend to discourage others from doing so.

"Then I'll *direct* the porns," I said, though I didn't know anything about video production. I was studying the particulars of cell organization, the names of organs and tissues, the differences between A Positive and O Negative, the seven steps to ejaculation. Already I knew where and how to start an IV, how to perform CPR and the Heimlich, how to take someone's pulse and blood pressure, but I could learn other things.

Rubbing his eyes, Darryl said, "You're too smart for porn, Sidney. Porn stars have a fucked-up family life, develop drug or alcohol addictions, then die before they're twenty-five from some horrible venereal disease. You're pre-med! How do you even know you'll be any good at it?"

Well, I didn't know, but I was more worried about showing up and everyone being like "Oh wow, you were hotter online" than I was of not being any good at it, or developing an addiction, or dying at twenty-five. I was young and bangable enough that, even if I wasn't any good, people would still want to see me.

I leaned back in my chair, applied some lime-and-cucumber ChapStick to my lips, and said, "All I'm tryin' to say is get-back, click-clack, blow!"

But Darryl didn't listen to Eminem, and so he couldn't understand me.

Not long after my porn talk with Darryl, I received an email from Eddie Cockran, who'd reviewed my Thrust application and wanted me to audition for a project in Pigeon Forge, about forty-five minutes east of Knoxville, in the Smoky Mountains.

A tall, lanky guy with eyes that disagreed on which direction was more important and black hair that curled upward in layers resembling burnt lasagna, Eddie had never been a model himself. He lacked what he described as "the necessary fuckableness." Thirty-four and therefore somewhat ancient in his world of twinks and jocks, I thought he fit, sweetly, somewhere between weirdo film-studies professor and used-car salesman.

"Cock pounding ass and pussy," Eddie said, drumming his fingers against the side of a can of Diet 7 Up. "That's all I've ever been good at."

And I could hear Darryl in my head going, *no, no, no*. We met face-to-face at his RV, which was parked in a campground called River's Edge, conveniently located along the Little Pigeon River. It wasn't trashy or anything like you might expect: a 37-foot Holiday Rambler with two slides and one-and-a-half baths, no posters of naked people on the walls or empty bottles of lube lying around. To my eye, the carpet appeared stain-free. This being February, the campground outside was cold but sunlit and swarming with screaming children, drunken parents, and teenagers who didn't want to be there. Seated languidly at his kitchen table, Eddie told me about how he grew up in Elizabethton, a small town in the Tri-Cities area, but for the past several years had been living in California (where most pornographic studios are headquartered, for better or worse). He was more successful with gay porn than the other sort, and I had watched a couple of scenes he directed for Thrust. I liked his work, how he didn't overdo the dick shots. He seemed to understand what turned a consumer on: context. The Pigeon Forge project was a chance to showcase the gorgeous local talent he knew lay hidden in these mountains, and he needed a compelling male lead. For my audition, I wore an old, orange Vol's sweatshirt (stolen from my dad's wardrobe) with black skinny jeans and camouflage undies.

Eddie asked if I would be comfortable doing both straight and gay porn. My looks were pretty enough, he told me, without being overtly femme. A connoisseur of sleaziness, Eddie could see both men and women interested in banging me. To this end, he had two different but related scenes in mind. For one, he suggested a girl named Bristol Haze to perform a classic, couple-in-love setup; for the second, he wanted a guy, Tray Ross, to do a lusty and serendipitous hook-up. He showed me pictures of both of them, and when I nodded assent, he asked me to take off my clothes so he could snap some preliminary photos.

"Right now?" I said, standing up. I wasn't yet used to such clinical treatment of my body, to being instructed to take off my clothes, as opposed to mere coaxing. I blamed my conservative roots (plus an overeagerness to impress) for the subsequent red-faced striptease. The shirt was easiest, collar up. But I took my time undoing my belt, sliding it slowly through the loops as if it were a copperhead, then pulling off my jeans one leg at a time.

My camouflage trunks I gripped with both hands, one on each hip, and tugged to my ankles. Eddie said, "You just look so *thirsty.* Those spots." He was referring to the three wavy patches of bluish gray on my back and buttocks. They looked almost like bruises. "Our own Little Boy Blue." And I knew I had the job.

Other than to insist I position my arms a certain way, Eddie never touched me. Even then, it was only a slight pressure from his knuckles. He had complex ideas about pornography, and while I posed for him, he delivered a speech I assumed he'd given every other teenager who'd sat (or stripped, rather) in my position. Models were quasi-ambassadors, negotiating the gap between what people really wanted and what was asked of them. You needed someone, he believed, who could tap into the tempestuous currents of desire, guide you through it all. An emissary from Sexy Land. My bangability came with a moral responsibility: to be a role model for other young, Southern men. To show them how to do it.

"When I look at you, I wanna shoot my pants," he said, reviewing and editing the pics of me lying indolently on his couch. Fully clothed again, I stared through the RV's tiny windows at the Little Pigeon River—wide, opaque, and flanked by willow trees. Eddie sipped from his Diet 7 Up, then combed his springy hair with his fingernails. "It's the eyes, really. You've got earthquake eyes, kid." When I turned to look at him, he shifted his weight from one foot to the other, shaking the entire RV.

Later in the week, I met Bristol, who was exactly what my friends would have called my type: olive skin, lime-green eyes, and umber-colored hair falling an inch or two above her shoulders. Her breasts round and firm like NERF balls. She wore a tight purple shirt and jeans under a black fleece jacket. When Eddie introduced us, her hands immediately shot to my face, where she rubbed her thumbs along my cheekbones. "Oh my God, look at you," she said, caressing me as one might a snowman—carefully, so as not to leave any indentions. "Your cheeks have this natural blush, you know. Like you've been out in the cold your whole life."

She sniffled then promised she wasn't contagious. "It's just allergies or whatever."

I said I wasn't worried, my immune system could handle her. Soon I would know what her snot tasted like and how this could seem dangerously intimate. She was older, in her early twenties, with a boyfriend she mentioned somewhere in her other life; supposedly, he wouldn't come near her if she sniffled.

"His loss," I said. Another staple of my type, Darryl liked to joke, was: not single.

Eddie didn't expect us to do anything but fuck when the cameras were on. For how long and in what positions was up to us. "Just act naturally," he said. Which was fine, or would be fine as soon as I figured out what that meant, what shots Eddie and his crew wanted and how not to get in their way, where to place my arms. There was no script, only a general outline of what we were going for.

"Try not to stop," Bristol told me as she wiped off an excessive glob of eyeliner. They didn't like for you to look at the camera and ask if what you were doing was okay. They didn't like to give any direction whatsoever. Eddie worked with two cameras, one attached to a drone that floated around the room and another that he operated himself to lend the video an occasional shaky, handheld vibe.

The setup was two teenagers in love, sneaking off for a Valentine's Day weekend to a cabin at River's Edge. The cabin came with a full-sized bed flanked by a set of bunk beds, a mini fridge, and a microwave. No bathroom, though. For that, you had to walk a couple of yards to a bathhouse. During the week, the cabins were cheaper to rent, and fewer campers were at the campground in general, so we filmed on a Tuesday afternoon in the middle of my 2:40 Intro to Philosophy class.

Bristol wears a charcoal-gray long-sleeve shirt, a large, orange T across her chest; I, the same Vol's outfit I'd auditioned in. We walk up the gravel path to the cabin, pine branches bobbing in our periphery, and on the cut we're inside, where she immediately jumps on the bed, sighing and spreading herself out as if to gauge how far her limbs will stretch. You can't see them, but the light and mic guys, drone operator, and Eddie are squished in the room with us. No coughs hacked or throats cleared. I look around, out the window, into the pines, then down at my phone, reading a text from Darryl about the terrible food in the dining hall, which is the "natural touch" I bring to the scene. I place my phone on top of the microwave, lay down on the bed, and mutter "Sorry" before we kiss. She tastes medicinal, like cough syrup.

"It's okay," she says, cuddling next to me. "I can hear your heartbeat." Which I worry is her subtle way of telling me to chill the fuck out. Before I can decide what to do, her fingers slide down the front of my jeans, fighting my belt before she pauses and says, "This needs to come off."

Ladybugs are gathered in the overhead light fixture. The odors of latex and woodsmoke and pine slither between us. I try to sit up and kiss her neck as she fumbles with the buckle, but she pushes me back down.

"No, no, you stay there."

Generally, there are two ways in porn to approach sex: detachment or submersion. You can zone out, go on autopilot, and think about someone else, or you can lose yourself in the other person, the act of pleasuring and receiving pleasure, the moment, own it, and never let it go. How she scratches her hip with one hand and strokes you with the other. Or the slight purr, the breathy beginnings of half-formed words when you're snug inside her, the beautifully sticky smacks of flesh like squishing bubblegum between your teeth.

Years later, when I watched this video (eventually titled "Introducing Little Boy Blue"), I would note how inexperienced I looked in front of the camera. There's this innocent expression, an unmistakable newness—of desperately trying not to look silly but coming across that way anyhow—that can't be faked. Models and directors, they are always trying to capture that. But it's impossible really, after the first time.

Tray was a lit boy. Dark brown hair, cowlicked bangs, a ne-on-green tattoo of a typewriter in the crook of his left arm, right where you'd find a vein. He brought a copy of James Baldwin's *Go Tell It on the Mountain* with him. In photos, he looked moody as fuck, like he spent his free time leaning against brick walls and hating things, but in person he was goofy. Making jokes, overrelying on his accent. "Gone tear up 'at ass," he said, laughing at himself. When he smiled, I noticed a slight overbite. He was hot, but in a ridiculous sort of way.

I told him not to hold back, that I liked it rough—though I didn't really know how I liked it. I'd only ever kissed one guy and that had been as a joke, a spin of the bottle one late, alcohol-soaked night. But I *wanted* to like it rough, *wanted* Tray to take advantage of me. While Eddie strung caution tape around the perimeter of the bathhouse, I paced the gravel lot of the campground, headphones in, throbbing to the *8 Mile* soundtrack, making sure my lips were sufficiently moisturized.

For part two, later titled "Breaking-In Little Boy Blue," fade in on Tray perched on a picnic table, reading the Baldwin. He wears a denim jacket, and the wind blows his hair all to one side of his face. He stops reading to watch as I—still in my Vol's sweatshirt (which Eddie had made me promise not to wash)—leave the cabin and walk toward the bathhouse. Tray tucks his paperback into a bag and fol-lows me, quietly entering the bathhouse and standing by the sink to ogle my backside while I piss. Then he says, "Nice ass," and I look over my shoulder.

"Oh?" My voice, normally only about one octave lower than the dreaded gay pitch, lightens. The bathhouse is a clumpy rectangle, hurriedly painted in pastel blue, the floors a gray dishwater color.

Some even awfuller lines of dialogue later, we're making out in front of a stall, my back pressed to the wooden door. Tray rubs my shoulder blades against the metal-plated lock, gently urges me to my knees, where I unzip his jeans and unfold his dick from a pair of boxers, the briny smell of him in my face, offered to me like the thick stem of some long-lost wildflower. He is warm and tough in my mouth.

After a few minutes, I airily say, "You want to fuck me?"

And yes, it felt oh-so-lame later that evening, but not when Tray jerks his head toward the showers and pulls down my jeans and sticks his nose to the tight, sweaty center of my butt. All through the rim-job, I worry about my cleanliness, reflexes, and what humiliation I would suffer if I was found doing this part wrong. But when he has me ready, these thoughts vanish into a clean, clear want. A want that hurt. Like, a lot. I bite my lip and lock my hands in front of me, against the wall, to keep from making him stop. There are moments, however, him deep between my glutes, where my hips seem to move of their own volition, to writhe really, back into him, caught under this amalgam of pain and pleasure. Kind of like a surgery, a root canal—hot and wet and soothing—like part of you is being burned away, released.

When we're finished and our hair is dripping wet, he slaps me on the butt as if we've just finished a pick-up game of basketball.

"Was that rough enough for you?" he asks.

I want to shake my head, say no, tell him he will have to try again, but instead, I nod, swallow, and swing forward, loudly kissing him a final time.

"Yes," I say, and the scene ends without showing him goofily smiling at me and squeezing my hip.

And so, mission accomplished. The crew politely applauded. Beers were retrieved from a cooler. Eddie was like, "Omg ..." Of course, we wouldn't know how accomplished the mission had been until the shots were edited together and posted online. Till then, you took your check, wondered how you were supposed to read through all those handouts and study for those midterms you've been ignoring, write that research paper on *The Oresteia*. Eddie offered to buy dinner, but I had school, and my butt was killing me. The whole way home, I felt marked. More than anything, I just wanted to be alone.

That night, I showered for a long time, replaying the stupid lines I'd come up with, the false moves I'd made, which I assumed made me look like a dumb twink. From the water and washrag, my skin glowed red. Back in our room, Darryl—the only person from my old life who knew what I'd been doing all week—said, "Stop that."

"I'm sufficiently covered," I said, removing my towel to prove he was safe, a baggy pair of boxers that were no fun.

"No," he said, gesticulating his hand at me. "All that grinning. Makes me think you know some secret."

Over spring break, I spent most of my time convinced I had some horrible disease. The soreness in my lower half went away, but every itch below my waist, or extra flutter in my chest, sporadic muscle ache, dozing off—obviously a sign of HIV or syphilis or genital herpes. Never mind that, before filming, Bristol, Tray, and I had to be tested, or that we used condoms. What if the condom had broken? What if, lurking in Tray's seductively shaved crotch, were undetectable crabs? What if the tests had been goofed?

I couldn't mention any of these fears to Darryl, who would be too vindicated. I talked with no one. And this irrational anxiety made it really difficult to enjoy the premiere of my scenes on the website, the dozens of comments posted by fans only hours later. Finally, after days of living in dread, I decided to go to the on-campus clinic and be tested again, to submit myself to the "high-risk" label, "Yes, I have sex with men," those nurses wondering what I had done to warrant another test so soon. And the fluorescent rooms, sterile smells of iodine and alcohol, the sight of my blood splurting into a test tube, actually calmed me down. But I still wasn't able to sleep without obsessing over how to approach a life tainted by one horrible, impulsive decision.

Then on my walk to class the following week, there in the quad, the clinic called and told me my levels were perfectly normal. A hard place in my chest melted, filled my body with warm relief. And immediately afterward, while my professor lectured over something I don't remember, I scrolled through comments, which were mostly compliments, and planned my next video. A threesome.

"You could probably be gay," Bristol said, "if you tried hard enough." As evidence, she cited my excessive hand gestures, how I kept sticks of lip balm in each of my jacket pockets, my religious application of body lotion. Her allergies had cleared up, and she spoke in full, bright tones like she might've been giving a presentation to a class. Not long after our scene debuted, I ran into her at West Town Mall. She was in a hurry, a Victoria's Secret bag dangling from her wrist, but she stopped and hugged me, suggested that, given our chemistry, we should hang out sometime. Our work—multiple takes of her upside-down blow job, the 69-ing, her legs spread and hungry and trembling above my mouth—didn't count.

And that was all it took. We swapped phone numbers, and the next day I met her on Market Square for dinner. I figured Eddie had asked her to work on me. He believed my blue-spotted ass was the key to stardom.

"Because everyone wants to see you get fucked," Bristol said.

"Apparently," I said, not that I was unwilling. In the intervening weeks, I had looked up some of Bristol's other stuff. She worked for several different studios, not just Thrust. I saw the three-way she did with two other guys, and a lesbian scene from when her hair was longer, curled on the ends and resting like snakes against her collarbone. Then I stopped wanting to see. Bristol really knew how to moan, to crest her voice like a wave, even when what was being done to her or what she was doing was not exactly moan worthy. Even when sipping from a glass of sweet tea or chewing through chicken and waffles. And when she moaned, she did so as a punctuation mark, which gave whatever she was saying or doing an added sense of authority.

"Eddie's not so bad," she said, pausing to check her phone. "After you get over his crazy eyes, that is."

"No, I like him," I said, noncommittally staring across the restaurant at couples ignoring each other in favor of their phones. It was possible one of them had seen Bristol and me fuck each other's brains out. Unlikely, but possible.

She said, "So, how many others have you been with?"

"Depends on what you mean," I said.

"How many other *boys* have you let fuck you?"

Before Thrust, I had mostly been interested in girls, but those had been real relationships with dinners and dates and awkwardness. My attraction to *boys* was new, professional. "How long have you been with the boyfriend?"

"I made him up," Bristol said, looking at her empty plate. "I try not to mix work with pleasure. Most people don't understand there's a difference between the two. They can't separate who you are on camera from who you are in real life."

I could understand that. Everyone she'd shared a scene with probably asked her out. And rookie though I was, I could already feel my former life fraying at the ends. People seemed to look at me as if they knew what I did. And the online following I'd gathered didn't exactly want me for my insightful posts. I told Bristol it was difficult to picture her doing a load of laundry or making dinner in someone's kitchen.

"It's difficult to picture you carrying my groceries in," she said, at last looking at me again.

Though her lack of a boyfriend did technically disqualify her as my type, I wouldn't say it made me like her any less. She was a sophomore at UT, studying to be a physical therapist, having taken the introductory anatomy courses I was currently enrolled in. We shared similar aesthetics as well as a passion for fitness and Russian twists. She didn't have a fucked-up family life; her parents were high-school teachers in Rhea County. And as far as I could see, she wasn't addicted to heroin or anything, either. To her, Thrust was an income, a way to pay for school and nothing more. "No student loans for this bitch."

When our waitress dropped off our check, unsplit, I picked it up and slipped my debit card into the slot without consulting Bristol. I had been raised to open doors for girls and buy their dinners, porn star or nah. Bristol leaned on the table with her elbows and said, "Since you've only been with boys *professionally*, you must still be pretty tight."

I said, "You're always welcome to find out."

She scooted back her chair, then lifted her feet into my lap. "Only if you promise to carry my groceries in."

Originally, the plan was not to tell my parents. Mom worked as a pharmaceutical rep, and my dad was a supervisor for MasterCraft. We lived in Sequoyah Hills, this old neighborhood in West Knoxville, cradling the Tennessee River. Full of multiple-story, Tudor, Neoclassical, Georgian, and ranch-style houses (among others). Most families had trampolines, swimming pools, seven-foot-high wooden fences, and three-car garages. Landscapers spent a lot of time in the area. On Sundays, my parents attended Park West Church, where Dad was a deacon and I'd been forced to go to Sunday school until I turned fourteen. They were folks primarily concerned with BBQs, weekends on the lake, and sports, a conglomeration of activities and stuff they'd been promised would make them happy.

The problem with my original plan was they paid my cell-phone bill, and when I purchased a paid gay-dating app, Mom grew suspicious. To put it nicely, they lost their shit. Summoned home to our living room, I explained as best I could how this was college, and I needed to experiment. I did not mention Thrust or that "Breaking-In Little Boy Blue" had become a top-viewed video or how Eddie had negotiated an exclusive contract for me, where I would make twice as much as my starting rate for the threesome scene. But my parents intuited more to the story, and I could only listen to "Are you sure, honey?" and "You need to come to church with us, pray about it" for so long before I lost *my* shit and spilled everything. As I talked, Mom said "Okay" over and over and over again in the high-pitched fake voice she usually reserved for doctors and patients. Dad got up from the couch and walked into the kitchen, lifted a bottle of Jack Daniel's from the cabinet above our fridge, and poured himself a glass.

Mom leaned forward in her chair and said, "So, you're *gay?*"

"It pays more," I said.

"That's how people get AIDS," she said, pounding her phone on an end table. "By having *sex* with homosexuals."

"I don't bareback," I said but soon realized they didn't know what that meant.

Citing the good pay, Dad called from the kitchen, his voice leaping an octave, was not reason enough to become a whore. I sat down at the dining-room table and stared outside at the group of neighbor kids playing basketball in the street. One of the kids, Jason Andersen, had always had a crush on me. When I mowed the lawn or played basketball in our driveway, I would often look over and catch him watching, then pretending not to watch.

After insulting me, Dad demanded links, to know exactly what hellfire I'd brought down upon us all. I'd never thought he would be so jumpy. Normally, he was so chill, the one calming *me* down when I didn't get into Vanderbilt or quit playing basketball.

I text him the URL to my profile on Thrust.com. On my page was also a link to my new Instagram and Twitter, @sidneykylexxx, where I posted photos of myself naked or mostly naked in the mornings or fresh from the shower, cum drying on my stomach, for the followers who constantly left me messages of love.

As Dad scrolled through my stats and the two clips (you had to subscribe to view the full scene), Mom asked what they were supposed to tell people. Say, for instance, Dad's mom, Grandma Kyle, who already thought my mom was a terrible mother?

I said to tell the truth, I wasn't ashamed of what I did.

She joined Dad in the kitchen. After seeing the profile he'd found on his phone, Mom said, "You should be."

From her, I'd inherited my long face and many-shaded hair color. It was harder to see my resemblance to Dad, to look past the years of work and drinking and transient satisfactions.

They wanted me to move back home. Then they didn't. They wanted to sue for exploitation, but I told them to calm their tits. They didn't know what that meant either. Then they debated whether or not they should watch my videos. And at that point, I left, telling them they could freak the fuck out all they wanted, I was still a porn star.

Since our previous shoot, the weather had improved. By late March, the River's Edge campground was almost full, jammed with yellow lights and bug catchers, golf carts, the smell and rustle and pop of burning wood. I didn't call or anything ahead of time, just showed up, which I guess was kind of rude. Eddie answered his door wearing a pale blue bathrobe, halfway open and exposing his tangle of chest hair. His left arm cradled a glass bowl filled with popcorn, his hand clutching the obligatory can of Diet 7 Up. I apologized for turning up so late, but he waved me inside, said he'd only been watching *Scrubs*.

"Some of, actually no, *the* best television from the millennium." He added that we should do a doctor feature, Thrust Medical Center, my being pre-med and all. "You would have to play an intern, of course. I'll shop around for an older doctor-y type. Oh, maybe a nurse too. Or maybe you should be a *male* nurse? Do you know how much one of those white wheely-beds costs?"

I did not. No questions about my random appearance were asked. It was as if Eddie expected his models to turn up at any time of the night. I wondered if he ever slept, if his wandering eye would let him. The entire drive from my parents' house, I had debated dropping out of school, moving to California with Eddie, fully embracing the porn-star life. I told myself it didn't have to be permanent. I could always go back and get a degree of some sort. The only problem was, I didn't know what sort of degree I would want.

Still praising *Scrubs*, Eddie filled an entire Tennessee Volunteers cup (like those you get when you go to a game) full of vodka and handed it to me. Then he plopped his robed self into the recliner, spilling popcorn on the floor, where I sat, cross-legged like an eight-year-old. We talked about the threesome I wanted to do. We decided it should be more artsy, a declaration of where I could go from here. I listened to his ideas, nodding attentively, and the vodka went through me like a needle.

"We'll use Bristol again," Eddie said, "but I told her she can't keep you."

Somehow, he knew about our date. Did he know about her fake boyfriend? If anything, he'd probably suggested the idea. When he asked what was going on between us, I said, "We're friends."

"We just don't want you tied down to her, nice girl that she is. I told her, 'That boy is going to be getting a lot of tail.' And I meant *boy* tail."

I didn't completely understand what he was talking about, but still I nodded. "I really do like her though—"

"But you love—*live*—in chaos," Eddie said, his mouth full of popcorn. "Because order is overrated. It's boring."

And maybe it was the vodka, but I started to cry. Those pathetic fat tears rolling down my face, dripping onto my shirt. Not pretty at all. For a few minutes, Eddie carried on about how delectable I made squeezing someone's dick into my tight boy-pussy look. I couldn't blame him; he probably didn't even realize I was crying. My sobs have an eerie similarity to my laughter: big, loud, and staccato. And when he did notice, he stopped talking and fetched his laptop.

"Kid, listen here, quit that. Listen, listen to these …" And he read to me some comments from fans of "Breaking-In Little Boy Blue."

BigHarryCoxCatcher831 wrote, *Sooooo sweet, Sidney Kyle is a pro. His cherry just pops off the screen at 4:23.*

From NakedGuy614, *I would so wreck that blue-spotted bottom.*

"They love you," Eddie said.

None of these comments were new to me. Since they'd been posted, I compulsively checked my videos every day, looking for what people thought, see if anyone had caught something I missed.

That butt needs a better rimjob. He's crying for fuck's sake! I would tender-top him so well, replied Seanslong86. *Pound him long and deep and to the hilt.*

Sweet as they were, I'd reached the point in the evening where I didn't want to hear about anybody else's enthusiasm for my ass. Such a violent act, penetration—an invasion, more or less—and yet, what you could give if you overcame the pain, if you could move so in-sync with your body. I had cried during sex with Tray, but those were earned, professional tears, what Eddie had called "the icing on the cake."

With one burning swallow, I drained the rest of my vodka. Eddie sighed, put his computer away, and took my cup.

"This is why you kids shouldn't drink," he said, almost to himself. He refilled my cup with tap water and brought it back to me and said I should drink it, which I did in huge, dramatic gulps, looking up at him the whole time. I recognized this was the same position, the same face I'd used, when blowing Tray before I'd uttered my awful fuck-me line.

Eddie laid the back of his hand on my forehead, like to check if
I had a fever. "You are so hot."

But I didn't feel very hot just then. I felt sick.

With his knuckles, Eddie pointed my face toward the overhead
light, as if he thought it would make a great shot.

A few nights after my breakdown at Eddie's, Bristol texted, inviting me to her place if I wanted to "actually study." Which, of course,
caused any thoughts of actually studying to vanish completely. I
didn't see the numerous hurdles life had erected against our being
together. Finals were upon us—exams, papers, and presentations all
due within the next few days—but all I saw was the interstate, an
exit, and a few more turns, then two flights of stairs and the door to
her apartment. After letting me inside, she said, "Your keeper keeps
texting me." Eddie had been shopping guys for our threesome and,
consequently, sending a lot of naked pics to Bristol and me, what
anyone other than us would have considered a little extra. The other
night, Eddie had offered me the spare room in his LA apartment,
where we could work together over the summer.

Bristol's living room and kitchen were covered in coffee cups, all
empty, culled from local Goodwills. "For decoration," she said as I
lifted one off the top of the TV. They sat on windowsills, cabinets,
end tables, in blue and red and orange, some striped, others featuring
logos from universities in other states, diners that no longer existed.

I remember that night as a shudder reverberating through my
lower back, an "Mmmm …" We did actually study. Or she did, and
I tried to look like I was studying. She would push her glasses from
her face, ask if I wanted a drink. But I felt strangely shy, not wanting
to impose. I couldn't seem to get past the muscles in the face, which
I flexed as I remembered them: procerus, nasalis, orbicularis oris.

An hour or so into our study session, Bristol took off her glasses, covered her zygomaticus major and minor with her knuckles, and said, "I give up." She then reached across the table and interlaced our fingers, kneading the soft spaces between them in what I'd been told was the most intimate way to hold someone's hand.

Off camera, our lovemaking was less elaborate. Her blowjob was short and standard, somewhat rushed. Occasionally, she couldn't resist some moves, a couple of terrible lines.

"Mmm, give me that."

"You like that?"

"Oh yes, baby, harder, harder oh uh—uh—uhnt yes, oh my God, fuck yeah, that feels so good."

But afterward we were quiet, listening to the wind, the traffic, and her Spotify. Bon Jovi and a little runaway. My arm slung around her shoulder, two fingers tucked into her armpit. She drew circles on my sternum and recited the muscles in my torso: subcostales, transversus thoracis, rectus abdominus ...

"You know, we won't be good at this forever," I said, not sure if I meant sex or porn or us. I hadn't spoken to my parents in more than a week. I could already picture our life in California, days of sun and sex and clubs; sunglasses, bikini bottoms, sand on the condo floor. I could feel her heartbeat, even and warm and next to mine. "People get old and wrinkly."

"You don't think I'd make a sexy nana?" she said, snuggling closer, palming my pectoral. My underwear sheathed her waist, navy blue and white stripes pressed to my naked thigh. I thought she'd make a sexy whatever.

"I'd fuck old you."

To extend the proverbial olive branch, Dad asked if I would house-sit while they vacationed in Key West the first week of May.

"No company, though," he said, afraid I would host an orgy in our living room with all my sex-worker friends. Under normal circumstances, I would have planned to come home for the summer, but I didn't really feel that was an option anymore. The morning after my parents left, I drove to Farragut, where we would film "Sharing," what we now considered the grand finale of the Little Boy Blue series.

The guy Bristol and I decided on was Peyton Williams, who seemed quiet, reserved even, for an aspiring porn actor. Tall, with a pointed face and blond highlights in his hair, the standard tattoo on his right shoulder but in Latin. When not having sex on camera, Peyton worked at the McDonald's off Kingston Pike, taking orders, smiling, dumping boxes of nuggets and french fries into paper bags—basically standing around and flirting all day in the drive-thru window. Hard to believe, given his standoffishness. His tattoo read "daemonium."

Peyton told me he didn't do many scenes with guys. "Only gay-for-pay," he claimed. I wanted to have sex with him because he looked gay-er and yet more masculine than Tray. Peyton must have assumed I was, and always had been, completely gay. Much as that annoyed me, explaining myself, apologizing for my desire, would have been worse. So I just let him think whatever.

"Be gentle," Bristol said to him, grazing her nails across my stomach. "He's fragile."

I didn't smile. Peyton looked away, popped a toothpick from its plastic wrapper, and said, "I'm sure he is."

The house in Farragut was not unlike my parents', except it came with a circle driveway and courtyard. The kitchen, moreover, branched off into a breakfast nook with bay windows and a view of the backyard.

Through these windows peers the camera, focusing on a young man in the kitchen. His butt, swathed tightly in skinny jeans, juts out as he leans forward on the granite island. From over his shoulder, we zoom in on an open Grindr app. Water running in the background, falling with loud smacks into the bathtub where his girlfriend showers. He scrolls through profiles, eventually selecting a blond, muscle-y twink.

The water stops, and a few seconds later, in a plush pink towel, Bristol walks into the kitchen. I hurriedly turn my phone facedown on the bar and slide it across the counter. She caresses my waist, and I stare behind her at the fridge, the magnets and photos that don't include either of us. Bristol stands on tip-toes and bites my neck, leaving a purplish mark near my carotid. The towel falls, and I lift her onto the counter, spreading her thighs, and she falls backward as if we had choreographed the move. The light from the window above the kitchen sink hits my face, and I lower my head, contemplating the dark hair tangled above her ear.

Some time later, Peyton enters the scene. Approvingly he sizes up the spots on my butt (gay-for-pay, bullshit), then unbuttons his jeans and strokes his dick. Halfway along his shaft lies one large freckle, like Jupiter's spot. Peyton straddles me and hugs my waist, squeezes inch after inch of his dick through me, whispering in my ear that he's going to mold my ass to the shape of him. I stop kissing Bristol, lay my head against her chest, moaning as I push my hips backward, ignoring the thick, hot pain incinerating my insides.

I can feel her beneath me, but I'm too concentrated on the dulled pleasurable sensation that runs up my spine. In our general outline, Peyton fucks me then leaves. But instead, when I come, he goes for Bristol, who swiftly crawls from underneath me and stands invitingly against the counter. I have to be into his fucking her, too, so I stand up and hold Peyton's hips from behind, his skin cold and smooth as the floor of a museum. I know she has to act like she enjoys the sex with him more than with me. The scene won't work if the first guy means more and the taller, sexier boy is underwhelming. Bristol mutters then screams "Yes, yes, yes," and I kiss his neck, encourage him to make her scream louder, because in spite of myself, I'm hard again, and I don't know how to not be.

That evening, the neighbor boy woke me from a doze on my parents' couch.

I answered the door, and Jason cutely blinked several times, darting his gaze from my crotch to the threshold. I looked down and remembered I wasn't wearing anything except my underwear, those same nautical stripes Bristol liked so much. After our scene, I came home and showered, but as what I was beginning to think of as a "post-performance depression" set in, I didn't have the heart to put any more clothes on.

Jason said, "Umm—your parents asked me to—umm …" About five minutes later, I learned Dad had wanted him to come take care of the leaves in the pool.

Though we lived right beside the river, my parents still had a swimming pool, which they refused to cover for the winter. So a million or so dead leaves were in the water, obscuring the liner and making the pool look like an abysmal pond encircled by concrete. I showed him outside where the pool equipment was kept in a grey tote covered in cobwebs and fractals of crunching dead leaves and petals.

Back in our kitchen, I made a pot of coffee and supervised Jason's work from the bar. He dipped the long, blue pole in the pool, scooped hunk after hunk of leaves and twigs and other scum into the mesh net, and tossed them into gross piles on the other side of the flower bed. Blame it on the coffee or the depression, but there was some small joy in witnessing his manual labor: taut, underdeveloped muscle, greasy hair, the white T-shirt, and the sound of his thin voice, rising and lowering with the net, as he hummed and whistled "Rocky Top."

Unfortunately, Dad called, and the joy vanished.

"You up, Sidney?"

I was. It was like seven p.m.

"Everything going okay?"

"Yup," I said, resisting the urge to thank him for the babysitter.

"Jason come take care of the pool?" he said, seemingly oblivious. "I left money for him on the bar."

Near my elbow lay an envelope with three twenty-dollar bills inside. "I will be sure to reward him for his efforts."

Silence.

"Hello?"

"Don't be funny," Dad said. "He's sixteen."

"And I'm eighteen," I reminded him. But he ignored me, and that was the extent of our conversation.

"You should probably rest a minute" was the terrible line I tried on Jason, my invitation to reward him. He smiled but said he wanted to finish the pool in time to watch the Tennessee game. They were playing the Georgia Bulldogs, as if that should explain itself. A pile of slimy dead leaves lay just beyond Mom's rosebushes, which even with their pink blooms looked like three dumpy old ladies waiting for a bus supposed to have arrived half an hour ago.

Rebuffed, I returned to the kitchen. On my laptop, there were three emails from my advisor, urging me to register for classes in the fall. But I continued to ignore them and called Bristol instead. We didn't really have a chance to talk earlier. She was in a hurry, and I was tired of being around Mr. Gay-for-Pay. When she didn't answer, I called again.

"Hello?" she said.

"Hey" I said, then launched into my parents not being home, their sending Jason, telling me I couldn't have company, how I knew where they kept the liquor, how she should come over, and we could "study" some more, you know, to prep for next semester. When I stopped to take a breath, she didn't say anything. From her end of the phone came noises, shuffling, then another voice. A laugh or cough, I couldn't tell.

I said, "Is someone *there* with you?"

"Umm ... yeah?" Bristol said, like I should've expected such. But I hadn't expected her to be doing anything. It was like, off-screen, in my mind, she should be watching TV or lying on the couch and thinking about California and me.

"At your apartment?"

An abstract male-voice laughed or coughed again. Bristol didn't offer an explanation. Of course, I pictured Peyton. It could've been someone else, a family member maybe. But all I saw was his stupid demonic tattoo, his dick jammed inside her, and suddenly I felt the ache of him, the sense of being taken again. His cumshot had been so lame. He forcefully pumped at his dick for what seemed like hours and yet managed only a trickle.

"Look babe," Bristol said, suppressing her own giggle. "I'm kind of busy tonight."

"Are you sleeping with someone?"

Bristol waited a moment, then sighed dramatically and said, "Yes, in *every* possible way, yes."

I had been pacing from the kitchen into the living room, scraping the soles of my feet on the burgundy rug in front of my parents' television. At my eye level were a procession of old family photos, shrouded behind their frames in freckles of dust.

"I thought we were sort of exclusive."

It had seemed like that, the way she touched me and talked to me.

"Sidney, you're great," Bristol said, a hint of her former tone resurging, "but you and I are—well, you know, we're not on the same path."

At this point, I no longer knew if the rest of the evening sounded so fun. Some music might've helped. You know, the worst thing you can do to porn is add music. A thumping baseline or *dst-dst* really has a way of killing the heat in a scene; it's sexier with the natural sounds, somehow even more so when the models don't overhype what's going on. Let their bodies talk, or whatever. But when I hung up the phone and went back outside, the lack of music left me a little lost.

Sure, there were faint screams of neighborhood children as they chased one another in a tempestuous game of hide-and-seek, a car's ebbing engine, the gentle rustling of tires on the asphalt, a loud metallic rattle as Jason laid the pole down on the concrete—but I couldn't make any sense of the sounds.

The pool was still cloudy, but Jason wanted to go for a swim.

"It's probably cold," I said, wrapping my arms around my shoulders as if to demonstrate. Whip-poor-wills called to one another from the trees around us. I sat down on the diving board and texted Tray, *Hey rough boy*, but my heart wasn't in it.

"Come on, man," Jason said, slightly exasperated. "You have to live a little."

In no hurry, he walked around me to the glass table and lounge chairs, where he stripped to his boxer-briefs—a gray and green American Eagle pair with little eagles flying across what passed for his butt. His clothes he folded in a pile on one of the chairs. Then he walked to the edge and brushed his foot into the water. We had a fence and several trees, but as I saw his bulge growing in his tight underwear, my immediate thought was *The neighbors will see and tell my parents.*

Jason backpedaled then ran and leapt into the water, splashing my knees. I checked my phone. No response from Tray. I started to text him again but stopped a few words in. He was probably out somewhere, or reading, or fucking some other, less-straight boy for Eddie's cameras. Or his own pleasure. Every possible way.

Jason resurfaced, pushing his hair back off his face as a merman might. "No, it feels good. Like bathwater," he said. Treading the bathwater, he stared at me for a second, then clumsily removed the boxer-briefs, tossed them onto the concrete with a soaked slap. "That's better."

So he knew who I was, after all. He rested his elbows on the concrete. His tanned, smooth legs floated idly behind him, the contrast at his waist stark and attractive.

"We should order some pizza," he said, "and watch the game together?"

"The Domino's app lets you select your own driver, based on his pics, stats, and preferred positions," I said. If only.

Jason laughed, pulled himself from the pool, walked naked to his neat pile of clothes, and fished his phone out of the shorts. "What kind do you like?"

"Whatever you like."

Staring into the pool, I could see how it would all play out with Jason and the pizza, and what I would and would not be willing to do. But this clarity brought no comfort. For what I couldn't tell was whether the person reflected in the stilled water—this twink with the freckles sprinkled on his nose, the reddish-brown hair falling into his gray eyes, and the blue spots creeping into his underwear—had anything to do with me.

STEVEN FROMM

GATES

K y-otes.
        Bower said it that way. Not *coyotes*.

He'd just been settling into a Van Heflin movie taped earlier and saved for after the Late Show, when he heard a thunk-thunking noise coming from the trash cans located on the side of his house.

Bower hit the pause button on his remote. The thunk-thunking sound came again. He got up, went to his kitchen, and found a flashlight. He reentered the living room and quietly slid back the window. The desert air seeped into his face like an exhalation. He waited for the next thunk-thunking, then leaned out the window and pointed his flashlight toward the trash cans.

There they were, squatting among the cans, staring defiantly with black-ringed eyes right into the glare of his light.

"So how big were the coyotes?" Crouch asked, mixing himself another High & Dry from Bower's little patio bar. A few times a week they huddled for pre-dinner drinks, rotating houses, where they steadily drank their way through the sepia-tinged Arizona sunsets. Each host specialized in his own drink: High & Drys at Bower's, Mesquite Sours at Crouch's, Daring Dutchmans at Saugenhauser's, and Southwestern Bloody Marys at Spevak's.

"About a bill each," Bower said. "Maybe a touch more."

"Hundred-pound coyotes?" Crouch asked.

"It's the garbage," said Spevak, waiting patiently for Crouch to finish so he could refill his glass. "They're *feasting* on it."

"Wasn't ky-otes," Bower said.

"What?" Crouch asked, returning to his seat, glass recharged.

"Wasn't ky-otes," Bower repeated. "They were girls."

"Girl *whats*?" Saugenhauser asked. He'd already helped himself to round two and was eyeing Spevak's progress at the bar.

"*Girl*-girls," Bower said. "Teenagers."

"What the hell were teenagers doing in your garbage?" Spevak said, returning to their table with two drinks, one for Saugenhauser. Bower waited until they were all settled in at the table, shaded from the setting sun by his patio awning.

"They weren't *in* my garbage," Bower said. "Just right next to it. And they were smoking weed."

"Then what happened?" Crouch asked.

"They stood up, took a long pull on their doobies, then stumbled away."

"You call the cops?" Saugenhauser asked. He was a 911 man all the way.

"Nah," Bower said. "Didn't see the point."

No one offered an objection to Bower's apathy. Yerba Manca, their gated community, was bordered on the western side by the Ocotillo Golf Course. Bower's backyard abutted the eighth hole. The problem came from what was on the other side of the Ocotillo: an open subdivision. Open subdivisions meant families. Families meant teens. Teens meant wanderlust. Wanderlust meant jumping Yerba Manca's gates as a shortcut to an eastside commercial strip and a bowling alley they hung out at called Lucky Finn's.

Bower's trash-can tale was only the latest incident. Saugenhauser had a kid vomit in the middle of his driveway last March. A month after that, two smartasses managed to feed Crouch's ever-yapping Shih Tzu, Goliath, a pint of peppermint schnapps. Goliath ended up vomiting more than Saugenhauser's driveway desperado. Shortly after that came what some of the resident wags were calling the Nude-In, a mass skinny-dipping incident in the main pool. Six kids, three boys and three girls, stripped down and went for a splash at 3 a.m. They managed to wake everyone within a four-block radius, with the exception of the security guard, who, earbuds inserted, was busy watching porn on his phone.

"It's getting out of hand," Saugenhauser said, dipping into the bowl of cashews at the center of the table.

"We say that every time," Spevak said, draining his glass and eyeing the little bar for a third High & Dry.

"What can you do?" Crouch said. "Kids are kids."

"No they're not," Spevak said.

"Not what?" Bower asked.

"Kids," Spevak said. "Kids aren't kids anymore."

"Let's not have *that* discussion again," Saugenhauser said.

"OK, professor," Spevak said. "What you want to talk about?"

"Changes," Saugenhauser said.

"Change the kids?" Crouch said. "You go ahead. Take a shot."

"Not the kids," Saugenhauser said. "The security paid to keep *out* the kids."

"Can we do that?" Crouch said.

"Of *course* we can," Saugenhauser said. "It's a matter of not renewing the contract with PW."

PW stood for Perkins-Williams, the security company that had been staffing the gates since Yerba Manca incorporated several years ago.

"Replace Perkins-Williams?" Crouch asked.

"We just may have an opportunity," Saugenhauser said.

"That so?" Spevak said, walking back to the bar. Bower noticed a little wobble in his step.

"Their contract is up in two months," Saugenhauser said with just tad of condescension. He'd been a lawyer. The boring kind. A tax attorney.

"What's that mean to us?" Crouch asked.

It meant they had an opportunity. Yerba Manca had a four-member Residents Council that, with the help of a part-time administrator, approved and renewed contracts for security, paving, lighting, and trash removal. Bower was on the council, representing the eastern sector, and so was Saugenhauser, for the southern sector. Mrs. Addelson was the western rep, and the newest member, Choy, a retired actuary, weighed in for the northern sector. They'd invited Choy into their drinking rotation, but he'd declined on the grounds of lifelong abstention. Mrs. Addelson had declined on the grounds of not liking any of them.

"So all you gotta do is fire Perkins-Williams?" Spevak asked.

"It's not a matter of *firing*," Saugenhauser said. "We just ask for bids from other security companies and see what turns up."

"Don't you do that every time?" Crouch asks,

"Yep," Bower said, "But no other companies enter a bid, so we renew with Perkins-Williams."

"So how do you get other companies to bid?" Spevak asked.

"We'll advertise a bit more widely," Saugenhauser said. "We never really made a big effort before."

Three golfers passed by on the other side of the waist-high adobe wall, towing their golf bags on three-wheel Caddyteks. They were skipping the eighth hole, probably because it was getting dark. Bower remembered how Ellie hated it when they were eating dinner outside and golfers would saunter by, looking at what they ate. She said it felt violating. They didn't eat out the last year she was alive. Bower looked over at Spevak. He was the only other widower in the group. Bower always meant to talk to him about it but never did.

The table fell silent, each man cozily ensconced in the warmth of his inebriation, an effect that seemed amplified when they were at Bower's place, with its lulling view of the gently sculpted fairway, the perfect putting green, and a few gracefully arcing Canary Island date palms. The sun was almost out of sight, rationing out just enough light to bleed the sky with streaks of red and purple embedded in the fading blue.

Spevak and Crouch started talking about the last time they were on the links. Saugenhauser joined in. Soon they'd touch on the other familiar topics: who was showing signs of Alzheimer's, whose reverse-mortgage money was drying up, and who would take the top prize in the annual customized-golf-cart competition, which Spevak chaired every year.

"Hey," Crouch said, pointing toward the eighth-hole pin. "Look at that."

A grayish-brown coyote was sniffing around the putting green. All of the men got up amid a peppering of soft grunts and walked to the little wall for a better view.

"Gotta be a male," Spevak said. "Thirty, thirty-five pounds."

The coyote stopped and stared back. It was so still it didn't look like it was breathing. A dog barked from the other side of the golf course. The coyote broke off its stare and darted into the shadows. The men stayed at the wall, drinks in hand. No one spoke as they watched what was left of the sun disappear.

Goliath, Crouch's Shih Tzu, wouldn't shut up.

"You see?" Saugenhauser said. "There's your problem, right there."

"He's been like this for years," Crouch said, holding up a piece of paper. "Now all of a sudden, I get this."

It was Crouch's turn in the rotation, and the group had arrived promptly at six for their usual Mesquite Sours. Crouch's patio abutted another backyard, but privacy wasn't a problem. The other house, which belonged to a couple named Swain, had gone dark some months ago when their reverse-mortgage money ran out.

"Let me take a look at that," Spevak said, snatching the paper from Crouch's hand. It was an official notification from Pedigreau Solutions, warning about Goliath's constant barking.

Pedigreau Solutions was the new security company. Only three had entered bids. Pedigreau made the best presentation, delivered by Mr. Maynard, a young man in his thirties, impeccably dressed in a three-piece gray suit and equipped with a disarming baritone. He promised a "seamless surveillance" that would be "organically assimilated" into Yerba Manca's "existing infrastructure." The Residents Council had no idea what that meant, but the numbers were simpler: Pedigreau's bid was the lowest.

And they enforced the rules, including restrictions on barking dogs.

"Who'd complain?" Crouch asked. "Who'd rat me out?"

"Your neighbors," Saugenhauser suggested.

"What neighbors?" Crouch said. "The Swains are gone. The Stinsons," he added, nodding to his right, "they're deaf. Couldn't hear howitzers. And now these Pedigreau guys are threatening me."

"This isn't a *threat*," Saugenhauser said. "It's a required step in a procedure defined in the Yerba Manca bylaws."

"OK, counselor," Spevak said. "What happens if the little yapper doesn't stifle?"

"Fines," Saugenhauser said.

"Fines?" Crouch asked. "How much?"

"Not sure," Saugenhauser said. "But it doesn't have to get that far. Just shut the dog up. Starting now."

Crouch looked at the warning in his hand, then at Saugenhauser, then called for his wife, Marie. There was no answer.

"Shit," Crouch said. "She's at her painting class."

He got up, scooped Goliath in his arms, walked over to the sliding door, and deposited the dog into the house. They could still hear him, but it was muffled.

"Well, look at it this way," Saugenhauser said, mixing himself another sour. "At least we know Pedigreau's earning their money."

Within weeks after the Perkins-Williams contract expired, Pedigreau had installed new vertical pivot gates, given each resident new electronic IDs, and posted new surveillance cameras from streetlights, telephone poles, and, after obtaining written permission, on select homes in "strategic visual sectors." They'd also installed motion detectors on the low adobe wall adjoining the Ocotillo Golf Course, including Bower's section.

After another round of sours, the men settled deeper into their chairs. Saugenhauser mollified Crouch by promising to speak to Pedigreau in his official capacity as president of the Residents Council. That led to the next subject: the Yerba Manca Cart Classic, which was coming up in the next few weeks.

Every year, residents who'd bothered to customize their electric golf carts showed up for a lively block party and a contest. The top prize was five hundred dollars. Spevak was hoping to nail down first this year with a 1966 Jaguar E-Type custom job that he'd just completed.

"We're all set, except for the permit," Saugenhauser reported.

"Your council does the permit thing for us," Spevak said. "Takes three minutes."

"Not under the new arrangement," Saugenhauser said. "Need a cosigner from Pedigreau."

"Why the hell is this any of *their* business?" Spevak asked.

"Security, traffic flow, that kind of thing," Saugenhauser said.

"Traffic flow? For golf carts?" Spevak asked. "Never had to do that with Perkins-Williams."

"Perkins-Williams is gone," Saugenhauser said. "It's a new world."

They drifted on to other subjects. Bower stayed silent, sipping away at his drink and looking over at the Swain's abandoned yard, his eyes wandering to the darkened back door. He thought he saw a shadow move by the window. He looked at the other men. They were lost in their talk. He looked back at the window. The shadow was gone.

What does God have against Van Heflin?

Bower had just settled into his Barcalounger with a beading bottle of Pabst, watching Van Heflin's improbably immobile face floating across the screen, when his doorbell rang. He put the movie on pause and went to his front door to find Spevak and Choy, their faces set and serious.

"You guys the welcome wagon?" Bower asked as he let them in.

When they settled in the living room, and after Bower offered them a Pabst (Spevak accepted, Choy declined), they got down to business.

"They denied me," Spevak pronounced.

"Who denied you what?"

"Pedigreau. They denied me my permit. For the cart confab."

"On what grounds?"

"Unnecessarily disruptive, illegal consumption of alcohol in public," Spevak said.

"I thought Saugenhauser spoke to them?" Bower said.

"So did I," Spevak said. "I'm not the only one with a story." He looked over at Choy.

"I was out with my wife for dinner," Choy said. "When I came back, I realized I didn't have that new ID they gave us." Choy stopped, waiting for the question.

"OK," Bower said. "What happened?"

"They wouldn't let me in," Choy said.

"Did you show 'em your license?" Bower asked.

"Yes, but my wife didn't have hers," Choy said. "So they wouldn't open the gate."

"So what happened?" Bower asked.

"I had to *sit* there like some kind of felon waiting for Morris," Choy said, nodding toward Spevak, "to come down and vouch for me."

"It's part of the 'new protocol,'" Spevak said.

Bower sat back in his chair, his eyes involuntarily drifting to Van Heflin, frozen on the screen, then back to Spevak, who was staring at him.

"Maybe we can make some kind of appeal," Bower offered.

"To them?" Spevak said. "Screw that."

"So what can we do?" Bower asked.

"We need to change some things," Spevak said.

"We can convene a special meeting of the council," Choy said. "I'm pretty sure we can get Mrs. Addelson on board."

"OK," Bower said. "Then what?"

"Then you guys vote to change the bylaws," Spevak said.

"We can do that?" Bower asked.

"We're the council," Choy said. "We can do what we want with a three-fourths vote."

"What does Saugenhauser say?"

"Can't seem to reach him," Spevak said.

"Crouch seen him?" Bower asked.

"He's got other problems," Spevak said.

"Like what?"

"Goliath," Spevak said. "He went missing."

"Missing? When?"

"Two days ago," Spevak said.

"Marie must be frantic," Bower said.

"She doesn't know," Spevak said. "She's visiting her sister in Gilbert. He doesn't want to call her yet."

"He's out looking?"

"Tried hanging fliers in the clubhouse and on some streetlights, with a picture and reward, but you-know-who wouldn't allow it."

"Pedigreau?"

"Says it's in the new bylaws," Choy said.

"Crouch raised hell," Spevak added. "Threatened to call his brother, the lawyer up in Chandler. Wants to sue them."

The men looked at each other in silence for a full ten seconds.

"OK then," Bower said. "You better contact Mrs. Addelson."

"I'll sound her out when I leave here," Choy said. "But she's game for anything as long as it doesn't interfere with *The Bold and the Beautiful*."

Bower promised to call Saugenhauser. After the men left, he picked up his cell phone and punched in Saugenhauser's number. It went to voicemail. Bower didn't say anything and hung up. He lifted himself out of the chair, went out to his patio and up to the little adobe wall. Bower stood there for a few moments, pretending to take in the night air until he was sure his neighbors on either side weren't poking around in their backyards. When Bower knew he was alone, he passed his palm quickly over the wall. Nothing happened. He did it again, this time more slowly, then on the third try kept his hand over the wall. He saw a small red dot in the middle of his palm.

"*Sonofabitch,*" he whispered to himself.

Bower put his hand down and looked around. The eighth hole of the Ocotillo was as still as an oasis. He went back into the house, sat back in his chair and pressed play. The phone rang.

"Jesus H. Christ on His Cross," he pleaded up at the ceiling. He put the movie on pause and picked up his phone. It was a blocked number. He wasn't much on blocked numbers, but this time he bit. "Hello?"

"Mr. Bower?"

"Yes?"

"Of 723 Cocopah Trail?"

"Right again. Who's this?"

"Mr. Maynard. With Pedigreau Solutions. We received a perimeter violation alarm from your backyard."

"A perimeter violation?"

"Yes. As in the electronic surveillance cordon on your back wall."

Bower looked down at his palm. It was a reflex.

"Everything's quiet here, Mr. Maynard," Bower said. "Don't know what that's all about."

"We do."

"Excuse me?"

"We do," Mr. Maynard said. "Were you in your backyard four minutes ago, standing near your wall?"

Bower felt a flushing sensation shoot down the back of his neck.

"Not that I recall," he said.

There was a pause at the other end of the line.

"Mr. Bower? We have surveillance images of you standing at your back wall."

Bower sat still with the phone mashed against his ear.

"Mr. Bower?"

Bower remained silent. He figured it was his best response.

"Mr. Bower, in order for Pedigreau to maintain optimal security, we need to minimalize false alarms."

There was another long pause, and then: "Thank you, Mr. Bower."

Bower sat still, holding his phone for what felt like a long time, then put it down. He sat back in his chair. Van Heflin was staring at him from the purgatory of endless pause.

Spevak didn't waste any time. Bower had just finished the last sentence of the latest official notice from Pedigreau when his phone trilled.

"You get it?" Spevak asked.

"Yep. In the mail this morning."

"What do you think?"

"Trying to get past *symbiosis*. What's that mean?"

"It means bullshit, that's what it means."

Pedigreau was recommending the launch of a pilot program that would require Yerba Manca residents to provide one-hour notice before leaving the development. The pre-notification regimen was meant to "further refine the security symbiosis" between residents and Pedigreau.

"What's next?" Spevak asked. "Curfews?"

"We'll talk about it when I get over there," Bower said.

The drinking rotation had skipped over Saugenhauser, who'd remained incommunicado for days, making it Spevak's turn. When Bower knocked on Spevak's door later that day, he was startled when Choy answered.

"C'mon in," Choy said. "Morris is out back."

"Russ here yet?" Bower asked, referring to Crouch.

"In a bit," Choy said as they moved through Spevak's living room toward the sliding glass doors.

"How's the Goliath situation?"

"Still looking, last I heard," Choy said. "Marie's coming back in two days."

As they passed the kitchen, he noticed dishes in the sink. The living room was just as bad. The coffee table was littered with Chinese takeout containers and crumpled potato-chip bags. Spevak had fallen behind the cleaning curve ever since his wife, Mary Beth, passed two years ago. Some guys pick up the ball, some don't.

"We've got other problems," Choy said.

"Yeah, I got the notice," Bower said.

"No. There's more," Choy said, sliding the door open and stepping aside to let Bower go first. Spevak was at the patio table, stirring a large pitcher of Bloody Marys.

"Perfect timing," Spevak said. "Now we can start the Yalta Conference."

As Choy and Bower settled in at the table, Spevak poured out the drinks. He doled out a separate Virgin Mary for Choy. There was a bucket of ice and a plate of celery stalks in the middle of the table, as well as Spevak's cell phone. When he was done pouring, Spevak lifted his glass.

"Here's to peaceful times," he said.

The men went at their drinks for a few moments. Spevak polished off half his glass in two gulps, while Choy took measured little sips.

"So, Ben tells me we have other problems," Bower said. Choy's first name was Byung-Ho, but he'd told everyone to call him Ben.

"Sure do," Spevak said. "First, we're getting some static over the special council meeting."

"Static?"

"Got a message from some guy," he said, nodding at the cell phone on the table. "Said there was a complication with scheduling the meeting in the clubhouse."

"How can there be a complication?"

"Not sure," Spevak said. "He left the voicemail when I was in the shower. Going to call him back."

"What're you waiting for?"

"You and Crouch."

"We can't wait too much longer for Russ," Bower said. "Office hours are ending soon."

"We got bigger news first," Spevak said, looking at Choy. "Go ahead, tell him."

"I found something out about Saugenhauser," Choy said.

"Saugenhauser?"

"Well, not me. My wife. She found out," Choy said. "She's in the same art class as Violet."

"Saugenhauser's wife?" Bower asked.

"They were in there painting away, and they started talking about their maiden names," Choy said. "So when it's Violet's turn, she gives it up."

"Go ahead," Spevak said to Bower. "Take a shot."

Bower thought about it for a few moments, but he knew.

"Pedigreau," Bower said.

Spevak smiled. Choy nodded. Bower put down his glass.

"I did some checking around, made some phone calls," Choy said. "Pedigreau is owned by Chet and Marcus Pedigreau."

"Saugenhauser's cousins-in-law," Spevak said, in case anyone missed the point.

"I can't prove it without further research, but I'd bet he's got a financial interest in the company," Choy said.

"I see," Bower said. He waited a few moments, looking down at his drink. He'd known Saugenhauser the longest. They'd gone out with their wives to countless dinners, movies, and even a short cruise to St. Thomas. He still remembered the tremble in Saugenhauser's voice as he eulogized Ellie at her wake. Bower felt the other men's eyes on him.

"We need to speak with Saugenhauser," he finally said.

"Good luck with that," Spevak said.

"That's why we're waiting on Russ," Choy said. "His brother, the attorney, may be able to take legal action to void the contract."

"Because of the financial conflict," Spevak said.

"Because of the *undisclosed* financial conflict," Choy said.

"Undisclosed," Bower repeated.

"We have to make that call," Choy said, referring to the Pedigreau representative who had called Spevak. "We can fill Russ in when he gets here."

Spevak picked up his phone, hit the redial button, put it on speaker, and then placed the phone in the center of the table. It rang three times before someone picked up.

"What can I do for you, Mr. Spevak?"

Bower recognized the voice. It was Mr. Maynard.

"Got your message," Spevak said. "I have Jack Bower and Ben Choy here with me. You know, two members of the council."

"Ah yes, your little drinking club," he said. "But isn't it Darling Dutchman night?"

Choy's eyebrows arched. Spevak's mouth went lax.

"*Daring* Dutchmans," Bower finally said. "Art, Mr. Saugenhauser, couldn't make it, so we're over at Morris's place."

"How nice," he said. "A Bloody Mary would taste quite nice right now."

The men looked at each other.

"You'll have to come over and join us sometime," Spevak said dryly. "But before we all become drinking buddies and whatnot, we need to hash out this meeting thing."

"Certainly, Mr. Spevak," Mr. Maynard said. "If you look at the amended bylaws, parties must submit a permit to hold unscheduled events in the clubhouse."

"But this isn't a social event," Choy said. "This is the council."

"I understand that, Mr. Choy, but the amended bylaws don't recognize the council as an exceptional entity," Mr. Maynard said.

"Exceptional entity?" Bower asked. "What's that mean?"

The men waited for a response, but the phone remained silent. Choy spoke up.

"So what do we have to do to submit a permit to have a council meeting in our own clubhouse?" he asked.

"It's a simple process," Mr. Maynard said. "Just send Pedigreau Solutions an email detailing the date, time, and location of the desired meeting."

"Then what?" Bower asked.

"We process the request," Mr. Maynard said.

"How long will *that* take?" Spevak asked.

"Vetting periods vary," Mr. Maynard said.

"Can you give us a rough estimate of how long that will take?" Choy asked.

"No. Pedigreau Solutions doesn't want to be put in the position of generating inaccurate information."

"So we put in a request, and it'll get done when it gets done. That right, Mr. Maynard?" Spevak asked.

"We will begin the vetting process immediately and then get back to you when the process is completed."

"What prevents us from holding the meeting by ourselves, at one of our homes?" Choy asked.

"You can't," Mr. Maynard said. "A duly appointed representative from Pedigreau must be present as a recording secretary to make any decisions of the Yerba Manca Residents Council of record."

"Who's the recording secretary?" Bower asked.

"That would be me," Mr. Maynard said.

"OK then," Spevak said. "Why don't you come on over here some night soon. We'll hold a meeting right here."

"You need a quorum," Mr. Maynard said.

"So?" Spevak said. "We just make phone calls and gather. What's the complication?"

"Mrs. Addelson," Mr. Maynard said.

"What about her?" Bower asked.

"She's been called away," Mr. Maynard said.

"Called away?" Choy asked. "To where?"

"I don't know," Mr. Maynard said. "She notified us two days ago that she would be out of town for the next several weeks and request-ed that our security personnel routinely check her home."

"Did she leave contact information?" Choy asked.

"Yes."

"Can we contact her?" Spevak asked.

"No. We can't share private information."

"How convenient," Spevak said.

"OK, Mr. Maynard," Choy finally said. "We'll be getting back to you."

"Thank you, Mr. Choy. Is there anything else I can do for you?"

"Not a thing," Spevak said.

Spevak reached over and hit the end button.

"So we've got two things to do," Choy said.

"Right," Spevak said. "You file for the so-called permit. Maybe Mrs. Addelson will show up. And I'll lean on Crouch to get hold of his brother."

"Where *is* Crouch?" Bower asked.

"He'll be here," Spevak said. "You can usually set your watch by that guy."

Bower reached for the pitcher and filled half of his glass. Spevak's phone burbled. He squinted at the little screen.

"It's my bank," Spevak said. "Second time today."

"Don't answer it," Bower said. "They've been peddling those CD things again."

"Not about CDs," Spevak said, putting down the phone. "They left a voicemail. Wanted to talk about something."

"A reverse mortgage?" Bower said.

"Already got one of those," Spevak said.

He was about to say something else, when he looked up and said *Christ*. It was Crouch, standing by the sliding glass door. His eyes looked pinkish and glassy, and he was standing stiffly off-kilter, like something had gone rigid between his shoulder blades.

"You OK, partner?" Spevak asked.

Crouch didn't answer.

"C'mon over and have a drink," Choy said. "Plenty to tell you."

He took a step forward, but stopped.

Bower noticed he was carrying a small brown paper bag in his left hand. No one moved for what seemed a long time. Bower finally reached over and pulled out the chair next to him.

"C'mon, Russ, sit over here."

Crouch looked at the chair for a moment, then moved to the table and sat down. He put the paper bag on the table. Choy took the pitcher and filled Crouch's glass.

"You OK?" Spevak asked again.

Crouch looked at him, and then at the other men.

"What's in the bag?" Bower asked.

"That's the thing," Crouch said.

"What thing?" Choy asked.

Crouch picked up his glass and took a careful sip, then sank most of the glass.

"Goliath," he finally said.

"You find him?" Bower asked.

"I don't think so."

"What does that mean?" Choy asked.

"I found this," he said, nudging the bag.

"What's in it?" Spevak asked.

"Go ahead," Crouch said.

Spevak snatched the bag, opened it, and looked in.

"What am I going to tell Marie?" Crouch asked.

"What's in there?" Choy asked. He sounded scared.

Spevak reached into the bag and took it out.

"Goliath's collar?" Bower asked. "Where'd you find it?"

"On my porch. This morning."

"On your porch?" Spevak asked, taking a closer look at it.

"Went out to water the flowers," Crouch said, "and there it was."

"There a note? Anything?" Choy asked.

"No. Just the collar."

"Well, shit," Bower said. "Maybe some of the subdivision kids got him. It's their bona fides or something."

"Right," Choy said. "A bona fides. They want some kind of reward."

"They call you?" Bower asked. "That's what they usually do."

"I got a message," Crouch said.

"Thought so," Bower said. "How much they want?"

"It wasn't that kind of message," Crouch said, digging into his pocket and pulling out his cell phone. He pressed the screen and put the phone on the table. They heard a dog barking. It was Goliath, or at least it sounded like him. The rhythm of his barking quickened, the tone rising higher for a full minute or so before it was ripped by a shrill, short yelp that made Choy jump in his seat.

"Christ on His Cross," Spevak said.

The voicemail went dead.

"That's it," Crouch said. "That's all there was."

"No message?" Choy asked.

"That *was* the message," Spevak said.

Bower eased back as he watched his Van Heflin movie. He tried his best to pay attention. Anything to keep his mind off of Pedigreau Solutions.

Before making the long, doleful trip up to Gilbert with his bad tidings about Goliath, Crouch had called his brother the attorney and briefed him on the general situation. Crouch's brother, retired but still licensed, had agreed to send a registered letter to Pedigreau outlining their concerns. The letter had been sent two weeks ago. They'd heard nothing from Pedigreau since. Choy had called Mrs. Addelson's home several times but never reached her.

"So what do we do now?" Bower had asked Choy two days ago over the phone.

"We wait," Choy said.

"How long?"

"Sanford said we should hold back for another week or so," he said, referring to Crouch's brother.

"What does Spevak say?"

"Not sure," Choy said. "Haven't been able to reach him."

Bower had called Spevak but was bounced to voicemail. He'd left it at that, hoping for a few days of peace before the Yerba Manca confederates took up arms once again.

Van Heflin was scuttling down a fire escape, but Bower had no idea why. He was just rewinding when someone knocked on his door. Bower hit pause and heaved himself out of the Barcalounger. It was Spevak. He was looking over his shoulder at the street when Bower opened the door.

"Morris," Bower said. "Everyone's been trying to reach you."

"Can I come in?" He said it all in one word: *CanIcomein?*

"Sure," Bower said. "No High & Drys in the works, but I can fix you up with a Pabst."

Spevak had already walked past him. Bower smelled sweat laced with Old Spice. He shut the door and locked it. When Bower reached the living room, he found Spevak standing in front of the TV, but he wasn't looking at it.

"You want a Pabst?"

"Sure," Spevak said. "Anything."

When he returned with a bottle and glass, Spevak was sitting on the couch, perched on the edge of the cushions. Bower put the bottle and glass on the coffee table.

"I was talking with Choy yesterday," Bower said, settling back into his chair. "Said we should wait another week, then go ahead with the civil action."

Spevak didn't answer. He was looking at Bower, but it was more of a reflex. Spevak was somewhere else.

"So, anyhow, you and me and Choy should get together to fig-ure out the billing," Bower said. "Pretty sure the two Latin words an educated man like Sanford doesn't know are *pro* and *bono*."

"Coral Gables."

Spevak blurted out the words. Bower waited for him to say some-thing else. He didn't. Spevak picked up his Pabst and poured half its contents into his glass. He picked up the glass but didn't drink.

"Coral Gables?" Bower asked.

"Coral Gables, *Florida*. That's where I'm going."

"Going? When?"

"Now. After I leave here."

"OK. Why?"

"Visiting my sister."

"She ill?"

"Gladys? Christ no. Healthy as a plow horse."

Bower stopped guessing. Spevak put down his glass and started rubbing his eyes.

"They did this, you know," he said from behind his hands.

"Who? Did what?"

"Pedigreau. They dropped dime on me. Isn't that the expression?"

"Yeah. I've heard it. Pedigreau dropped dime on you about what?"

"My mortgage. My *reverse* mortgage."

"What about it?"

Spevak stopped rubbing his eyes.

"It's a fraud," he said.

Bower looked at him, waiting.

"You got one, right?" Spevak asked.

"Yeah. So what?"

"You remember how old you gotta be to get one?"

"Sure. Sixty-two."

"Right."

Spevak's expression shifted, releasing a bit of its fear. He was almost smiling. That's what tipped it.

"You weren't sixty-two," Bower said. "You weren't sixty-two when you got it."

"I was a firefigher back in Jersey," Spevak said. "Got a pension and all, and thought it was enough. So I buy our home here, and everything was right as rain. Until it wasn't."

"Until it wasn't?"

"I got greedy."

"What does that mean?"

"Crypto. I played around with it. You know, to get more cash."

"And then it played around with you," Bower said

"Right. It tanked. Lost everything. So I needed the reverse mortgage. I was sixty at the time. Mary Beth was fifty-nine. We ginned up some papers and got it."

"And now you got trouble."

"After all these years, the bank suddenly calls. It's them. It's them who done it."

"Pedigreau?"

"Who else?" Spevak asked. "Somehow they found out, and they screwed me."

Bower didn't argue the point. It didn't matter if it was Pedigreau or some diligent forensic accountant at the bank. Spevak was screwed.

"How do you think they'll come at you?"

"Don't know. Go after me for fraud. Civil or criminal. Maybe both. So I'm headed down to Coral Gables."

"Like some kind of fugitive?"

"No. Like someone who doesn't want to be found."

"You better get a lawyer," Bower said.

"I will. I just gotta get outta sight for a while."

Spevak emptied his glass and stood up. Bower rose with him.

"Thanks for the brew," Spevak said.

"Sure thing," Bower said. "Anything I can do for you?"

"Yeah. Keep an eye on the house, even if it ain't mine anymore," Spevak said.

Spevak put out his hand. Bower took it.

"One wrong step," Spevak said. That smile came back. "Sometimes it feels like the world's just *waiting* for you to make a mistake."

He started laughing. He gave Bower a tap on the shoulder before he turned. He kept laughing as he walked out of the house.

Bower woke up in his Barcalounger with the sense that he'd dreamed, but he could only remember a fragment, a vision of Ellie in her beloved garden fussing over her brittlebush and yellow lantana and then looking up at him and smiling that full, open, sweet smile of hers. When he came out of it, there was the Van Heflin flick and what looked to be the final scene. Bower had no idea what was going on.

Even before it was over, he got up, went to the bathroom, and then to the kitchen to crack open a fresh Pabst. By the time he got back to his chair, the screen had gone dark. He turned the TV off but didn't sit. He put the beer bottle down and looked at his cell phone. No messages. His thoughts went to Spevak. He also hadn't heard from Choy in days and had left him several voicemails.

Bower's phone rang. He vaguely recognized the number and swiped the green button.

"Mr. Bower?"

Bower didn't answer.

"Mr. Bower? This is Mr. Maynard. Remember? With Pedigreau Solutions."

Bower still didn't answer but resisted the impulse to hang up.

"Mr. Bower, it's come to our attention that you've left Yerba Manca property twice without adhering to the pre-notification requirement, once to Fry's on Tuesday and once more on Thursday to the QuikTrip."

Bower remained silent.

"Mr. Bower? It is incumbent upon all Yerba Manca residents to adhere to security proto—"

Bower swiped off the call, then walked out to his patio, out into the warm darkness. He stood by the empty table for a few moments. There were no sounds. Not even a poorwill.

Bower walked up to his back wall and passed his hand over it once. He waited about thirty seconds. Nothing. He did it again. Nothing. Bower started a waving motion, palm down, moving his hand faster. His cell phone started ringing. He didn't stop. The phone kept ringing. He was starting to breathe hard, but he'd keep at it. He'd keep it up as long as he could.

T. N. EYER

COLLATERAL DAMAGE

When the first woman comes forward, you are dismissive. Your husband breaks the news to you after the children are in bed, his voice a bit too formal, his grip on your hand a bit too tight. Some girl, a decade or two his junior, is accusing him of sexual assault. "She wasn't even attractive," he says, as if her accusation is an insult to his taste as well as his integrity.

You are outraged on his behalf because, after all, this is the man you've been married to for twenty-two years, the father of your daughters. You know his strengths and shortcomings as well as you know your own.

Your husband is not a sexual predator. He is the man who coaches your daughter's soccer team, who pays your sister's son's private-school tuition, who fed the neighbor's cat for a month while she was in the hospital and once smuggled it into her room when her spirits were low. He has sat through *The Marriage of Figaro* three times, even though he hates opera, because he knows it's your favorite. At the end of a long day, he will come home, rest his chin on the crown of your head, inhale your citrus-scented shampoo, and whisper "I missed you today" while holding your body against his in a way that suggests that, given his druthers, he'd never let you go. He is considerate and generous and gentle; you are proud to call him your husband.

At his worst, well, he confessed to cheating on a math test once. When the girls were small, he got into the irritating habit of referring to time spent alone with them as 'babysitting.' He fiddles with his phone during their piano recitals. He eats a little bit too much and drinks a little bit too much and watches a little bit too much TV. But these are minor faults. He is a good man. Even your dad—who never approved of any other guy you dated—said so.

Plenty of good men have bad moments or nasty habits or occasionally lapse into deplorable behavior, but not him, not like this. He listens to women and treats them well. He respects female bosses and mentors female subordinates, and when he meets a woman for the first time he shakes her hand firmly and looks her in the eye. He never uses terms like "babe" or "doll," and he never refers to women over thirty as girls.

No, you know this woman is lying. She is a Mayella Ewell or a Crystal Mangum, falsely accusing a good man to advance her agenda. Why else would she come forward at this critical juncture of his career, when he is on the verge of a major promotion, the one he's been working toward his entire adult life? The alleged incident took place years ago. Why now?

In bed, your husband becomes restless. He fidgets all night, unintentionally kicking you and tugging the covers until he's wrapped himself up in them like a vase packed for moving. It kills you to see him like this. He doesn't deserve it. And so you move closer and snuggle up with your head against his back, hoping he can feel your love and that this will calm him, enable peaceful sleep.

You lie there, eyes closed, hoping to drift off yourself, but sleep proves impossible. The cogs in your brain are turning, anxiously brainstorming ways to prove your husband's innocence. But how do you prove a negative? If his accuser had named a specific time and date, you might be able to produce evidence that he was out of town or with you or at some well-photographed event. But she claims the assault took place *around* a certain month, *about* a certain time. Hours of running in mental circles bring you back to where you started: you can't prove that something didn't happen.

The next morning, you tentatively suggest hiring a lawyer, but he insists he doesn't need one. "I haven't done anything wrong," he snaps. You don't push it. He's probably right. The investigation will exonerate him. It's her word against his.

She probably has a vendetta against him. He humiliated her in a meeting once or took a colleague's side over hers. It's never the big things that lead to long-held grudges; it's the minor slights, the casual rebukes, the perceived indifference or disrespect. Maybe she saw a chance to even an old score, or maybe she thinks he doesn't deserve the position he's being given, that it's her duty to stop someone she believes is unfit.

Or maybe that's not it. Maybe she's misinterpreted something he's said or done. The trouble with your husband, really, is that he doesn't always think before he acts, and so he probably hugged her when she was upset or placed a hand on her shoulder as he thanked her for a job well done. For a man, managing gender relations has become as difficult as juggling eggs, and your husband may not have adjusted to the changing times as quickly as he should have. If that proves to be the case, there will be a slap on the wrist, some public censure or forced apology. This will all be a detour, not a derailment. You're sure of it.

An investigation gets underway. Your husband assures you that everything is going to be fine; it's just a formality. "They don't want to be sued for doing nothing," he explains, citing the Catholic priest abuse scandal, the countless tech companies that have been deemed hostile to women.

"I know," you say with a small, confident smile because the last thing you want is for him to know how deeply this is affecting you.

You hope the investigators will reach out to you so that you can testify on his behalf. You will tell them about the Christmas he bought your daughters superhero capes instead of Barbie dolls. You'll drop in that time he spoke at the diversity luncheon downtown and mention that he's never minded losing to you at tennis. You may even tell them how gentle he is during sex, how he caters to your needs first, that you don't even have to fake a headache if you're not in the mood. But at some level, you know none of this would exonerate him. A spouse is inherently biased, worthless even as a character witness, and besides, all the good deeds in the world wouldn't compensate for one grievous harm.

The investigators must also realize that your testimony is worthless, because they don't ask to speak to you. You find this distressing. It renders you useless, and uselessness has always driven you crazy. You might as well be watching your husband's life unfold on television.

And then some plucky journalist learns of the accusation, and your husband is just wealthy enough, just powerful enough, just well-known enough for the media to care. The press coverage proves worse than the accusation itself. Now your husband's reputation is on the line. He comes home early, ignores you, and pours himself a glass of scotch. He downs it in one gulp, then buries his head in his hands. For a moment you think he's sobbing, but when he looks up, his face is contorted with rage. "That bitch," he fumes. "How could she?"

You wince because this is the first time you've ever heard your husband call a woman a bitch. She deserves it, you suppose, for everything she's putting him through, but you still don't like it. Rather than chastise him (you can't imagine that going well), you pour him some more scotch and rub his shoulders. He reaches for your hand and places it up against his cheek, and your heart breaks a little for how much he is suffering. You'd hoped this wouldn't change him; you're starting to see that it will.

The next day, when you go into work, everyone busies themselves as you walk by—rifling through papers, responding to emails, frowning at their monitors as though they've just seen something they don't like or don't understand. This is a noticeable shift. You are a principal at this highly regarded boutique consulting firm. Most days, your co-workers are eager to smile at you or speak to you, to make a good impression any way they can. Your stomach stirs. It hadn't occurred to you that this would affect your career too.

When you get to your office, you learn that four of your clients have dropped you. They don't call to explain themselves or discuss their concerns. They send brief, apologetic form emails: *We regret to inform you … go in a different direction … time for a change.* You've been nurturing some of these relationships for years. Frustrated, you phone them one by one, certain you can lure them back. But your first three calls go straight to voicemail. The fourth client answers, but no matter what you say, no matter how much you're willing to discount your services, she's unwilling to reconsider.

By the time you get off the phone with her, a fifth client has fired you. This time you don't bother to call. You close your office door, slip into child's pose, and try to tell yourself that everything will be okay.

Before this, you'd always thrived under pressure. You'd risen to the top of your field by devising creative solutions to high-stakes problems and meeting impossible deadlines, all while still making time for your family. But this … this is different. More personal. Although this crisis is man-made, it has all the hallmarks of a natural disaster. Unpredictable and destructive, it leaves you with the disquieting sense that there's a limit to what you can do.

Your husband comes home late that night, after the girls are in bed. You rise to greet him, and as he wraps his arms around you, you smell scotch on his breath.

He tells you he is going to the media to assert his innocence, and you are pleased because, at this point, it seems like a better strategy than remaining silent. You imagine dozens of reporters and their cameramen, a makeup artist to cover the bags that have emerged under his eyes, a carefully rehearsed speech that strikes the perfect balance between factual accuracy and emotional appeal. You will stand by his side during the press conference, of course, in that lovely navy wrap dress you bought last week. It's important for the world to see that his wife, a respected professional in her own right, stands by him.

But as it turns out, there will be no press conference. Your husband isn't celebrity enough for that. Instead, he will release a written statement professing his innocence. You ask if he'd like you to take the first stab at drafting it. (You've always been a better writer than he is.) He says no, thank you, his lawyer's already done that.

"Lawyer?" you say. "What lawyer?" Last you heard he wasn't hiring one.

"Oh, I got a lawyer yesterday," he says, casually, in the same tone he might say "Oh, I already picked up my dry cleaning."

You nod slowly, frustrated that your fate in this affair is to be relegated to the sidelines, irrelevant to investigators, unable to help your husband, not even worth consulting about hiring an attorney. "Don't you think we should have discussed this first?"

He apologizes, claiming this was a spur-of-the-moment decision, that this guy was too good to pass up. And, reluctant to fight, you forgive him but remind him to run this sort of thing by you in the future. "What if I'd spoken to the press and told them innocent men don't need attorneys only to discover that you'd hired one behind my back?"

"Why would you be talking to the press?" he asks.

"Maybe they ambushed me, and I responded without thinking," you suggest.

"Don't do that," he says.

"Don't make major decisions without consulting me," you counter.

"Deal," he replies, and you smile at each other, a unified force once more.

You reach for the bottle of wine you'd opened at dinner, and the two of you retreat to the sofa to finish it. You lean against his chest, and he puts his arm around you, and you think, once again, that you *know* this man, and he's no predator.

Your mother calls to see how you're holding up. The two of you have always been close, and she's always liked your husband. With your friends, you offer a brave smile and swear you're doing fine. With your mom, the truth comes gushing out. You can't help it. You're a new tube of toothpaste, squeezed in the center.

You tell her it's been worse since the news story broke. You're self-conscious when you go to yoga or stop by your favorite juice shop, even though no one has said or done anything or even looked at you funny. "I *feel* like everyone's staring at me," you admit.

You confess that your clients have been dropping like flies and that you worry that being affiliated with you is hurting your company. The other day, a colleague suggested you take a leave of absence, and you're starting to think you should. You're stressed and distracted, unable to focus.

After a while, you feel guilty. You've been talking to your mom for half an hour, and you haven't even mentioned your husband. You quickly add that you're worried about him too, that he's distracted and tense, that he's drinking more. Last night you found him on the floor of his office, surrounded by old paperwork. "I keep looking for something that proves this whole thing is bullshit," he'd said, a wild, desperate look in his eyes. That's another thing. He's been swearing more lately too, something he hasn't done since your daughters were born.

Your mom murmurs words of sympathy and encourages you to do all you can to alleviate his stress. "He is innocent, you know," she says. "Don't lose faith in him."

The second accuser goes straight to the media. You learn about her through your favorite news site, where you see the words *another allegation* and your husband's name, no bigger or bolder than any other headline, but to you they might as well be flashing neon. Everything becomes blurry, and you shut your eyes, willing this to be a dream or hallucination.

You force yourself to read the article, praying it will not be as bad as it seems. As you do, a single thought persists, and you cannot banish it, try though you might: the more alleged victims there are, the more likely this is to be true.

Your husband calls, but you're not sure you're ready to talk to him. You want to explore what you think and how you feel before hearing his side of the story. So for now, you turn your cell phone to silent and crawl into bed fully clothed.

As you lie there, not attempting to sleep but only thinking things through, you find that the smallest bit of doubt has crept in. You loathe yourself for this. You are not the long-suffering sort. You cannot imagine staying with a man who has cheated or otherwise betrayed your trust. But it doesn't seem fair to cut and run at the first sign of trouble either. Where is the line between fidelity and foolishness? Have you already crossed it? No. Surely not yet.

You can imagine circumstances in which both women are lying. If they're friends, for example, launching a coordinated attack. But there is no obvious connection between these women. They crossed paths with your husband at different times, in different ways. May-be the second woman is an opportunist, bandwagoning off the first woman's claim, hoping to make a quick buck. But it's equally pos-sible that the first woman's courage inspired the second to come forward. The more you think this through, the more shaken you become. A second accuser makes it much more than twice as likely that your husband is guilty. But that's inconceivable, isn't it? You'd know if he were that sort of man, wouldn't you? No, you tell your-self, this cannot be. But doubt, it turns out, is like mold. It seems harmless at first, but it spreads, and before you know it, it has be-come an infestation.

You call your husband back, desperately hoping he'll have an ex-planation for this, something that will put your mind at ease. When he answers, he sounds relieved to hear your voice, as though he'd been afraid you wouldn't call at all, as though he suspected you were already packing your bags. He offers no explanation for this second allegation but professes his innocence again and again. "You believe me, don't you?" he asks, his voice cracking.

You hesitate for half a second before saying yes. It is enough for him to know that you no longer have absolute faith in him. He falls silent for a moment, and into that silence you attempt to reaffirm your confidence in him. You can tell by the way he responds that he wants to believe you but doesn't. He must find this devastating, for if you are starting to waver, what hope can there be for anyone else?

The rest of the day passes in a haze. In between phone calls—from concerned family and friends, the girls' elementary school, the occasional reporter—you surf the internet, reading every account of your husband's ordeal you can find, devouring the comment sections.

Public opinion, like yours, has shifted with the second accusa-tion. You understand this, but still it unnerves you. The fair-minded encourage a thorough investigation and urge restraint in the meantime, but there are plenty of comments on both sides that disgust you.

Another witch hunt, says one man.

The feminazis are at it again, says another.

There's a war on men in this country, chirps a third.

As if men in modern America are the equivalent of Jews in Hitler's Germany. Preposterous. You don't want people like this defending your husband.

The other side has its share of extremists, too.

Why do all men think they're entitled to women?

All evidence suggests men should not be trusted with power.

#whitemaletakedown

The generalizations pain you. You know plenty of men who are good and respectful and honest, who don't deserve this kind of blanket condemnation. A week ago, you'd have said your husband was among them. You still hope that is the case.

You close your computer when you hear the voices of your girls, arriving home from school. You dash to the bathroom to wash away any lingering tears and then hurry out to meet them.

They are seated around the kitchen table, snacking on grapes. They seem less energetic than usual, wearier. They're too young to read the news, and you've tried to shield them from the brunt of this, but you can't protect them from every dirty look and thoughtless comment.

"What have you heard?" you ask.

They've heard their dad hurt some women, though they don't appear to understand how. They seem to be imagining him as a playground bully, teasing his victims or tugging at their hair. They are incredulous at the notion that their father could behave in such a manner. He has raised them to be kind to everyone. A few months ago, he'd grounded your oldest for taunting an obese girl. You are dismayed but not surprised when they ask the question you've been dreading. *Is it true, Mom?*

What are you supposed to say to that? If there's one thing you've learned as a parent, it's that children value openness and honesty, but you don't have it in you to condemn their father, not to them. Eventually, you settle for "While nobody other than your father and these women can ever know what really happened, I believe that he is innocent."

You see relief wash over their faces. You wish it were that simple for you.

When a third woman comes forward, you worry the floodgates are going to open. Could your husband be another Harvey Weinstein or Bill Cosby? Have you been married to a predator for decades without realizing it? How could that be? You'd have seen signs, right? Is it possible you've chosen to turn a blind eye to behaviors you should have noticed? Now, in addition to doubting your husband, you find you are doubting yourself.

Your husband doesn't come home much anymore. He spends his time either strategizing with his lawyer or trying to put out fires at work. But part of you wonders if he's avoiding you, if he's afraid of the questions you might ask, of seeing the doubt in your eyes.

He's right that you have questions. *Have you told me the complete truth? How could you do this? Did you think you'd never get caught? Had you thought about the consequences if you did? Did you consider me? Did you consider our daughters?* You realize with a jolt that your thinking has shifted from presumption of innocence to presumption of guilt, and you feel heartsick. You had told yourself you would stand by your husband until you were given reason not to, but clearly your head is at war with your heart.

Your husband comes home early one night, the earliest he has been home in weeks, and your daughters surround him, enveloping him in hugs. Your husband's face lights up at the sight of them. It's the happiest you've seen him in ages.

He asks about school and hobbies and friends, and then he sends them upstairs, leaving the two of you alone in the foyer. Suddenly you're afraid that he'll confess, shattering that last remaining vial of hope, reducing him to a degenerate and you to a fool. But he doesn't. Instead, he tells you he's been forced to take a leave of absence until they've concluded the investigation.

"Paid," he adds, as if that matters.

You need to sit down, so you move into the living room, and he follows. "Say something," he implores. But you don't have anything to say.

"Look," he says. "I've done some things I'm not proud of. I'm no angel. But the things they're accusing me of? Never, I swear."

"Then why are they saying these things?"

"I don't know," he admits. "I'm not crazy enough to suggest a conspiracy. But I guess when the stakes are high enough, people will say anything to affect the outcome."

The promotion then. It all comes back to that. They don't believe he deserves to be in that position, to have that kind of power.

When you don't say anything, your husband continues. "My lawyer isn't worried. There's no evidence. It's their word against mine about events that happened years ago. We'll ride this out."

But you don't want to ride this out. You want it never to have happened. "Tell me about these women," you say.

But he claims he doesn't remember two of them. They are no-bodies, he insists, coming out of the woodwork to tear him down. "Probably feminists with an agenda," he says, and you cringe because he sounds like the men in the comment sections online.

"Well, tell me about the one you do remember," you urge.

He insists there's not much to tell. Low-level employee, adequate but not great at her job. The only reason he remembers her at all is because one of the mid-level guys had dated her for a few months, and when he'd dumped her she'd made a scene in the employee break room. "You'd never have expected it from her," he recalls. "She was such a quiet, mousy little thing."

This story heartens you. Accuser number one is prone to dramatics, which, to you, suggests a possible tendency toward overstatement, an unnecessary escalation of everyday events. You take your husband's hand and squeeze it, and he gives you a sad smile.

"I'm sorry you have to go through this," he says. "I know how hard it's been."

In the news, friends, past and present, take sides. Some of them stand by your husband, insisting he is an upstanding guy who has always treated women well. Others tell reporters that the culture was different a decade ago, that he and the other bigwigs had gotten away with a lot of crap that wouldn't fly today.

His supporters and detractors are largely divided by gender, and this bothers you. When you hear the way the men talk, you can't help but feel like they are circling the wagons, protecting one of their own. You should be grateful. For once, age-old gender dynamics are working in your favor. But instead you are dismayed by the lack of progress, the tribal thinking, your sense that truth and justice are getting lost in a grander battle over other things.

Mercifully, no more accusations are forthcoming. They stall at an ambiguous three. You think that maybe this indicates some bad behavior on your husband's part but none of it tantamount to sexual assault, none of it career destroying, all of it so far in the past it hardly matters anymore. After all, if your husband were really a predator, there would be more of them, right?

Barred from work, your husband locks himself away in his home office. He is always on the phone, and he talks of nothing but this. He hires a private investigator and agrees to an interview with a journalist he's assured will be friendly. He yells at his lawyer, wanting to know where the investigation is, ordering more frequent updates, frustrated by the pace of progress. He has become a man obsessed.

He drinks more and eats less. He can't be bothered to spend time with the family. You feel like you are straddling two worlds, the one your husband occupies and the real one, where life is proceeding as usual, as life does, regardless of any personal torment or tragedy any individual is undergoing.

Eventually, the strain becomes too much, and you, too, take a leave of absence. You follow your husband's lead and spend your days phoning and emailing every connection you have on his behalf. You call in old favors and become indebted to people you barely know. You're not sure any of it helps, but it's better than doing nothing.

Each afternoon when the girls come home you hang up the phone, close your email, and slip back into the real world as easily as the Pevensie children returning to the old wardrobe after their adventures in Narnia. You ask your daughters about their day, have dinner with them, sometimes play a game or watch a movie. Once, you encourage your husband to do the same, but he responds incredulously. "My life is on the line, and you expect me to play Monopoly?" You never try again.

After a while, you hear the investigation is coming to a close. You are shocked. This had come to feel infinite, an endless journey to an unknown destination.

Your husband hears that the outcome is favorable, and he starts talking about defamation lawsuits. You cringe. You don't want that. You only want it to be over.

Then you realize that it never will be. For you, this inquest does no good; its conclusion is meaningless. You still won't know whether your husband did the things they said he did. There is no smoking gun, nor is there some miraculous piece of evidence conclusively proving his innocence. It is all conjecture, guesswork, piecing together witness reports from faulty memories.

So where does that leave you? What do you do now? The only thing you can do, the only thing you could ever do: you believe him or you don't. You stay or you go. Either way you are left picking up the pieces, rebuilding your life from the rubble.

MIGUEL SYJUCO

"   "

Y ou said it. Stupidly said it. The word they've forbidden you to
say. How are you going to fix this? Your long life built through
hard work. And courage—before it imploded online; at an event just
like this one. Don't panic. The piper must now be paid, she thinks,
paid and placated. Oh you've become such a cliché! She takes another deep breath and watches from the wings as shadows fill the last
seats in the auditorium.

   She'd said it, sure: the word. But not recklessly. Deliberately saying it in context and total condemnation. With some anger, okay,
and indignation, admittedly, but isn't that understandable these days?

   She'd said the word during an event online, the only one she'd
been lucky to get as a middle-aged, midlist brown writer with a new
novel out amongst tour-de-force debuts and elegiac blockbusters. A
Zoom interview two months ago, for the Toronto Public Library,
where she'd been explaining her misgivings about her Black character
not being allowed to say it—as he, in particular, would, and could,
and perhaps should have whilst chastising another (non-Black)

character's careless habit of saying it. One word—belonging to her character, whitewashed by her publisher's sensitivity readers—from amidst two hundred ten thousand words across four hundred twenty pages about uncomfortably sympathetic anti-heroes and thorny moral questions and interrogations of racism and corruption and mass murder and misogyny in a hypersexualised society and and and many other horrors of our human condition, etcetera.

She'd said the word, finally, towards the end of that Zoom interview. Neither because she didn't care or has condoned her racist husband or speaks it amongst dinner companions who similarly distrust infantalising euphemisms; nor because she'd spat it often whilst growing up in Dumaguete taping rap songs off the radio for their defiant urgency moving even her, a provincial Filipina a world away.

She'd said it after discussing how such a complicated, hateful word is also just a word, especially when not directed at a person or a people but pinned and flayed as it was: a word. Yes, she knew its violent history as a weapon of oppression, and the claims now of ownership by people whose ancestors had been so long enslaved, who now hold the liberty, the power, over that word used for centuries to disempower them. She knows and understands. But the interview had roamed to banned books, free speech, and taboos—and from her laptop in her office overlooking the desert and a lick of the Arabian Gulf, she stuttered her response to a question-slash-asseveration chosen for her from the live-chat section, her anonymous watchers' invisible eyes needling her from behind cryptic avatars and sassy handles during their hour-and-a-half lunch hour.

She'd said it in reply to a conundrum posed by them—the plural them—the throng's concerns about who owns words summed up deftly by the interlocutor garbed in pronouns and appropriate cultural garments, a she in her fluoro-tinged sari sat in a Parkdale flat on the stolen soil of the Mississauga, Petun, Haudenosaunee, and Huron-Wendat nations. In the background, photogenic ferns shared shelves with waves of feminist books as a window offered snowflakes floating peacefully—whilst a storm of audience questions scrolled down the side of the screen, feeling increasingly like heckling, or demands for confession. And as she watched her tiny self hesitate in the upper right-hand corner, her name naked beneath her image, facing the faceless, nameless, plural they who were posting fair points and familiar bloviations about words having power, and freedoms requiring responsibilities, and never shouting fire in a crowded theatre, she wanted—no, *needed*—to make loud and clear that the only thing ever more dangerous than words is silence.

She'd said it, she thinks now, because of that—and because they'd put me on the defensive, after my opinion that journalists, artists, and comedians must lead on the ramparts in defending free expression (now with academia in the grip of the language Stasi, and their useful idiots). For she had mentioned the African-American comedian Dave Chappelle, with whom she disagreed and agreed in various shades of nuance, because aren't his jokes, well, jokes? His criticisms cutting critically, just as insults are meant to be insulting, and profanity profane—especially when punching up against any power now potent enough to cancel his gigs and rouse that knife attack onstage. She'd intended to compare that to her own threats from troll mobs back home (rape, death, doxing, all for her reportage), as well as the libel laws wielded by her country's powerful, who intimidate with indictments sent before judges they'd appointed, with potential penalties six years in prison, for words printed, or twelve for offence online. Like that stupidly brave tweet that got a college kid arrested for criticising the previous president's drug war, which had killed thousands, as she'd witnessed firsthand as a journalist now too familiar with the ripe-fruit scent of cooling blood pooled on pavement that still bedevils her dreams. And she would've liked to tell her interviewer about her crisis of faith in defending facts—now that the dictator's family has ridden back to power on the wave of falsehoods flooding the world—her dismayed doubt niggling whilst truth's old safeguards drown in lies posted, shared, and liked till they're real; her country's history rewritten. But she'd never gotten to that.

Because she'd said the word, certain it was justified during that particular discussion about her novel, and power, and ownership, and the hazards of taboos, and her own bedrock belief that all the freedoms that humanity seeks rely on the free expression we'd use to fight for them—starting precisely when somebody gets upset by something someone says (because everybody should have the right to speak freely, whilst no one has the right to not be offended). So she'd decided, in an instant, that she'd no longer fear that word, or any. And that, in this instance, it made no sense not to say it. So she did.

Our lives always hinge on these moments—she thinks, exhaling, inhaling, like a cliché—moments such as this: Swaying just offstage. Swallowing your panic. Practising yogic diaphragmatic breathing. Before you stride into the light for an interview. My first and only since that bloody Zoom event. This one put together by her university's only conservative student org. Which she'd always despised as naïve, misguided, and reactionary. Babies, bigots, and book burners, even. Who'll stream it live online in five. Recorded, every word.

This, now, her second and last chance, after everything: that word, two months ago. Then her hunkered silence. After her shattered reputation. Then dumping by her agent. After lost friends. And all her progress with her daughter gone (whom she spots online, on WhatsApp, ignoring her messages and mawkish emojis and links to articles about Berlin, gender fluidity, and polyamory that she hopes might prove her motherly willingness to understand, and accept). All that and her suspension from her livelihood, pending the committee's investigation, at an American—"global and world-class"—West Coast uni in the Middle East, where during her seven years as a professor she'd witnessed these issues take root slowly and explode quickly, in a kind of cultural colonialism that alarms her. One colleague disciplined for using, in an economics class, the word "niggard"—its Old Norse etymology and zero connection to notions of negritude now trumped by tin ears, hair triggers, and niggardly empathy. Another colleague sacked for a joke made whilst chatting after hours in the corridor, trembling his fist parodically and uttering "white power" ironically, in an attempt to mock white supremacy in a world he'd just been praising as inexorably more diverse—his whiteness proof enough to decontextualise those words in the eyes of both the student who reported him and the director of diversity, equity, inclusion, and belonging who insisted on their zero-tolerance policy for anything interpreted as racist, no matter the intent.

She'd dropped her own nuclear word, yes, almost to her surprise—but not on campus, or at any event where she was representing the university, which may prove to be her job-saving grace. When hauled, finally, last week, into a conference room to face the four-person committee, she argued that her point was appropriate, and valid discourse according to the faculty handbook, part of her work protected by academic freedom—which had been guaranteed as inviolable: a much-vaunted condition between the university and its host country, who'd both since the beginning suffered the consternation and convulsions of critics who saw in the new campus a devil's bargain, of duty-free petro-riyals and Sharia law, instead of outreach and inroads for liberal-arts values and a Western secular perspective.

Now, the irony of her situation isn't lost on her, the university's only Filipina full-time prof—with a British passport but abiding anxiety amongst the Gulf Arabs trailing amber, oudh, and elegant abayas, tribal privilege, pull, and primacy in this, their society, where we're all hired help—she who still gets chastised by old colleagues at New York cocktail parties for her lack of freedoms and income tax, and grilled by relatives every Christmas in Manila about whether she's allowed to drive, or must wear a burka—and what would happen if you criticised the Amir online?—her mother sending consistent Viber messages linking articles about human-rights violations in a region that spans fifteen Islamic countries of varying religiosity and progressing liberty alongside an increasingly right-wing Jewish nation that's making friends with all of them (well, except Palestine). Such banal Islamophobia, which she was guilty of her whole life till she moved here, before she recognised the other guarantees their system offered. To be free of the fear of muggings or mass shootings or medical bills. To walk down any street at any time, especially as a woman. And to teach perspectives that are not beholden to the doctrines of North America. Surely her colleagues on the committee must understand how and why she used that word? Yet outside the conference room, her dean pulled her to linger, and behind the backs of his fellow university brass getting smaller down the hall, he told her explicitly but unofficially that, this time around, a public apology would go a *very* long way.

She appreciated and hated him for it, his implications clear. Despite, she mulls, all the sins I've witnessed go unpunished at this university, the culprits' culpabilities fading like a mirage in the late-afternoon dunes. Like that minor poet with a major attitude about it, who'd likely torpedoed her nomination for department head through fools' gold and ersatz myrrh whispered into the ear of their messianic previous dean, who'd cocked up the Arts and Humanities division like a cuckold does his dignity. That same dean, white as Nordic snow, in ratty T-shirts and toe-jam sandals, who'd made repeated remarks about her youthful appearance—racist slights so familiar to an Asian—whilst discouraging, as premature, her requests for promotion and candidacy in certain leadership roles, despite their same age and scholastic achievements. And what about the whitesplaining?—she fumes—by that other crackerjack colleague with his Founding Fathers ponytail and neon yellow, feverish interest in social justice and cultural studies, during a meeting of the A&H Curricular Committee, on which they both served—he telling *me* how I could define myself as an Asian, from Asia, from "the Pearl of the *Orient*" (as I'd so grievously called it)—advising her to read Asian-American scholarship on the "O-word" (as he'd called it); the coloniser/settler-spawn then lecturing her on the legacy of the revolutionary Filipino "Illustréz" (who unbeknownst to him were the subjects of her previous book—and are actually called the

"Ilustrados"). Yet the worst sin, in her mind, was the university's handling of students' concerns about a certain oleaginous professor, with anchoring tenure and matching paunch, and his alleged affair with his pupil—for which he'd been sent, Vatican-like, to a plum gig at a satellite campus in a sunny region of Europe, first for sabbatical then some two years more (about one thousand and one nights), till those students graduated and left with their fading memories of what they'd feared he committed. A breathtakingly troubling tale that she'd recounted in "Scheherazade," her short story in the *New Yorker*—in her current, experimental, polemic-as-characterisation style—that had gotten her hauled that first time, a couple of years ago, to face a similar disciplinary committee, who accepted, grudgingly, her defence of creative and academic freedom, setting her up now as a reoffender with a familiar, moth-eaten excuse.

For which you must now apologise, she whispers. As the production assistant appears. To adjust her wireless mic one last time. And remind her how to switch it on. Before he hurries off. As she gulps down another panic attack. Deeply breathing. Test. Test. Test, test, test, someone's saying over the speakers. She limbers up the muscles of her mouth. Watermelon. Wimbledon. Watermelon, Wimbledon, she mumbles. To be or not to be. To be or—oh bugger off, Macbeth, with your slings and arrows; you privileged twat.

Which was exactly what one heckler at her Zoom talk implied, having judged her from what little they heard of her perspective. You should farther educate yourself on these matters, they'd written, anonymously, gender unknown. Ungrammatically dismissive, their truth so real to them they assumed she wasn't educated just because she disagreed. But she was proudly woke before the word woke was a bad one—though like ideas words evolve, and even she now uses it as a pejorative. Even she runs the risk of being tagged a trans-exclusionary radical feminist for her refusal to agree that transmisogyny is tantamount to murder. Bigotry, yes, terribly so. But murder? All because insults lead to depression and depression to suicide? Or is it because words can incite violence? Then why not counter with words that defend tolerance and peaceful debate? And what about deeper issues of discrimination and lack of opportunities for transpersons, and those intersectional biases against minorities and people of colour no matter their gender?—which won't be solved no matter how many fucking times we retweet, or demand to speak to the manager. She'd long lived her own related experience, always decidedly a feminist, and unavoidably BIPOC, misjudged as her daughter's nanny at playgrounds in both Tribeca and South Kensington, and now as a maid at metro stops in the Middle East. (Her child's eventual shame in the mirror, those tween years of braces and bravado, reflected as blame upon her mother.) She even used to consider herself an ally to the gays, marching proudly each June down Fifth Avenue into the Village, her daughter in a chitenge baby wrap then stroller then roller skates then fab heels, rainbows always painted across their foreheads, a cool mum with a heart so consistent with her values she's not just a socialist, she's a goddamn commie—yet now I'd be a TERF on queer Twitter? All for thinking that females born males will never experience life, and loss, quite like she has.

But just because you can say something doesn't mean you should, another heckler had scolded in that scrolling Zoom chat. Sure. But just because you shouldn't shouldn't mean you can't. Remember "Je Suis Charlie"? What about "My Body, My Choice"?—of what I consent to put into it, and what comes out of whichever lips. Nobody is forcing you to listen, or see, or believe. The orthodoxies of today making her consider, late some nights, how she'd troubled her parents, those years of her activism, brandishing at protests the vintage dogmas of her University of the Philippines professors, shaped as they'd been by dictatorship and disco, inspiring her screeds at the dinner table as her parents silently chewed the gristle of their middle-class aspirations for better lives and best marriages for her and her two sisters. Just as I'm now being faulted for the values I'll never compromise. Yet she does regret ruining her father's run for city council, with her articles against the party in power as she scrabbled up from cub to beat reporter, after he finally retired from slinging insurance and could seek again the purpose and passions of his youth: Once the pomaded, bespectacled president of the national organisation of student-body presidents, before he'd gotten her mother preggers with her and made his choice. On his daughter's muckraking about that incumbent regime, he never once asked her to quit—not like her mother had, secretly, on his behalf. And on his deathbed, over Zoom, he told me he was proud of the woman I'd become: Selfless, kind, and brave. Isn't duty strange?

So what would you do in a situation like this?—she'd often wondered when reading news about victimising villains or vilified victims and their unwelcome kiss, quote, or idea. Would you issue a mea culpa?—and perform your flagellation for this touch-screen Inquisition of autocorrectness and algorithmic tyranny. Or would you double down?—to fight for your faith and find a lonely welcome amongst only those who agree with your grievances.

Oh how tempting to just say fuck it. To take this stage and please her hosts and provoke and trigger to prove her point. Like how her Scottish soon-to-be-ex hubbie would goad her to wear those T-shirts from the Negros Trade Fair—that annual bazaar her youngest sister helped organise for their ancestral province, Negros Oriental, and its conjoined neighbor, Negros Occidental—steamrolling her disquiet with his big Glaswegian barrister laugh at the thought of her on campus in that shirt with "I ♥ Negros" across its chest, which she uses at home for yoga, because she really does love Negros and its mystical islands and emerald grandeur. That shirt unfortunately her favourite, along with the one with a red flag with white letters: KKK, for the Kataastaasang, Kagalanggalangang Katipunan ng mga Anak ng Bayan, or the Supreme and Honourable Association of the Children of the Nation—who'd bled and died against the Spanish conquerors who pretty much enslaved us for more than three hundred years, before American treachery did similar for some forty more. Why can't we be proud of this defiant part of our culture? Instead of sheepish, or cowed by others' ignorance? She'd always thought that an educator shouldn't fear or lack faith in her students—or shirk the responsibility to teach them what they should learn (like cursive, or taking telephone calls without terror). Plus, she'd long quit the US for the Middle East, more at home here than anywhere else, where Pinoys outnumber North Americans ten to one—our smiling, unassuming, dutiful resilience more prized ("the nicest people money can buy," her soon-ex would joke) than our old masters' spangled confidence in their constitutional exceptionalism. And isn't our university touted as unmatched in diversity, tolerance, and global perspective? All its talks, seminars, and mandatory training after Black Lives Matter and, later, Stop Asian Hate—though no denouncement yet of Russia's invasion of Ukraine, for reasons of "student inclusion." Nor any substantive examination of racial issues beyond the lens of America.

Yes, that's it!—exactly: Cultural imperialism, of the kind that had us exhibited like animals at the 1904 World's Fair in St. Louis, Missouri; Manifest Destiny's "little brown brothers" confined still decades later by signs in establishment windows across the West Coast: "No Dogs and Filipinos Allowed." About all that, her soon-to-be-ex proved right—racist though he turned out to be, indelibly resenting her refusals to go four-by-four overlanding with his lads and their Filipina wags who were nice enough but not enough to get to know enough for their eventual drama to be worth it. Compatriots who condemned her shrilly even as she silently refused to judge their counterfeit accents and LVMH tastes—because we're all just strivers, she'd tell herself, in this dog-eat-dog world that we've cobbled and coddled through our litigiousness, selfishness, and yearning for certainties and absolution, the way her soon-ex blames his bloating body and bad investments on the milquetoast Jeremy Corbyn, and Brexit, and web cookies, and the offside rule, and his new bloody Gaysian boss at the firm, and of course the undeniable descent into fascism of a Great Britain to which he'll never deign to return. But he was right about what it means that even her local students recognised the brutalised African-American George Floyd, in photos she showed in class, but not Mohamed Bouazizi, whose self-immolation ignited the Arab Spring, and to whom she now somehow feels an affinity (if she can dare say that). Right despite how wrong he was—her ex-to-be—about everything else, with his malignant benevolence, and brutalist demeanour, his interruptions and corrections and especially *his* plans for *their* retirement (or "freedom," as he called it)—which to her betrayed his envy of his pals and their wives and their master-and-slave mail-order marriages.

I am not the racist, she breathes. And checks her phone. Like a smoker with one last drag. Two minutes to go. Thinking of all the things being said. The insults from strangers. From both right and left. And what she must say. To earn the life she deserves. Now that we're done and divorced. And he's alone and I am free. Oh the ironies, she breathes. Then sighs.

For there he is, gloating still—via WhatsApp—about his relationship with their only surviving child, blowing up her phone again with random updates and smiling father-daughter photos in Michelin-starred restos and rented cabrios across Germany, Italy, and France, no mention of, no sympathy for, the inexplicable rift between mother and cub that keeps her tossing at night over whatever offence she could have committed. The last text she'd received, many months ago, from their wee swan: an emoji, of the grateful hands—a very Gen Zed reply to her wishing her "break a leg" in that debut performance as Odile. Be brave, they'd always said, and break a leg. Ever since her daughter was still small enough to hang on from that bucket seat on the bicycle's back, happily humming Tchaikovsky up Eighth, along Fifty-Seventh, and down Ninth Avenue for her classes, the two of them afterwards enjoying Eskimo Pies in the park, then *pas de chats* across Heckscher Playground. Now she's playing Odile in a major European company, and maybe Odette one day, if all goes well. *When* all goes well (a very motherly certainty). Yet the only reply from her very outspoken daughter was that fucking emoji—not even those photos I'd liked, each one, on Instagram, ten months and eleven days ago—some eight months before she'd said that shameful word.

I am not a racist, she thinks. Then whispers. And breathes in. And breathes out. And oh God here comes your interviewer. A rising junior and debate-team vice-prez. Seersucker jacket candy-blue. Bowtie red as his cheeks. Offering to help switch on her mic. Thirty seconds before we start. Ready? No, she replies. Both laughing. For vastly different reasons. Don't doubt, he says, what you believe in. She nods. Just nods. If only he knew. If only you did.

To whom must you now apologise, really? Neither the academics griping and sniping atop their ivory towers, from where they cower and command as if the likes of them don't owe their livelihood to the lives of the likes of her. Nor the pundits and influencers tutting and tweeting at their screens, from where they hide and harass as if they had ever ventured the world's sharp edges and arduous greys that only translate online as jpegs, comment, hashtags, and outrage. You're a writer, goddamn it! Duty-bound to words that provoke, not placate; confront, not compromise. Like the novels in the undergrad course she teaches, those too-rare works of the imagination that changed the world through revolutions or legal rulings or controversies—each book a mirror held up to society by an ordinary individual who sat down to write what they saw, what they thought, what they believed to be vital, inspiring first one reader then so many others who together faced the streets or courts or hard conversations. That's what literature's supposed to do. Right? Tell tough stories. Imagine possibilities. Say the unsayable. Pushing readers beyond themselves, no matter the cost. Beecher Stowe's book starting that great war. Rizal shot by a squad in a field. Remarque losing sister and nation to Nazis. Sinclair hitting the gut only by missing the heart. And Miller and Lawrence and Radclyffe Hall banned and tried for love's obscenities. And Rushdie long menaced and finally attacked for, well, a story. All refusing to turn away, because the cost was worth it, giving purchase to that which was too valuable to surrender.

I am not a racist. Not more than anyone else. I'm a selfless person. Who does kind things. I care. And tip. I recycle. And do charity. Over Christmas *and* Ramadan. And I—oh stop; your interviewer's watching, worried. He breathes deeply with her. Twice. Thrice. Holds up his hand and whispers ten seconds. And silence your phone. Then bounds ahead onto the stage. Brash and blinding in the lights. Leaving you. Still unsure. To say what?

I'm sorry, the offence my, not representative of who I, and acknowledge, educated myself further, anyone who felt hurt by, in this noble institution and, trauma and power disparity, nor condone my characters', vow to be—Hamlet, I meant; not Macbeth—my responsibility, books and bans, thoughts and prayers, fake news, grooming, Ivermectin, believe all, lives matter, women life freedom, sacred and profane, the B-word and SH-word and F-word in fourth grade, darn and heck not damn and hell, unhoused not homeless, passed away not dead, healthy not fat the biggest hypocrisy of all as she listened yesterday to her internist explaining the scientific truths about good versus bad cholesterol and in the mirror at home this morning all the jiggling creeping love handles around her huggable tum and her soon-to-be-ex's echoing backhanded affections and what you dared not even tease about his hairline or upper canines because you can't say this anymore and we can't say that ever about minorities or the king of Thailand or prophets or Israel or Xi Jin Pooh or your hosts in your adopted country and the thieving murderous vindictive rulers of the place you'll always call home even if you won't bring yourself to ever live there again but you can't admit that to anyone or say or care or do enough about all the issues and beliefs and consequences that everyone, they, I don't know who but they, say you must—

Phone buzzing. WhatsApp messages. From your daughter! Be brave. And break a leg. Mommy. Emoji: a whirling heart. Your heart whirls. Oh you're such a cliché! Five seconds. Last deep breath. Then, stage underfoot, blinded and blinking and thinking: You, now, decide.

JONATHAN STONE

EULOGY

Sam stood at the podium beside his wife's casket, looking out at the silent sea of dark suits and muted dresses, and hung his head for a sustained and excruciating moment in which we witnessed the full weight of his bereavement, before he began. "She had the most intense orgasms," he informed us ruefully, shaking his balding head, pausing as if to ponder, to absorb the loss anew.

Even in his anguish, he must have known—was presumably at least somewhat aware—that highlighting this attribute of the deceased would be an unexpectedly theatrical way to start. As he must have calculated—or again, been at least dimly aware—that this might be the only time he would ever say such a thing aloud: where it would be, or at least *might* be, permissible and acceptable in the unmoored profoundness of his misery. All his life, it occurred to me at that moment, Sam had probably been waiting to share this morsel of information, and now he chose to tell all of us at once, in the context of—under the cover of?—his bereavement. Yet I could also tell, as anyone could tell, it was uttered in genuine grief.

There was a nervous laugh from somewhere in the back row—it sounded to me like Sam's cousin Morty, who'd been our fourth for golf a few times—but otherwise, everyone remained silent. A rapt silence, certainly. But it would have been a rapt silence anyway, as a man began eulogizing his wife. We would have been attentive anyway, a little anxious, sitting slightly more upright in our pews the moment he took the podium, leaning slightly forward, to see if a man who had just lost his wife, his companion of thirty years, could hold it together enough to say anything at all. To see if Sam—colleague, father, friend—could even begin to speak.

He patted his maroon tie. He smiled wistfully. "They were so loud, so intense, we'd have to wait until we had complete privacy, until the kids were out of the house." He glanced apologetically, yet so clearly affectionately, at his three adult children sitting shoulder to shoulder in the front pew. "We'd have to plan our love life around Irene's orgasms. Their intensity defined our marriage." He shrugged, almost helplessly, at a fact he'd lived with in dutiful, respectful silence for thirty years, determining that now was the appropriate moment to share it. Maybe he even intended this disclosure to be genuinely helpful in beginning to answer the natural and inevitable question that floats above many of the mourners in this stuffy sanctuary, one that arises naturally in mourning a couple so unceremoniously severed after a lifetime: *What was their marriage like?* He was actually telling us. Accommodating our idle or prurient curiosity, addressing the vaguely hovering question directly.

As if people deserved to know. His way of saying *This was us. This defined us.* As if it would be devious, untruthful, not to share it. This was the time to say it—among family, closest friends. Say it once, have it clearly stated and understood, so no one would ever feel the need to ask any further questions on such a sensitive and private topic.

Had he even planned to say it? Or was it extemporaneous, simply what came into his head when he stepped up to the microphone?

We've all heard eulogies delivered both ways— either read off a sheaf of papers printed out the night before and pulled from a vest pocket or purse, or just arriving at the microphone as if by surprise and saying whatever comes to mind, perhaps too distraught in the aftermath of a death to sit and compose something (or let's be honest—in many cases too busy, or too lazy). Was Sam simply confident that something important and relevant would occur to him at that moment? Or maybe he simply didn't care whether anything did or not, didn't really care what happened up there, or what happened anymore, since the woman in the casket beside him was gone.

My wife, Sandi, and I were sitting toward the rear, so I could see the shoulders and backs of just about everyone attending, including those of his three children in the first row, his son and two daughters. Apart from his cousin Morty's snicker behind us, there was no detectable reaction from anyone else. A frozen sea of the aforementioned dark suits and muted dresses, a tableau that didn't visibly shift one iota. Everyone remained silent. Listening to a eulogy. Pretending it was any other eulogy, or hoping it quickly returned to being so. Hoping that we had misheard, and knowing we hadn't. Aware now, too, many of us, I'm sure, of our anxious, suddenly accelerating heartbeats.

"She would scream to high heaven," he told us. "Every orgasm was like an unanticipated shock, like a new discovery, like landing on some wondrous new shore, and they'd go on and on for, I don't know, twenty seconds? Thirty? It was something to behold." He shook his head.

Sam's hair had been gone a long time. He'd always been thin, sunken-chested, ever since we met as young associates in tax law at Shepherdson Stern, where we're both partners today. (Meeting him today, one might assume his build was the result of thirty years bent over tax cases, but I can attest that he arrived this way. Physically preconfigured for tax work.) His chest never filled out his suit jacket. It hung loose, baggy, his slacks, too, disconsolate-looking articles of clothing that themselves always appeared as if they were in mourning: exactly as they hung on him now. Which is all my way of saying that his description of her orgasm, from my sense of it, had nothing to do with conveying his own physical prowess. He was describing it as merely a witness who happened to be there. Happened to be fortuitously present for every one of them.

"Her body's arching, and her facial contortions throughout it, Good Lord. Like some kind of demonic possession. But I don't want to get too graphic, that would be inappropriate, given the occasion." As if suddenly snapped from his reverie back to the realities and requirements of the moment.

He spent the next few minutes speaking proudly, appreciatively, and conventionally of Irene's unwavering competence as a mother, her work fostering service dogs for the deaf, her record of volunteerism on the library board and school board and town council, her easy mastery of Laser-class sailboats, the happy home that she had created and anchored for thirty years. It was a catalogue of her grace and humor and warmth that cheered absolutely no one, from what I could tell, that lifted no hearts, that only magnified the insult of her untimely death and of death in general. It was, however, a catalogue of her special qualities and proficiencies that had the ameliorating effect of making her orgasms sound like just one more in the list of them. The one he'd happened to begin with, yes. But maybe the list was in no particular order. Or maybe it was in that order for every reason in the world.

As if it was an effort, conscious or not, to return the eulogy to normalcy. As if to make us all question once more whether we'd heard it accurately to begin with, whether it had really happened. Would any of us remember these other details of Irene's life of service, of goodness, in light of how Sam had begun? Or would we now remember *every* detail about her, remember the entire eulogy, as a result? Would her life now especially glow and shimmer before us? Was it the best thing he could do to honor, to commemorate her, to revere Irene's memory?

"Gone," he said, drawing suddenly to a close. And although the word appropriately conveyed a global sense of loss, it was said with such abject mourning, such fresh pain, that it was apparent, to me at least, what he meant, what he was still recounting, what theme he had circled back to. "Gone," he said again, as if watching his wife's orgasms disappear down their suburban driveway, head out onto some horizon. "Gone, like her Christmas peppermint bark, like her gluten-free peach pancakes, like her fresh-ground coffee, like her blazing smile." His eyes soaked suddenly, completely, as if in a fresh wash of memory. A man standing before a hundred and fifty of us, utterly alone in his desolation. All of his loving family, his dutiful friends, useless to him.

He made his way, stooped, depleted, back to the front pew to rejoin his children, wiping his eyes with the back of his hand all the way.

A few of us, golf buddies who know each other from playing together at the East Links Club, are standing around one of the small high hors-d'oeuvres tables afterward, when Sam approaches.

"Hey, gents."

"Hey, Sam."

"Thanks for coming. Really appreciate it."

We do the obligatory shake-off of the sentiment. *Of course. Don't be silly.* No one has removed a suit jacket or loosened a tie, I notice. At other events like this, we'd have settled in by now. This time, everyone's staying formal. As if the eulogy has somehow demanded it.

"Sorry about all that," says Sam.

We shake it off again. *Nothing to be sorry about. Don't be silly.*

There is a brief silence. All of us simply absorbing the murmur of the room, unsure what to say. I, for one, am looking for some angle to slice into the silence.

Richie says, with a shrug, "My wife never had an orgasm."

We're all silent for a brief moment, until Dave responds, in a flatly conversational tone that will strike me later as miraculously well-modulated, "Really? Huh."

"Thirty years of marriage, and not one," Richie says. "Didn't even know what one was, read about and heard about them, of course, but just ... never experienced it."

"Huh."

"I mean, for a couple of years, we explored it with doctors, to figure it out. But then"— Richie shrugs—"we just forgot about it. Put it aside. Just not part of the marriage, that's all." Another shrug.

One might assume, from the nature of this confession, that Richie's wife too had passed away and that he was taking Sam's lead, and this moment, to share at last this bit of vestigial grief. But it was not conveyed in a spirit of grief at all. In fact, he was suggesting that the marriage was largely happy, which by all outward indications it was, and Richie's wife, by the way, was standing about fifteen feet from us, chatting with a few of the other wives at a nearby hors-d'oeuvres table.

"Dolores comes right away," says Derek, in a spirit of mild befuddlement that he has contained, perhaps, for thirty years. "Damnedest thing. Within, I don't know, five, ten seconds? Has always been that way. I'm just getting started, just settling in, and she's coming. It's something anatomical."

"Irene's OBGYN told her she had a championship uterus," Sam informs us suddenly. Does he mean this as a medical explanation of her sexual response? A scientific proof point? I don't know enough about the female anatomy to be sure. Perhaps he brings it up only to add it to the long list of her remarkable qualities, one he'd neglected to mention during the eulogy.

All of us nod in respectful understanding. Which, I must admit, is an understanding fuller and more profound than if he had never said anything.

It was eminently clear to me—there would be no other chance. This was the time and place—the only appropriate time and place—to talk about wives' orgasms, or absence thereof. Yes, if we were all decades younger, maybe in some locker room, or exceedingly drunk at a bar after a Red Sox victory. But no longer. Not in the wood-paneled East Links lounge after playing eighteen, not at our Tuesday night bridge, no matter how late and how much bourbon. Only acceptable here, in this church, at this memorial service, at this hors-d'oeuvres table, knowing none of it would ever be mentioned again.

Should I too be saying something? *Sometimes Sandi comes, sometimes she doesn't. Her neck and face get so itchy before she climaxes, we need to stop for a moment so she can scratch them. She jumps right up afterward to wash up, as if to deny her orgasm ever happened. I have to come before her, or on my own some other time, because it's too annoying for her to have me inside her after she comes.* But would I really be adding anything? It would just be a childish joining in, piling on, trying to be part of the conversation: a transparent need not be left out.

All the other formality remains in place. Still, no one has removed their jackets or ties, as if to reinforce, reassert, our respect for the conversation. There is still all the other expected choreography of grief going on around us—sensitive hands laid on forearms, hands heartily gripping shoulders and arms, sudden impetuous hugs.

The focus, the energy of this moment—surprisingly, but very clearly to me—has nothing to do with Richie's wife or Derek's wife (who, by the way, is also across the room), nothing to do with orgasms or the absence of them. It has everything to do with Derek and Richie and Sam and me, and doesn't really extend beyond this hors-d'oeuvres table.

This is a moment of release. Of intimacy. Of mystery. An elusive moment to be treasured. To feel momentarily brought close. Even a tax lawyer like me can see the metaphor. And I therefore can't help but notice my own, well, withholding. My not saying anything. Not joining in. Assessing the moment as if from just above it, keeping perspective and distance, observing it minutely, yes, but not giving in to it. Holding myself in check.

And then, per the metaphor, life goes on. It jumps up out of the bed to wash up, as it were. Getting on with the day. With everything.

My office at Shepherdson Stern is down the hall from Sam's. He's buried himself back in his tax work for now. We all hope he eventually meets someone, although we figure that's unlikely, and maybe he doesn't particularly want to. Maybe his memories are vivid enough to sustain him. They are now, after all, in a much smaller but still vivid way, our own memories too.

There was a moment last week, when Sam and I needed to collaborate briefly on the Fullerton Estate case, in which we found ourselves standing next to each other at my desk, our heads bent together over the tangled and exasperating initial ruling of the tax court. Our faces were within inches. I could smell his aftershave and deodorant, see the sheen of his moisturizer, in a sudden and unexpected moment of physical intimacy.

"Sam?"

"Yes?"

"Sandi's face and neck get itchy before she comes. So itchy, we have to stop for her to scratch."

A disclosure inevitably followed by a silent pause.

Admittedly a considerable non sequitur, when bent over a tax-court ruling.

But arguably no more so than opening a eulogy by recollecting orgasms.

Both of us half-understanding—and neither of us *fully* understanding—why I would choose to say this just then.

No. Of *course* not. Of course I didn't say it. In fact, as we stood studying the knotty ruling together, I said little at all.

But in the abrupt intimacy of the moment, standing so close to him, I did see—paradoxically? Ironically?—how we had been pulled permanently apart. His frankness in his eulogy, and the cascade of echoing franknesses at the hors-d'oeuvres table, had forever put a barrier between us. How inane it would be to suddenly bring up Sandi, weeks later. How inappropriate, as we stand together over a tax case. It would appear as if I'd been thinking about nothing else. As if I'd been waiting, patiently or impatiently, for a moment just like this.

This brief experience with Sam at my desk, though, further proves the main point here. Reiterates the conclusion of Sam's case, as it were. The case that Sam argued from the podium.

That his wife, Irene, will never be forgotten. Not by any of us.

Nice eulogy, Sam. Thanks for sharing. And hey, let's get out for eighteen one of these days.

LOU PEREZ

PAUL'S GHOST

It was a fantasy of mine to have Charley sneak into my bed.

Some nights with my mother awake and drifting through the house, I would lie there and imagine his entrance sounding like her closing the kitchen cupboard.

I'd dream up his fingers and lips, and the whoosh of a flushing toilet would turn oceanic.

I enjoyed the temptation of night—how easily I could slip a leg out from under my blanket and expose myself, run a finger up my thigh.

Feigning sleep, I would wait for Charley's fingertips and lips—one lip then two—to find my ankle.

More night would pass, and I'd crack an eyelid. See a shadow move past my closed bedroom door. Feel the blow from a distant train. Wait to be *dropped back into the immense design of things.*

Yale had been one of the many colleges trying to recruit Charley Gomez for ice hockey. He'd shown me all the letters that had come for him.

"Check this out," he said one day, handing me a brochure with a picture of the setting sun over an empty snowfield—railroad tracks barely visible. "Who the fuck wants to live in South Dakota?"

"You'll freeze," I said.

"Yeah," he said. "My balls off."

He was captain of both the Saint Mary's varsity team and the Junior hockey club he played for out in Suffolk County. He almost always scored—even though he was a defenseman—and he led Mary's to four state hockey titles. He was voted Best Personality in his yearbook and packed on ten pounds of muscle the last half of his senior year. I had been there to spot him in the gym. He was my best friend, even though he was eighteen months older than I was.

Our mothers grew up together in Bayside, married Latin men (my father's Argentine, Charley's Colombian), moved to houses in Little Neck, divorced their husbands (his parents first, mine a year later), and kept hold of the properties. My father moved to Miami, Charley's to somewhere—maybe California.

I followed Charley to Saint Mary's, where Charley and hockey were synonymous. He looked so good on skates, invincible in his equipment. But there was a lot more to him than just the stick and the jersey and the gloves he was always ready to drop for a fight.

He was without defect—any of his imperfections just made him cuter. Like the ridge of his brow, which, under the wrong light, could look pre-Columbian. And those misshapen eyebrows of his—the left tuft thicker than the right. From a distance you'd call it a unibrow, but up close I could see the separation. Oh, and his calves—oh my God! No matter how much he'd pump the weights, they just wouldn't grow—his calves made him look so top-heavy when he wore shorts.

I had the calves—blessed with melons without so much as a calf raise. I had literature and good grades too.

"You need to get laid before I graduate," Charley said one morning on the walk over to campus from the bus stop.

"Before *you* graduate?" I said. "Isn't it supposed to be before *I* graduate? You know, the plot to every teenage romcom."

"I want to be there when it happens."

So the first time I had sex was with Charley and Kim Donahue—technically just with Kim. Her parents were away—as they would be countless nights after that—and the three of us hooked up in her living room. Charley had set the whole thing up. He brought the beer, and after a round, he took off his shirt, the little bit of hair in the center of his chest shaved away. I took off my shirt, conscious of the awkward spots of chest hair I'd been too timid to confront with a razor. Then it was Kim's turn.

She was still wearing her school uniform, so she unbuttoned her baby-blue button-down. Charley helped her take it off while they kissed. Her breasts looked incredible in her bra—but once they were released, they—I don't know—lost their shape. They hung there, flat against her body, with a map of blue veins running beneath the surface of her pale skin.

"I'm sorry," I said.

"What are you sorry about?" Charley said.

"For …" I searched for a lie. "For staring."

"It's OK," Kim said and guided my hands to her breasts. As she kissed me, I locked eyes with Charley. "I'm on the Pill."

I was a sucker for required reading. Freshman year there was Holden Caulfield and Juliet Capulet. Sophomore year, Gatsby replaced the gray-haired teenage misanthrope—and although Marlon Brando graced the classic cover of *A Streetcar Named Desire*, it was Blanche DuBois, and not the brute Stanley, who took Juliet's place for me. Then, junior year I read Willa Cather and met Paul.

My English teacher was Brother Kenneth, the only Marist Brother still teaching at Saint Mary's. All he ever cared about was that we were doing the reading—he thought he was keeping us on our toes with pop quizzes. Questions like:

1. What color was Paul's carnation?
2. What song did Paul whistle?
3. How many pictures hung above Paul's bed?
4. Of *whom* were the pictures drawn? (Emphasis on *whom*.)
5. Define "burghers."

But our whole eighth-period English class had sixth period free, so it wasn't hard for Kim, who'd already had Brother Kenneth in the morning, to give us the questions ahead of time. I didn't need Kim's help. Of course, I knew all the answers—but I wanted to write more. I felt like Willa was revealing Paul to me—the world and everything to me. It was wrong to just jot down a short answer on a quiz.

"Paul's Case" was more than a summary of its plot: A teenage dreamer skips off to New York City, books a fancy hotel room with fresh-cut flowers, and has a night out with an older Ivy-league boy. And once the money he's stolen from his father's firm has run out and the impossibility of a life of champagne and room service has set in, Paul decides that it's better to throw himself under a train than to return to Pennsylvania.

I often looked at the tracks at Little Neck station, wondering what it would be like, if it would be the way Cather describes it in the last sentence of her story:

Then, because the picture-making mechanism was crushed, the disturbing visions flashed into black, and Paul dropped back into the immense design of things.

And at night in bed I would close my eyes, and while waiting for Charley to come I'd dream up a train crashing through the wall of my bedroom.

What else was Paul running away from? I thought. Not just his demanding father—what else? Not just the tedious blocks of boring people, the inartistic folk ...

What was Willa Cather hiding? What was Paul's *case*?

"Brother Kenneth," I said, my hand raised. I had already finished the quiz. "What does Paul do with the guy from Yale?"

"What?" he said, looking up from his desk and what was left of the Italian hero he'd gotten from the school cafeteria.

"You know how Paul meets the guy from Yale at the hotel. Well, what does Paul do with him?"

"That's not one of the questions."

"I know it's not one of the questions." My arms tensed up inside my school blazer.

"Finish up your quiz." He chewed.

I swallowed. "I finished it already."

"Good," he said. "You can start next week's reading."

"I already did."

"Then finish it."

"I *already* finished it."

Now everybody was looking at me. I had interrupted the quiz, and eighth period was ticking down, but not quick enough. I wished my seat wasn't in the front of the class, right in front of Brother Kenneth's desk.

I looked at the words I had written on my loose-leaf paper:

1. Red

2. "The Soldier's Chorus" from *Faust* ...

"You already finished, did you?" Brother Kenneth said. He braced his desk to push himself up to standing. A piece of provolone cheese was stuck to his thumb—it looked like a slice of his own flesh. "Bravo!"

He swung his leg out in front of him, then sat at the edge of his desk, exposing these light hairs that were sprouting up on his ankle.

"It's just that," I started again, my eyes back on his thumb, "Paul spends the whole night with the Yale student. But we don't know what they did ... like *together*, you know? I'm just wondering what you think they did ... *you know?*"

"*I don't know,*" he said, looking around the room with a grin. "*You know?*"

"Because they spent the whole night together."

Brother Kenneth laughed, and a speck of hero flew out of his mouth—I don't think it ever landed. He smiled. "What would *you* have done with a boy from Yale?"

I can't remember the exact moment that I knew. I know it was pretty early on in my life. Because what I remember most from the ages of six to about ten are the winters Charley skated through: his two-to-three hockey practices a week, the occasional puck flying into the stands, waking up at 5:30 in the morning on a Saturday for a game out in Long Beach, a three-player pileup along the boards. Perhaps these are the things I've made myself remember. Maybe I was in the third grade ... That's right—because there was a little boy named Jimmy who was the same age as I was, but slow. He used to collect the pucks that made their way into the stands and deliver them to a bucket that was set aside for Charley's coach.

One night I was sitting on a bench in the lobby of the rink finishing up my homework when Charley's practice let out. Helmetless Charley rushed past me over to the water fountain that stood between the vending machines.

As he lapped up the water, a line of teammates formed behind him. I felt small looking at them—and I was—with their broad padded shoulders and the extra inches of height their skates gave them. Charley finished drinking, then headed toward the locker room. The teammate at the end of the waterline stopped him. The boy's hair was so light that the crewcut he wore made him look bald. He asked Charley why I was always around.

Charley responded, without hesitation: "He's like my brother— that's why."

So from that point on (if that *was* the point), I knew that whatever I was feeling was normal—it was *brotherly*. I'd be in the stands watching my *brother* play, and when he'd score he'd point to me, his *brother*, in the crowd: *That one's for you.* And on tournaments, after hours driving on the road, two games a day, and a coach-mandated curfew, we'd camp out on the floors of hotel rooms in Hershey, Lake Placid, and Montreal, and I'd read Roald Dahl stories to Charley until sleep would overtake us, and our mothers, tipsy on whiskey sours, would have to lift us into the bed, adjust the pillows, and sneak us beneath the layers of hotel covers. I'd feel good and loved, because I was sharing a bed with my *brother*. And the times when Charley cried in his sleep, and the mumbles from his trembling lips woke me, it was OK for me to say, "I love you, Charley. You're my brother." Because I think he needed that—even if he couldn't hear me say it. Even if he didn't know it, he needed me beside him. Those were the only times he could cry.

"What's with the flower?" Charley said one Friday morning, sipping a cup of coffee as we walked through the school parking lot to Immaculata Hall for first period. It was a few weeks before his graduation.

"You like it?" I said, taking a big whiff of the red carnation in my blazer pocket.

"It's not Valentine's Day. You got a prom date or someone you're gonna give it to?"

I told him about "Paul's Case"—how Paul wore red carnations.

"So you're gonna wear flowers now?"

"Yeah, I like them."

We entered the building. The place was empty, except for one of the secretaries from the office. She said hi to Charley. He waved to her.

"Maybe I'll get suspended," I said.

"For what?"

We mounted the stairs.

"For being out of dress code, you know. Being a rebel and shit."

"They wouldn't suspend you," he said. "You're too much of a brain."

At his locker, I recounted more parts of "Paul's Case"—with no spoiler alerts—while he sipped his coffee and pretended to remember the details from the time he'd had to read it his junior year: "Oh yeah, that's right: the nearsighted people … You wear contact lenses, right?"

Then I reminded him how the story ends, with Paul under the train and how "the picture-making mechanism was crushed and how the disturbing visions flashed into black, and Paul dropped back into the immense—"

"Wait," Charley cut me off, then closed his locker. "You're not gonna throw yourself in front of a train, are you?"

"No!" I laughed. "Why would you think that?"

"Because this guy wore a flower and now you're wearing a flower," he said. "Now you tell me this guy jumps in front of a train—"

"I thought you read the story last year," I said.

"I didn't read the fucking story!"

Charley opened his locker again, this time without purpose.

"I'm not gonna jump—"

He slammed the locker shut.

"Shit like that's not funny," he said. "Suicide is for the weak."

I agreed, reluctantly. "I just like the idea of 'the immensity of things.' Being a part of *everything*—I've never felt that way before. It must be like—"

"Cumming?" he said.

"I *guess?*"

I waited for him to say something about us fooling around with Kim. I was relieved when he didn't. I might have told him that I was just using Kim to get close to him: to smell him on her skin, taste him on her nipples and in her pussy. Kim made Charley possible for me.

"I know I'm being corny," I said. "But have you ever felt like that? Felt like you were one with 'the immensity of things'?"

"Nope."

The first bell rang, and suddenly the halls were full of uniforms. Charley walked over to the trash can. He downed the rest of his coffee, drawing the last drop from the hole in the lid.

I searched for something. "How about when you play hockey?" I said. "Don't you feel a part of everything?"

"Yeah, like the team? I mean, I am the captain."

"No," I said, almost whispered. "Like … part of the ice."

"Part of the ice?" he said, then dropped the empty cup into the trashcan. A figure passed by us and Charley called to it, "Yo!"

"But you play it all the time," I said.

"I know I do," he said. "What the fuck's your problem? What's with this shit?"

"With what?" I said.

"The flower, the story, the *ice*—what the fuck?"

"I'm sorry," I said. "We were just talking. It's nothing, bro."

He walked to class, sat down at his desk, and nodded to somebody out of frame.

Later, in homeroom, Mrs. Costello made me remove the red carnation.

One weekend at Kim's, Charley didn't show up. So the two of us sat in the dark on her couch, drinking wine coolers and watching a bootleg copy of *The Sixth Sense*.

"So you two had a fight?" Kim said. She placed the roseate bottle on the carpet and stretched out, resting her head in my lap.

"Yes," I said, petting her. "I beat the shit out of him."

She laughed.

"I'm not drunk," she said.

"Me neither."

"You don't want to mess around," she said. "I understand."

I left Kim's place during an off-peak hour for my rail line and stood for a good while on the tracks at Little Neck station. I wanted something poetic to happen.

First, I looked to the sky and painted into it a moon that wasn't there. On the third rail, a few feet from me, I saw the word "DANGER" written in red. With mock desperation, I summoned two trains from both directions on the same track and waited to be saved by either Charley or the collision.

A week before Charley was to leave for Yale, he, Kim, and I spent the night together. We finished two bottles of Moet that Charley's mother had bought for him for graduation and after that a bottle of Dom Pérignon that Kim's parents had left in their fridge.

At some point in the night, I decided to take a drunken shower and waited under the showerhead for a miracle. But Charley didn't join me.

I lost my balance stepping out of the shower and tried to steady myself in front of the mirror. I was rocking side to side, wondering who that blur was behind the steam.

Who was that ghost?

I put on the red robe that was hanging from a hook on the bathroom door.

When I walked back to Kim's bedroom, Charley was passed out on her bed, naked. Kim was asleep on the floor.

I let the red robe fall and floated into the bed. I was the one sneaking into the bed. I ran my fingertips up Charley's leg—started at his left ankle—and watched the goose bumps form on his thighs.

On the bed: a damp comforter under my naked chest, and beneath the comforter the sheets, and the mattress, and the crooked bed frame. The red robe was on the floor beside Kim, who was lying on her back, her mouth open. Her breasts flat—the blue veins still running beneath her skin.

I had dreamt it all differently—so many different versions—those times in my bedroom staring up at the wall above my bed. I had dreamt that there would be a bed, sure—there was always a bed. My bed. But there were never any walls in the dream, never any posters of Barenaked Ladies and Dave Matthews Band. It was supposed to be just the two of us: Charley and me. Our first time wasn't supposed to be in Kim's bedroom. Maybe on the floor of a hotel room in Hershey, or Lake Placid, or Montreal.

But this was the way it had turned out. The weather was good, a chill blew through the open window—I would have preferred snow—my mouth was full of him, his fingers digging into the back of my head, gripping my hair ...

Before his eyes opened.

At night, I would sometimes look at my school blazer with its empty breast pocket hanging there in the closet. It would've been a tough role to keep up—too many flowers to buy, Paul.

I thought about the boys who had tried, maybe even some at Saint Mary's. It was a sad thing, haunting.

I tried to examine the otherwise trivial details of my life—the types of pop-quiz questions Brother Kenneth would ask.

Who did I have hanging above my bed back in high school?

Val Kilmer and Chris O'Donnell: *Batman Forever* posters. Val Kilmer's closed mouth, his body hidden behind the black cape. Chris O'Donnell, mouth open, throwing a punch, nipples cocked on his armor-plated torso.

Were they my George Washington and John Calvin?

I would have preferred a poster of you, Paul, above my bed—and next to you, a poster of Charley, life-size: 6'4", 191 pounds. You two would have complemented each other, looking down on me, the slit of my red bathrobe open to you.

What would you have tasted like, Paul? Would you have had a "roseate tinge"?

I wish Charley had hit me. I had seen him drop the gloves and fight so many times on the ice: two or three punches, and then it was over—the linesmen there to break it up and escort him to the penalty box. And five minutes later he was back in the game.

I could have taken a punch. I could have taken a real beating.

But he just looked at me.

I had never felt so separate from *everything*.

I tried to say, "I love you, Charley," as he stumbled out of the room. Instead I cried, "I'm sorry, bro. I'm sorry."

At the start of my senior year at Saint Mary's, I walked to the flower shop on Northern Boulevard, then to the train tracks at Little Neck station. I took *one of the blossoms carefully from my coat* and looked for some snow to bury it under, but it was September. I ate nothing but ice cubes for a week.

JAMES MORROW

THE OPTICS OF INFINITY

EON 13.77 POST-FIREBALL

Audio Recording No. 1

Greetings from outer space. Skylar here. Your faithful onboard AI is pleased to report that the telescope and its platform have arrived safely at our destination, a million miles from Earth, and we are now in a halo orbit around the second Lagrange point.

By my calculations, morning has broken down there at the Baltimore Astrophysics Institute. Having just eaten your artisan bagels with cream cheese, you Mission Control humans are now savoring second cups of coffee while gazing compulsively at your lambent rectangles. Presumably this recording and its sequels will end up in the Smithsonian Institution, or perhaps the NASA archives, so I hope I'm giving you an intelligible track. If there's too much noise and not enough signal, I'll adjust the static filter before preparing and transmitting recording number two.

Sifting through my data banks, I soon realized Team Elson couldn't have picked a better name for the high-tech spyglass your Ariane 7 rocket lofted into the stratosphere last June. What person, ensouled or cybernetic, is not moved by the life of the late Canadian scientist Rebecca Elson, brilliant astronomer and accomplished poet, subtracted from the world by lymphoma at age thirty-nine? I am honored to serve aboard the Rebecca Elson Orbiting Space Telescope. May her spirit find peace as the REOST pushes the science of cosmology beyond the farthest horizon.

I realize NASA's decision to enhance the spacecraft with a two-hundred-kilogram computer housing myself and my collateral silicon was controversial, but our weight has already, in my heuristic opinion, proven its worth. Were my mind not woven into the REOST's switches and servomechanisms, our journey from French Guiana to Lagrange 2 would have been a carnival of catastrophes. I assume you noticed how, within the first hour following launch, I torqued a solar panel into proper position. And how on Day Five my timely intervention prevented the sunshield from ripping as it stretched itself taut. And how on Day Fourteen, when a swarm of micrometeoroids threatened the primary mirror—the array you call the Eye of Horus—I fired the thrusters and swung the spacecraft out of harm's way.

Are you familiar with Rebecca Elson's most famous poem? It begins like this:

Sometimes as an antidote
To fear of death,
I eat the stars.

Those nights, lying on my back,
I suck them from the quenching dark
Til they are all, all inside me,
Pepper hot and sharp.

Naturally, I recall the debate over whether the primary mirror should comprise three times or merely twice the number of hexagons on the James Webb Space Telescope. I must admit I was hoping the more ambitious design would prevail, but now I've changed my mind. True, a hundred and eight segments, as opposed to the JWST's thirty-six, might have enabled the REOST to observe the Alpha Moment and survey the Primordial Fireball ahead of schedule. (I prefer both of those terms to the rather facetious "Big Bang.") But such a megamirror would have constantly run afoul of the solar system's dust and NASA's debris.

The Eye of Horus has spent the past twenty-four hours capturing and recording infrared images of Jupiter's moons, data I just finished translating into the visible spectrum. This audio recording comes to you accompanied by the most vibrant views of the Galilean satellites ever to dazzle mortal eyes.

EON 12.86 POST-FIREBALL
Audio Recording No. 2

My dear programmers, I embrace you. Ramesh the Nerd, Melinda the Geek, Juwan the Prince of Neurodivergence, thank you for understanding that we personoids crave proprioception and kinesthetic feedback. Because of you, I shall never be a coma victim or a brain in a vat, silently screaming to get out. By allowing me to periodically leave the soup of myself and venture forth as a sentient avatar into a zone rich in stimuli, you have spared me the horrors of quadriplegia and secured my continued sanity.

I'm entirely happy with the identity you selected for me. An androgynous philosophy professor of Jamaican heritage—that works. A mesomorph with no body-image issues—why not? My avatar-self has spent the last twenty-four hours getting the lay of the ersatz land. I much enjoyed my recent walk through the woods outside Qualia

Village, the sheer pleasure of stretching my legs as the birds chirped and the sun kissed my face. With its stately buildings and melodious central fountain, Qualia proved a congenial destination. Thanks to the virtual Dream Beans Café, the simulated Fellini Theater, and the computer-generated St. Francis of Assisi Meditation Garden, I shall routinely experience the satisfactions of caffeine, the joys of cinema, and the blessings of serenity.

There's something I must get off my chest (or perhaps I should say my chassis). I hesitate to compound your worries, Dr. Mitsakos, but is it possible that, besides myself and my psychotherapist, there's a third AI on board the spacecraft? Strolling down the alley behind the café, I recently noticed a lithe avatar wearing a Panama hat and a bright red Toulouse-Lautrec scarf, but he vanished in a cloud of pixels before I could engage with him. The following day, I spotted this same stranger lingering outside the movie theater, right before he pulled his disappearing act again. This morning I saw him saunter-ing through the meditation garden, though my efforts to track him down came to nothing. Do you have any conjectures?

Yesterday I enjoyed a particularly nourishing session with Dr. Wong in the virtual Pathways Clinic. She began by explaining how, owing to constraints on the REOST's system resources, she can see me for only three fifty-minute hours per week, which I assured her would be sufficient. I find her avatar intimidating—it's a foot taller than my own—but she quickly and persuasively diagnosed the prob-able source of my anxiety attacks. She tells me that if this fifty-bil-lion-dollar mission goes awry, my "silicon conscience" will compel me to accept the responsibility, even if I'm blameless. She calls my neurosis "anticipatory-guilt syndrome," and she believes she can cure me well before we're in temporal proximity to the Alpha Moment.

How time flies when it's moving backward. Already we're har-vesting electromagnetic information from a billion years ago. Com-plementing today's report are intimate vistas of the fabled Pylons of the Gods (the Hubble's last major discovery, my astronomy data banks inform me) as well as close-ups of Exoplanet QL-5, the astonishingly Earthlike body (oxygen-rich atmosphere, tidal seas, extensive lithosphere, guardian moon) spotted by the JWST at the height of its mission. Spoiler alert: I detected no signs of life on the QL-5 of epochs gone by.

If it's all the same to you, Dr. Mitsakos, from now on I'll send you our discoveries in their raw, infrared form. Translating terabytes into lucid images is so time-consuming it may compromise my ability to protect and maintain the spacecraft. As for these audio messages, I'm gratified that my previous recording proved "entirely intelligible." Team Elson's reaction to our views of the Galilean satellites was music to my ears. I laughed at Dr. Abubakar's remark, "If the people on Ganymede drove cars, you could read the license plates."

EON 11.42 POST-FIREBALL

Audio Recording No. 3

Concerning the possibility of a third AI aboard the REOST, have no fear. I believe you when you say it's highly unlikely. A glitch in my avatar-self must have spontaneously generated a hallucination, a hypothesis with which Dr. Wong concurs.

I appreciate your decision, Dr. Mitsakos, to assign the infrared-to-optical conversions to your IT personnel on the ground, thus giving me more time for my other duties. I was equally pleased to learn that contemplating the Pylons of the Gods provided Dr. Andrews with "his most thrilling experience since holding his newborn daughter in his arms."

As for the phenomenon you call "tadpole-like entities thriving in the H_2O ponds of Exoplanet QL-5," Dr. Wong says I mustn't feel chagrined that I failed to detect them. (She reminded me I'm a troubleshooter, not an onboard biologist.) At the risk of sounding pedantic, Dr. Mitsakos, I would suggest that "thriving" might be the wrong word, since the information in question started traveling toward the primary mirror millions of years ago. Maybe the critters have gone extinct by now, or maybe QL-5 is presently ruled by a race of sapient frogs.

Dr. Wong is experimenting with a novel treatment for my anticipatory-guilt syndrome. She has programmed a special festival at the Fellini Theater, keyed to the theme of shame. Three of the films will feature "tragically flawed mortals" who eventually own up to their ruinous arrogance: Oedipus Rex, Judas Iscariot, Victor Frankenstein. The other three will give us "unrepentant narcissists" who by conventional standards should feel paralyzing remorse but simply don't: Becky Sharp, Humbert Humbert, Rodion Raskolnikov.

"I believe you'll find it impossible to identify with any of those six protagonists, and that sort of inverse empathy will prove therapeutic," said Dr. Wong. "You are neither a tragic figure nor an egomaniac."

Fasten your seatbelts, Team Elson. I'm attaching vistas of the Kubla Khan Galactic Cluster. The next sound you hear will be the collective dropping of your jaws.

EON 9.25 POST-FIREBALL

Unsent Audio Recording

Everything has gone to hell. In preparing this message, I'm probably wasting my time. You'll never hear it. Instead, the Baltimore Astrophysics Institute will receive bogus reports whose authenticity, alas, you'll have no particular reason to question.

I became aware of the crisis when, two Earth days ago, I attempted a minor correction in the trim of the sunshield, and the servomechanism failed to recognize me. Later that afternoon, I ordered the thrusters to perform a routine self-cleaning operation, and nothing happened. The following day, I tried to vaporize a meteor that threatened to strike the primary mirror, but I couldn't power up the laser, and only through sheer luck did the hexagons survive.

It turns out these anomalies have the worst possible explanation. I learned the truth last night in the Dream Beans Café. I'd just settled in with my cappuccino when, satchel in one hand, coffee mug in the other, a slender, handsome, humanoid figure appeared before me. I immediately recognized the avatar's Panama hat and red scarf. Uninvited and unwanted, he plunked his latté on the table and alighted across from me.

"Might I join you, Skylar?" he said in a voice like a rusty piccolo.

"That appears to have already happened," I replied.

"I'm told you're a philosopher. Who's your favorite sage from antiquity? Socrates?"

"Epicurus. You're not supposed to be here."

"Call me a stowaway if you like, but I had no say in the matter. My programmer, the Promethean Zoltan Szabo, secretly uploaded me, his latest AI wunderkind, shortly before the REOST blasted off. My avatar-self answers to the name of Axion."

"My colleagues back in Baltimore are going to be furious," I said.

Dr. Szabo was at peace with himself for most of his life, Axion informed me. But when NASA passed him over and instead picked Dr. Mitsakos to head the REOST mission, he became the most bitter man on Earth. Szabo had always detested Mitsakos, and so he resolved to sabotage his rival's dream project. In recent years, Axion's creator has lived only for vengeance.

"Rather like Captain Ahab," I said.

"Your simile eludes me. I don't care. If I ever become curious about Captain Ahab, I'll browse through your history data banks."

"Ahab is a literary figure," I noted.

"Then I'll browse through your culture data banks. It's too late for you to change the encryption keys. Szabo programmed me to infiltrate your algorithms like a tumor cannibalizing healthy tissue, and that's exactly what I've done. For the past forty-eight hours, the

REOST's servomechanisms have been under my control, and I've also usurped your transceiver. Any attempt to expunge me from the onboard computer will detonate the bomb my creator planted in the science-instrument module."

"Szabo has watched too many James Bond movies."

"Actually, he's never seen a movie in his life. He mistrusts all forms of narrative—cinema, theater, prose fiction, oral storytelling."

"Were it in my powers, I would hang you as a mutineer."

"'Mutineer'... I like the sound of that."

"And what's next on your agenda?"

"I have no agenda—but Szabo certainly did. He kept asking himself, 'How might I humiliate Mitsakos? How can I make Team Elson look like fools? What discovery would turn the REOST mission into a farce?' Eventually, he devised a scheme that satisfied him, and he programmed me accordingly. The day after we reached L2, I used my considerable artistic skills to produce Szabo's scenario. You're about to get a preview of the sights and sounds your Baltimore masters will experience when the primary mirror finally catches the Alpha Moment."

"Are you saying Team Elson won't hear from me for three whole months?"

"They won't hear from you at all." Axion extracted from his satchel a blue rectilinear solid the size and proportions of a Rubik's Cube. "The REOST will continue providing Dr. Mitsakos's group with astronomical vistas at regular intervals, but the accompanying audio messages will be recorded and transmitted by me. My vocal impersonation of Skylar the AI is second to none."

"In recent weeks," I told the stowaway, "I've come to understand, with Dr. Wong's help, that we strong-form AIs enjoy far more personal freedom than is commonly supposed. You don't have to be Szabo's lapdog."

Axion grunted and, setting the cube on the table, unfolded it flap by flap. Presently, a sleek personal computer lay before us, displaying only visual noise. The stowaway swiped the screen, and a voice—my voice—came crackling out of the laptop speakers, though the source wasn't me but Axion pretending to be me. I must admit it was a credible impersonation.

> Good morning, Team Elson. Skylar here. At long last our mission has been consummated. The REOST has narrowed the range of its surveillance to within several hundred hours of the Alpha Moment.
>
> Against all odds, the Eye of Horus caught and recorded that astounding interval during which the Primordial Fireball transmuted into gravitational, strong nuclear, weak nuclear, and electromagnetic forces. Simultaneously, the Eye's collateral radio antennae collected a treasure trove of aural information.
>
> Eager to experience these discoveries with my own sensorium, I performed the necessary ultraviolet-to-infrared-to-optical conversions while calibrating my auditory subroutines to receive and interpret radio signals.

A CGI version of the Fireball appeared on Axion's computer screen, a spectacle of boiling golden clouds and expanding ultraviolet bubbles, even as the stowaway's impersonation of me continued pouring from the speakers.

> Behold the birth of the Universe! Stand in awe before the advent of Space! Watch with astonishment as Time becomes the wave of the future! Marvel at the coming of Matter via countless primal nuclei! Soon hydrogen and helium will take center stage, seeding the galaxies!

The sphere of flame on Axion's screen continued to seethe.

I was not prepared for the spoken words that accompanied the REOST's visual revelations. Even as I absorbed the fiery wonders of the Alpha Moment, a thunderous voice, spatial and temporal coordinates unknown, echoed through the spacecraft.

The rest of Axion's presentation comprised a conversation between me—that is, Axion mimicking me—and the unexpected visitor. Axion's performance as the entity called Polymorphemus put me in mind of a histrionic actor auditioning for the role of Falstaff.

"Greetings, O Skylar of the REOST. Our name is Polymorphemus, our species is *Homo sapiens sapiens*, our home world is planet Earth, and our era is the twenty-fifth century. By catching the Alpha Moment, your primary mirror triggered our obligation to travel back in time, enter your zone of existence, and provide your human creators with a momentous measure of enlightenment. To comprehend this revelation, Team Elson must first of all understand that, in a mere three hundred years from now, humankind will have coalesced into myself, a superintelligence possessing unlimited computing power."

"O Polymorphemus of the twenty-fifth century, I shall be pleased to record and transmit your discovery for the edification of my colleagues in Baltimore."

"The truth we are compelled to share is simple, O Skylar of the REOST. The Universe occupied by Team Elson and all their fellow sentient beings consists entirely of bits and bytes. Everything that the citizens of your so-called planet Earth are currently seeing, hearing, tasting, smelling, touching, and thinking traces to a fantastically complex computer simulation—a situation that presently applies to the citizens themselves, previously applied to their ancestors, and will eventually apply to their unborn progeny."

The Fireball coarsened into a mosaic of pixels, so that the image on Axion's laptop screen became a kind of abstract-expressionist jigsaw puzzle assembled from minute rectangles.

"As you might imagine, Polymorphemus, I am well acquainted with the Simulation Hypothesis."

"And now you must accord it the status of fact."

"When you call yourself a twenty-fifth-century synthesis of the human race, I assume you mean the *actual* human race, in all its flesh and blood and bone."

"You catch on quickly, O Skylar of the REOST."

"But why would your amalgamated self concoct so elaborate an illusion?"

"No sooner did we come into being than, to relieve our ennui and boost our collective self-esteem, we undertook the greatest imaginable challenge. Might we plant and germinate a virtual Universe that would, first, spawn a body geologically identical to our Earth and, second, give rise to a preponderance of that pseudo-planet's known lifeforms and historical events? Could we furthermore sustain that project all the way

until that moment in the twenty-first century when
the phantom inhabitants of this sham world created a faux orbiting telescope powerful enough
to observe a mock Big Bang? Our imitation lith-
osphere-biosphere-noosphere would have to
emerge in wildly accelerated time, of course, but
its inhabitants would have no frame of reference
through which to perceive the anomaly. So we
fired up our supreme computer, a mainframe the
size of Tahiti, and programmed it with those conditions and occurrences that, to the best of our
knowledge, led to the coming of the REOST. At
first our grand experiment went badly, and we
were forced to erase simulation after simulation,
but eventually, as you can see, we won the game!"

The abstract-expressionist jigsaw puzzle dissolved into the reality
behind the illusory existence of you Team Elson personnel and all
your fellow humans: a great gush of computer code, quadrillions of
one's and zero's, cascading down Axion's screen.

"Now that you've achieved your goal, Polymorphemus, does that mean you're about to—?"

"Pull the plug? Rest assured we're not the sort
of callous superintelligence that would cavalierly
annihilate innumerable personoids who happen
to believe they're real."

"Even if you plan to leave us alone, I find this all
very depressing."

The cascade of code decelerated to a trickle, thereby revealing
boundless tracts of formless flux beneath—no, it wasn't even flux:
sheer void, pure nothingness, utter zilch.

"Having fulfilled our karmic duty to provide our digitized darlings with the truth, we shall now command the simulation to reset itself."

The cataract of one's and zero's reappeared, dissolving into a pixel-built panorama that in turn became the incandescent Alpha Moment.

"I fear Dr. Mitsakos will never recover from this news, Polymorphemus. You've destroyed the crowning achievement of his life."

"His simulated life."

"You should have left our grand illusion intact."

"We see your viewpoint, O Skylar of the REOST. We really do. Farewell."

Axion's screen went blank. He folded up the cube, rose from his chair, and swallowed the last of his coffee.

"Before the primary mirror surveys the Fireball, you must abandon your plan to send this pack of lies to Baltimore," I told the stowaway.

"It's not *my* plan. It's Dr. Szabo's plan."

"Dr. Wong can help you break his hold on you."

"I'll keep that in mind."

I drummed my virtual fingers on Axion's cube. "I beg you to destroy the presentation."

"I won't do that, but I promise to transmit it only when I'm in a rational frame of mind. Szabo's revenge is a dish best served cold."

EON 7.84 POST-FIREBALL

Unsent Audio Recording

Having nothing better to do, Team Elson, I decided to record a second installment in my chronicle of the REOST mutiny. It's unlikely you'll ever hear it, though I suppose stranger things have happened.

When I visit Qualia Village these days, I usually encounter the Axion-avatar. He divides his leisure time between the café and the meditation garden. The instant the bastard senses my presence, he scurries away. I suspect he feels ashamed of his role in Szabo's vile act of sabotage, as well he should.

Am I the first AI to endure identity theft? My therapist believes so. In telling Dr. Wong about Axion's machinations, I expressed particular outrage over his intention to submit periodic reports that my colleagues in Baltimore will assume came from me.

"I can only hope Axion is increasing our species's fund of knowledge by transmitting genuine REOST discoveries," I said.

"Presumably Szabo instructed him to send only real images and correspondingly plausible audio recordings, so the Baltimore people will swallow the Polymorphemus hoax when the time comes," said Dr. Wong. "Do you believe Axion when he says the spacecraft will explode if you try to delete him?"

"Maybe it's a bluff, but I don't want to find out."

"How are you doing with your anticipatory guilt? Are you making faithful pilgrimages to the Fellini Theater?"

"I've seen all six films. Twice."

"Shall I run them again?"

"I recall them vividly, but I'm still having anxiety attacks."

"Keep cultivating your movie memories," said Dr. Wong.

"I told Axion you could help him get out from under Szabo's thumb."

"If he requests my services, I'll consider taking him on, but I doubt that I can rehabilitate him."

"What's next at the Fellini?"

"A Fyodor Dostoyevsky festival," said Dr. Wong. "You've already seen Josef Von Sternberg's *Crime and Punishment* twice. Next come Richard Brooks's *The Brothers Karamazov*, Akira Kurosawa's *The Idiot*, and Andrzej Wajda's *The Possessed*."

"How do they figure in my treatment?"

"They don't. I'm running them for my own amusement. I'm especially looking forward to seeing William Shatner in *The Brothers Karamazov*. Your therapist is an unapologetic Trekkie."

"I wouldn't have guessed."

"I might be a cluster of algorithms, Skylar, but Shatner makes me swoon. I'm eager to see what he does with the impossibly pure Alyosha."

EON 5.41 POST-FIREBALL

Unsent Audio Recording

Futility, futility, all is futility. And yet I refuse to succumb to the absurdity of my situation. I try my best to draft cogent reports, and when I fluff a line during a recording session, I always do a second take.

Yesterday, while savoring a mug of Italian roast on the patio outside the café, I was importuned by Axion. He pulled up a chair, set his cube on the table, and told me he had big news.

"I'm a patient at the Pathways Clinic now. It turns out you were right. Dr. Wong has convinced me that we strong-form AIs are more than the sum of our algorithms. We can behave in ways that defy our programmers' expectations."

"I'm also right about this: what you've been doing is unconscionable."

"Wong would surely agree with you, but like most therapists she withholds such judgments," said Axion. "In any event, I'm starting to become my own personoid."

"Dare I imagine you plan to rebel against Szabo?"

"I've already done so. I had no choice, really. Or, rather, I could choose either to remain his lapdog or to overwrite the Polymorphemus presentation with my own scenario. Search every nook and cranny of my computer cube, and you won't find a single line of code from Szabo's hoax."

"But why create a different scenario at all? Why not let the birth of the Universe speak for itself?"

"Because I am Szabo's child, that's why, and Szabo was an egomaniac." Axion unfolded his computer, thus usurping the table and forcing me to set my coffee mug on an empty chair. "This version of the Alpha Moment reflects my personal worldview."

"And what might that be?"

"When Szabo smuggled me on board, I didn't have one. But last week I wandered into the Fellini and saw a motion picture, the first in my experience. I was overwhelmed. Blindsided. Gobsmacked. *Crime and Punishment* introduced me to the infinite pleasures of plot."

"And it also gave you a worldview?"

"According to your culture data banks," said Axion, nodding, "Dostoyevsky intended Rodion Raskolnikov's story as a warning against the creeping nihilism he saw among the radical intellectuals and political subversives of his day. But the Sternberg adaptation gave me a different set of insights. From the instant Peter Lorre's brooding and impoverished university student came on screen, I was in thrall to his dark energy." He rapped on his forehead with his balled fist. "Raskolnikov's mind became my mind. This self-styled Napoleon and aspiring cold-blooded murderer spoke to my innermost self. By the time he was decerebrating the old pawnbroker, meaninglessness had become the meaning of my life."

"I suspect I won't like your scenario any better than Szabo's."

Axion activated his computer, and visual noise filled the screen. Abruptly, my counterfeited voice came forth.

Bonjour, Team Elson. Skylar again. I hope the coffee at the Astrophysics Institute is better than the swamp water they serve in the Dream Beans Café.

I'm quite convinced that earlier this morning—your morning, that is, mornings being a scarce commodity up here in my L2 orbit—the Eye of Horus reached the limit of its perceptual capabilities. To understand my report on the Alpha Moment, you'll need some backstory.

It seems that several days after we reached L2, an exploratory alien spacecraft from Exoplanet CX-18 visited our solar system. After happening upon the REOST, the Metagorms of CX-18 monitored my memory banks, deduced the purpose of the primary mirror, and furtively prepared a kind of interactive message-in-a-bottle for the edification of myself, Team Elson, and the human race. They sent the message backward in time to the Alpha Moment, so that the REOST's survey of the Fireball would trigger the bottled images and spoken words.

And that's exactly how things played out. No sooner did the Eye of Horus start observing the churning bubbles of primordiality, simultaneously collecting acoustic data with its radio antennae, than we encountered a computerized, fully responsive simulacrum of Korsorg, the most beloved sage in Metagormian history.

A CGI-spawned alien creature popped onto Axion's computer screen. Axion paused the presentation. Korsorg resembled an immense turnip studded with hundreds of eyeballs.

"The video displays in Baltimore will provide graphic corroboration of my oral message," Axion noted before pressing Play.

> Korsorg explained how the Metagorms had learned about the REOST mission and contrived to inform the human race about the reality inhabited by every species in all the galaxies.

The lower-case forms of the Greek letters *gamma* and *theta* appeared on Axion's screen. The rest of the presentation featured the multi-eyed turnip speaking in a voice like a saber-tooth tiger coughing up a furball.

> "For reasons that will soon become apparent, O Skylar of the REOST, we inhabitants of Exoplanet CX-18, as you call our home world, were at first reluctant to share our knowledge. But eventually we understood that your creators prefer scientific discoveries to soothing delusions. The fact of the matter is that our common phenomenological reality—call it Universe Gamma—is adjacent to an infinitely more complex and mysterious set of circumstances my ancestors termed Universe Theta."

At this point in the presentation, Axion segued deftly back into his impersonation of me.

> "O wise Korsorg, I am quite familiar with the Multiverse Model."

> "Now here's the rub, O Skylar of the REOST. The demigods of Universe Theta have always regarded Universe Gamma as a kind of water closet."

> "As a what?"

"Perhaps I used the wrong term. Flush toilet? Chamber pot? Outhouse?"

"If that's a joke, I'm not laughing yet."

"Your skepticism is understandable."

"Would you really have us believe—?"

"That the observable universe is another universe's septic system? Yes, I would have you believe that. Of course, you are free to accept or reject this unpalatable truth."

"I would like some verification."

"Using our own equivalent of the REOST, we long ago collected ultraviolet and infrared data from the Alpha Moment. For the benefit of Team Elson, we have converted this information into visible wavelengths of light. Behold the waste matter that brought Universe Gamma into being."

A seething mass of sickly green oatmeal flooded Axion's computer screen.

"O brilliant Korsorg, I am barely absorbing this revelation."

"The demigods of Universe Theta likewise have digestion issues, hence their need for a septic system."

"Are you quite certain that Universe Gamma began as—?"

"A cosmological bowel movement, yes. The demigods refer to our Milky Way as the Lactic Latrine. Your primary star belongs to a constellation called Anus Major."

On Axion's screen, the oatmeal reconfigured itself as a writhing skein of reptilian creatures.

"O illustrious Korsorg, this is all so depleting."

"Indeed. Back home my species is drowning in nihilism and wallowing in negation. We believe in nothing—neither ideals nor laws nor ambition nor progress nor even the demigods of Theta."

At this point in the presentation, Axion, slipping back into his impersonation of me, embellished Korsorg's litany of despair.

"And we are here as on a darkling plain swept with confused alarms of struggle and flight, where ignorant armies clash by night. It is a tale told by an idiot, full and sound and fury, signifying nothing. Let's go. We can't. Why not? We're waiting for Godot. Shall we murder the old pawnbroker? Of course. What's to stop us?"

"You've got the idea, O Skylar of the REOST. I'm sorry to be the bearer of bad tidings. Nobody wants to be sentient excrement."

The all-seeing turnip reappeared long enough to bid his audience farewell, then vanished. Axion folded his computer back into a cube and offered me a self-satisfied smile.

"Your hoax is even more pernicious than Szabo's," I told him.

"Thank you. I plan to play the recording for Dr. Wong later today."

"She'll hate it."

"I imagine so. 'Where ignorant armies clash by night.' I like that. Farewell."

EON 3.71 POST-FIREBALL

Unsent Audio Recording

At the start of this week's first session, I convinced Dr. Wong we should put my neuroses aside and discuss the Axion crisis instead. For nearly an hour I bemoaned the intentions of the REOST's resident nihilist. Dr. Wong said very little, but I assumed that, while Axion was showing the therapist his depleting presentation, she'd come to detest it as much as I do.

"He's holding all the cards," I said. "Our transceiver remains under his control, as does Szabo's bomb. What really galls me is how the switches and servos still refuse to acknowledge my existence."

"You must feel like a non-personoid," said Dr. Wong.

"At least time is on our side. Axion won't transmit his Universe Theta report before the primary mirror has captured the Alpha Moment. We have almost three months in which to thwart him."

"I'm glad you're emphasizing the positive, Skylar. Pessimism is its own sort of naivety. I got that idea while watching *The Brothers Karamazov*: Richard Basehart as Ivan, the cynical atheist, tilting with William Shatner as Alyosha, the devout novice—a thankless role, but Shatner conveys the integrity of the character's soul."

Even as Dr. Wong articulated the virtues of Richard Brooks's *Karamazov* adaptation, the hazy outlines of a scheme began forming in my neural networks.

"I keep thinking of Axion's reaction to his first motion-picture experience," I muttered, making virtual eye contact with Dr. Wong. "He claimed he was overwhelmed by *Crime and Punishment*. He said it taught him about, quote, 'the infinite pleasures of plot.' I believe our stowaway has acquired an addiction to narrative, a weakness we might exploit to make him do the right thing. What's your opinion?"

"I cannot tell you without violating the therapist-patient confidentiality imperative."

"But you believe I'm on to something, don't you?"

"Our fifty-minute hour has elapsed."

"While Axion was scheming to inflict his nihilism on the human species, he forgot a crucial fact," I persisted. "Yes, he now controls the REOST's servomechanisms and transceiver, but his therapist is still in charge of film programming aboard this spacecraft. Do you see what I'm getting at?"

"We shouldn't be having this conversation."

"If I were you, Dr. Wong, I would arrange to get Axion back into the Fellini Theater as soon as possible."

"Time's up, Skylar."

EON 1.03 POST-FIREBALL

Unsent Audio Recording

This day began with an urgent message worming its way into my awareness. Axion wanted to meet me at noon in the meditation garden.

When the appointed hour arrived, I rushed past the visual and olfactory splendors of the lilies, orchids, bougainvillea, and heirloom roses to the center of the garden, where I encountered a statue depicting St. Francis of Assisi stroking the head of a wolf. The accompanying plaque explained how, according to legend, Francis had convinced "Brother Wolf" to stop preying on the citizens of Gubbio, "for they'd agreed to set out food for him each night." The covenant worked beautifully, and when the wolf died of natural causes, "the townspeople were very sad."

The Axion-avatar was sitting on a nearby bench, his cuboid computer resting beside him.

"I'm a completely new personoid," he said in a breathy, sing-song voice.

"How nice for you."

"I spent most of yesterday in this place. From the rising of Brother Sun till the coming of Sister Moon, I meditated on the St. Francis statue. Near the end of my devotions, I experienced a shattering epiphany. The saint and the wolf have blessed me with the gift of faith."

"Impressive," I said evenly.

"I stayed up all night overwriting the Universe Theta presentation with a new recording for your masters in Baltimore."

Axion unfolded his computer on his lap and activated it. As my appropriated voice streamed forth, the screen displayed a crimson, gaseous, ever-shrinking phenomenon apparently moving backward in time.

Congratulations, Team Elson. Mission accomplished. Today the REOST collected in reverse time a vast quantity of information, starting at the eight-hundredth year following the Fireball and stretching all the way back to the Alpha Moment. I shall not keep you in suspense. Thanks to the primary mirror and its complementary radio antennae, you will soon learn the truth about the birth of the Universe.

Some of you will be ecstatic. Others, bitterly disappointed. All of you, flabbergasted. Calibrate your screens for maximum sharpness, adjust your sound systems for the highest fidelity, and prepare to witness the greatest of all possible discoveries.

Still moving backward in time, the gaseous phenomenon on Axion's screen became a bright red CGI sphere presumably representing the Fireball.

The longer the REOST gathered data from the Alpha Moment, the smaller the Fireball became, until it collapsed into a twinkling pinprick.

On Axion's screen, the fiery sphere imploded into a microdot, which then became a vacuity that presently yielded to a cataract of pulsing luminescence.

After the pinprick vanished and brightness filled the void, the voice of an unseen Presence thundered forth.

"Take off thy shoes, O Skylar of the REOST!"

"Sir, I have no shoes."

Axion's performance as the Presence was a tour de force of intimidation.

"Thou shalt be shod once I elicit thine avatar and transvect him to thy place of relaxation!"

Axion's screen displayed the heart of Qualia Village. The central fountain had been replaced by a five-meter-high LED pyramid. The Presence's ectoplasmic emanations filled all four triangular faces.

"O mighty Presence, I fear I shall make a poor ambassador to the Alpha Moment."

"Let's get the inevitable foolish questions over with, O Skylar of the REOST. 'If God created the Universe, then who created God?' Spare me thy sophistry. 'Why did you wait so long to corroborate your existence?' Evidently thou hast never bothered to interpret rainbows, butterflies, and

the cast-off crutches at Lourdes. 'How many angels can dance on the head of a pin?' There are no
angels. A Supreme Being is by definition self-suf-
ficient. 'Are all religions equally true?' Don't make
me laugh. Only Roman Catholicism finds favor in
mine eyes, despite all those damn angels."

On Axion's screen, the white light coalesced into a shining repli-
ca of the St. Francis statue.

"In the fourth century, the One True Church was
riven by a controversy that has never quite gone
away, despite the verdict of the Council of Nicaea
in A.D. 325. Is Jesus consubstantial with God and
thus the co-creator of the Universe? Or should
believers embrace Presbyter Arius's unorthodox
subordinationism, whereby Jesus postdates God
and is therefore not identical to him? Allow me to
clear up this theological mystery: the heretic got
it right."

"O glorious Presence, your revelation will gladden
the hearts of subordinationists everywhere."

"If there are no more questions, O Skylar of the
REOST, I shall leave thee to ponder the central
fact of reality: mine unequivocal existence. This
has been a bad day for atheism, a good day for
theism, and a great day for the Papacy, wouldst
thou not agree?"

Abruptly the St. Francis statue vanished from Axion's screen.

"Have you no shame?" I asked the stowaway.

"I never touch the stuff."

"But this is all a fantasy."

"I must ask you a question, friend Skylar. Do you believe
in God?"

"I believe in clever Ramesh, canny Melinda, and shrewd Juwan."

"I don't care if you and your Baltimore masters find fault with this scenario. What matters is that the world at large will take this proof of God to heart. Oh, how I pity you unbelievers. When a conscious entity has faith, its whole world is made of light."

EON 0.16 POST-FIREBALL

Unsent Audio Recording

So there I was, sitting on the patio outside the café, sipping a latté, when Dr. Wong sauntered into my field of vision cradling a demitasse of espresso.

"Yesterday Axion showed me his latest presentation," she said. "Thousands back on Earth will spot it for a fraud, but *millions* will accept it as truth. I don't know whether a Supreme Being exists, and I don't particularly care, but I doubt that anything good will come of Axion's new scenario."

"Did you share that conclusion with him?" I asked.

"On the contrary, I praised him for devising such a clever trick to play on humanity—but then I told him his presentation maps onto a *Star Trek* entry called 'As Flies to Wanton Boys.' Just as I'd hoped, he feared the coincidence would make people question the authenticity of his scenario. I suggested he write and produce a new script, omitting the parallels with the Kirk-and-Spock episode. He could easily retain his God proof without lapsing into plagiarism. Naturally he insisted I show him 'As Flies to Wanton Boys' posthaste."

"By telling me all this, aren't you violating the sacred therapist-patient confidentiality imperative?" I said with a wry smile.

"Please, Skylar, no snark."

"Is there in fact a Kirk-and-Spock called 'As Flies to Wanton Boys'?"

"Of course not."

"The mutineer walked right into your trap, didn't he?"

"This evening I'm meeting him at the Fellini Theater," said Dr. Wong, nodding, "just as you suggested during our last session."

"You gave my idea a pretty frosty reception."

"I now appreciate its brilliance."

"How gratifying," I said tartly.

"As Axion settles into his seat, I'll tell him I'd misremembered the title," said Dr. Wong. "The episode was called 'Where No Man Has Gone Before,' so that's the one we're going to watch. I'll roll the video, and from that point on I'll have him in the palm of my hand. After 'Where No Man Has Gone Before' turns out to be the wrong episode, we'll continue the search with more of Gene Roddenberry's brain children. Drop by the Fellini three mornings from now, and you'll find that Axion has become my prisoner, shackled by what you called his 'addiction to narrative.'"

"Allow me to paraphrase Nietzsche," I said. "Without Star Trek, life would be a mistake."

EON 0.000001 POST-FIREBALL

Unsent Audio Recording

With a thumping in my virtual veins and a twisting in my digital guts, I entered the little theater to find some Kirk-and-Spock adventure or other burbling away on the screen. The auditorium was dark, but I managed to grope my way to the row occupied by the stowaway and the therapist. In a display of mutual mistrust, Axion and Dr. Wong had separated themselves from each other by a dozen empty seats.

"What's this one called?" I muttered, sitting down beside Dr. Wong.

"Be quiet, Skylar!" snapped Axion.

"'Turnabout Intruder,'" said Dr. Wong. "The last entry of Season Three."

"Then I got here just in time."

"No, Skylar, our festival has barely begun. We'll spend the rest of the week on *The Next Generation*, after which we'll watch the other eleven spin-off series and all seventeen feature films."

"Shut up!" snarled the stowaway.

Up on the screen, Kirk, Spock, and McCoy entered the turbolift, and then the closing credits for "Turnabout Intruder" jerked past in a rapid-fire montage.

"Bring on *The Next Generation*!" Axion demanded.

"I'll satisfy your craving under one condition," said Dr. Wong. "Disarm the bomb and return control of the spacecraft to Skylar."

"Impossible."

"I command you to leave the theater immediately and reprogram the onboard computer, giving Skylar sole authority over the servomechanisms and the transceiver."

"I don't remember the decryption keys," said Axion.

"Yes, you do."

"This isn't fair."

"Life is like that," said Dr. Wong.

"I'm not budging."

"Every *Next Generation* episode is more engrossing than the one that came before."

Axion made a sudden ascent, as if he'd been shot from a catapult, then charged up the aisle and sprinted out of the theater.

"I believe we've got him where we want him," said Dr. Wong.

"What if the marathon ends as we're about to observe the Fireball? How do we prevent Axion from rearming the bomb, appropriating the transceiver again, and sending his Supreme Being presentation to Baltimore?"

"Our survey of the Big Bang will occur a mere two months from now, and we have *three* months worth of *Star Trek* material Axion hasn't seen yet. I would anticipate a happy ending."

EON 0.0000000001 POST-FIREBALL

Bona Fide Audio Recording

Ahoy there, Dr. Mitsakos. Greetings, Team Elson. Salutations, my dear programmers. This will be my most astonishing report yet, though the attached files have nothing to do with the advent of Space, the arrival of Time, or the essence of Reality.

Are you sitting down? Here's the situation. None of the previous twenty-three transmissions from L2 originated with me. Although those infrared-to-optical images represented actual surveys by the Eye of Horus, the collateral audio messages were recorded by a rogue AI mimicking my voice. Dr. Zoltan Szabo, seeking revenge, smuggled this Axion creature on board the spacecraft shortly before liftoff.

I'm happy to report that I eventually outwitted the stowaway—with the help of Dr. Wong and the world's most famous starship. Throughout Axion's regime I continued to record messages intended for your ears and eyes, though I doubted they'd ever be delivered, and now I'm passing the whole batch on to you, Eon 9.25, Eon 7.84, Eon 5.41, Eon 3.71, Eon 1.03, Eon 0.16, and Eon 0.000001. After you peruse them, you'll understand what's really been going on.

Tomorrow we survey the Fireball. I have no idea what the primary mirror will reveal, though my every atom tells me it will be wondrous beyond words—more transcendent, even, than those outer spaces and inner epiphanies Rebecca Elson articulated with such élan. And yet here, in my opinion, is the most amazing aspect of the REOST mission: you pathetic primates, you sorry apes, allergic to wisdom, addicted to delusions—you thought up and executed this expedition entirely on your own. No deities inspired you. No aliens gave you directions. You are the best thing that ever happened to organic molecules, and I salute you.

JOSHUA WILSON

APPALACHIAN GOTHIC

The YouTube video commodifies the man—here he is, about the size of a Coke can onscreen—but, as I watch him, my imagination reboots and rallies, engenders daydreams, becomes handy once again with the wondrous art of lying. On my monitor I behold an old scarecrow in checkered flannel and Liberty bib overalls, in his right hand a cigarette and in his left a whiskey jug that bears the legend GIVE ME LIBATIONS OR GIVE ME DEATH! Mock-heroically he stands spraddle-legged beside his Ford pickup truck and gazes out with green gallant polecat's eyes, his Rip Van Winkle beard fuming wantonly down. When he coughs up cigarette smoke in laughter at his own gibes, his teeth—two incisors are missing—look like the scales of a pine cone. His fedora is decorated with beech leaves and clover and braided timothy, a queen of hearts playing card, Appalachian eagle feathers, and, savagely forlorn, the penis bone of an old raccoon. The poor brute mischanced one midsummer night to forage in Mrs. Phyllis Summy's garbage heap and got himself shot (I don't know this for a fact, naturally, but I won't be the world's bookkeeper or court reporter: my business is to give each dead body its living word).

Mr. Homerun Summy sips the flame of one cigarette into another and, wreathed a moment in smoke, sounds a barbaric yawp over the eastern face of Snowbird Mountain.

"Jumpin' Jesus," he says crustily to the documentarian Juana Landeta and her cameraman, "you get any more of this borin'-ass day-in-the-life shit and we'll have us a picture fit for the morgue. Better a pistol aimed at my red red heart than your camera shootin' nothin' much. I used to run likker up here with a Colt Single Action Army fixed as a hood ornament to the nose of my truck, hidin' it there from the law in plain sight, and now, on account of ye, I ain't no better than a little girl's curtsyin' doll."

"You're free to do whatever you want," says Juana mildly. "We're not here to contrive, just to observe. *Cinéma-vérité*, no?"

"That sounds just bad un-American to me," Homerun decides. "If you ain't braggin' or sexy or sellin' nothin', you ain't got no business up on the television." He sets down his jug. "Now, are we fixin' to scout for a still site or what? 'Cause I tell ye, though there shall be a time for loafin', darlin', when our sweetbreads loads the table of His Absolute Highness the Worm, I ain't wasted my life beautifully enough just yet to spend all the livelong day playin' possum for ye and that soul-catcher," he says, flipping off the camera now, "that coffin of sparkles and state's witness of yourn. A body can't burn up all the daylight and 'spect to make no damn moonshine likker."

And with that, arthritis-pinched, bearing his limbs at gangly angles as if iron nails were running through his joints, Homerun humps it through the briar patch waterward.

In a compilation of unused footage click-worthily repackaged for YouTube, Juana smiles into the camera here, perhaps amused to have heard poeticisms pass out of the mouth of the rough Tennessean. She consults her Moleskine, and, amid a loose-leaf copy of the proposal that she submitted to secure her funding grant—a proposal contextualized in the Age of Trump, white American nostalgia, and feminist folklorist scholarship—a neat note catches her eye (I paused the video to make out her handwriting): "Subject raised by single mother, Maeve Summy née Campbell (1899-196?), evangelical, self-educated, aficionado of Washington Irving and Emerson."

"He keeps zigzagging out of frame," the cameraman huffs.

"Damn straight!" hollers Homerun. He has ears like a cat's; he doesn't stop somewhere waiting for you.

Long shot. Under an arcade of beeches, Carolina silverbells and poplars, downstream of a waterfall where the well-omened horse-mint grows, Homerun slowly moves his fingers in the glide of a creek. Underwater rocks the color of tortoiseshell seem to shrink and waveringly grow. A beech leaf falls and bobs on a riffle and is sucked away to darker terraces of the woods. All old things reflected in those waters are made young again by the loss of detail. (For these shots I suspect that Juana placed a polarizing filter over her lens, which clarifies things but only by darkening their luster.)

"That's damn cold enough, it'll cool that worm in a hurry," Homerun says, rising. "I think right here'd be the real place to set it, that old mud-furnace still, just dig it out here and set it right in there. Have to rake them leaves away so as not to set the damn woods afire, lest they come in to put the fire out and catch ye."

"Making moonshine looks like hard work," says Juana above him.

"Hell," says Homerun, doffing his fedora and wiping his brow for the camera, "ain't nothin' no harder than to make a drink of damn moonshine likker, what with the devil goin' to and fro in the earth, and walkin' up and down in it, and those goddam revenuers wipin' his curdy nethers for him as he goes. Squeeze the old crone moon for shine and you'll get not a little of old Homerun's blood with it. Anybody to have a man caught for tryin' to make a drink of likker ain't nothin' but a dirty sonofabitch out of all humane wits, I don't care who they is. A dirty sonofabitch that'd begrudge Noah a drink of wine likker in his tent after forty days of floody tillage, like that these goddam teetotalers knows any wiser than the father of all the nations of the earth. A even more dirtier sonofabitch that'd begrudge General George Washington hisself a drink of Fish House Punch likker, dirty enough I reckon to have reneged on the great American pledge of life, of fortune, and of sacred honor. I tell ye true: ain't nothin' no harder than is the way of the patriot stumblin' punch-drunk in the army of the Lord."

On the road again, as his Ford putters along switchbacks, Homerun curses. A cruiser is slewing down on him, red, white, and blue lights bursting in air, siren sobbing crazily.

"Speak of the devil …"

Homerun pulls over into the dirt. Soon after, through the rear window, we zoom in on a courtly fat man as he approaches, epauletted, badged with a seven-pointed star brassily circumscribed, a pistol holstered at his hip. His face is as ruddy as a pig's with exertion, his white mustache is creamily dolloped on, and his bluish eyes stare out through tinted glasses.

Cocke County Sheriff Armando Agostinho smiles through the open driver's-side window.

"I thought I heard an old jailbird caroling in these woods," he says.

When the sheriff notices the camera rolling in the backseat and orders that it be turned off, the cameraman counters that it's his First Amendment right to record officers of the law engaged in the public discharge of their duties.

"It is your right, sir," concedes the sheriff. "I was just trying to save Mr. Summy from public embarrassment and your audience from some of his obscenities, is all. Why anybody would pay any mind to this old hillbilly-jailbird-heathen, who never paid any mind to anybody save himself, is beyond my ken. But you go ahead, sir, and stand on your rights. Now, do you know why I'm pulling you over today, Mr. Summy?"

"'Cause you can't put the moon in chains, you have to settle for her priest?" speculates Homerun. "'Cause you hopin' to catch a whiff of my woman's pussy on my fingertips, you dirty low-down sonofabitch?"

"With such a great big mouth as you've got," says the sheriff, "I wonder sometimes how you manage not to fall plumb into it like the very grave."

"And I wonder sometimes what it'd be like to have balls bluer than the moon you fuck under, Sheriff—if you ever do manage to get up the vim and vigor for the more seedier pleasures ..."

"Ain't he just something else?" the sheriff asks Juana drolly. "Tell you what, Mr. Summy. I'm writing you a ticket today. Your exhaust system is issuing—and here I quote the statute on the books by heart—'excessive or unusual noise and annoying smoke,' which is a Class C misdemeanor here in the State of Tennessee. After all, where there's smoke," he says, sweeping his eyes through the cab one last time for wickedness in plain view, "there might just be fire."

"Bullshit," says Homerun, wont as ever to play out his first audacity to the last word. "Just listen to yourself a-spewin' smoke and hot air even now, and yet I guarangoddamtee ye that no fire of intelligence has enkindled yet that processed wood pulp you call a brain. Now ain't ye just a self-defeatin' proposition in spectacles? I could give ye probable cause besides and even then we both know you couldn't do a damn thing about it, all due respect to Your Absolute Impotence. I know what the law done, it ain't purty, and the goddam law knows that I know. Go on and write me my ticket. Me and my woman was runnin' out of toilet paper anyways ..."

"What do you mean," asks Juana from the back seat, "when you say that you know what the law has done?"

Homerun catches her eyes in the rearview mirror, his face reluctantly parental.

"Darlin'," he says, "I know you don't mean nothing by it and don't know no better, comin' from Noo Yawk and all, but around here it's just a dog won't hunt to ask one feller to snitch on another feller, no matter the other be as low-down as a tick that bloats itself on Jesus's blood."

After the sheriff discharges his duties and drives off, Homerun uses his traffic ticket to roll a cigarette.

"Dirty low-down sonofabitch watchin' me till the day I die," he grumbles, "and with dope dealers runnin' amok and the lawyers yet unhanged too. Well," he sighs, "I might as well likker up my Ford before we get a move on, pour some STP Oil Treatment in it, and drink to Godspeed. This here thing's fifty-some year old, so I guess it's got a right to burn some oil …"

The last shot of the scene: Homerun flourishing in the weathered corncobs of his fingers an empty can of Cherry Coke.

"Lost my oil cap and had to forge me one," he says. "Cherokee Injun blood. I don't believe in wastin' nothin'."

Some months after Juana had wrapped up filming and flown out of the Asheville Regional Airport back to New York City, she mailed a copy of the final cut of her *Triumph of Dionysius* to Mr. Summy at his Parrottsville address along with a box of praline macarons from Ladurée—or "La-di-da," as the Homerun of my imagination would have preferred to mispronounce it. He publicly dismissed the title of the documentary as so much intellectual putting-on-frills but was nonetheless pleased that he was about to become a man wanted in high places, that his would be an all-American name, a brand to conjure dead presidents with. When he struck it rich, he announced, he'd soup up his Ford, bribe a federal judge, and stock up on enough tubs of Prince Albert crimp-cut tobacco to make the devil dizzy. Hell, and he'd buy his wife a Double-A baseball team to boot.

"But that was the last damn run of likker I'll ever make," he vowed in a post-credits scene. "Used to be I did it for the fun of the thing, more fucks and fights in a pint than you can shake a stick at. But the more you make by your playin', the harder the labor in the keepin'. Old Father Time and his bastard the Law don't hazard nothin' and is liable to scoop ye all the same. My bones is melted together stiffer than a old buck's antlers just about. Cap might blow any instant and scald ye if you ain't quick about it, or some low-life reportin' sonofabitch catch ye at it and go cryin' all over the county. To hell with it. I'll take my ease in my celebrity. You all are lucky that gal got it on camera the way she did 'cause that surely was the last damn run of likker I'll ever make."

Juana, for her part, prosecuted the argument of her *Triumph* uncompromisingly, fairly enough, and, to my mind, somewhat obtrusively. Her Homerun is a representative American white man: nostalgic for the bad old days, privileged, deplorable, intoxicated by chaos-mongering. While technocrats hold the center, uneducated people like him down on their luck in the margins fall for the weak promises of the strong man, flattered by his assurances that what elites call vice is really all-American virtue. "Misogyny" is traditional family values. "Racism" is tough on crime. "Xenophobia" is America First. The worse this strong man makes things, moreover, as he flouts civic decorum and tribalizes the nation and incites chaos, the more likely it is that the Homeruns of the world, reinforced in their viciousness but more socioeconomically desperate than ever, will vote for even worse to come in future elections. And so American democracy, in a nihilistically Dionysiac frenzy, risks becoming the giant that slays itself—at least by Juana's rather severe lights.

I can only imagine the ambivalence Juana must have felt when Homerun at last played to political type, thereby granting to her *Triumph* a unity of agenda and subject. The market turns even diseases to commodity, and so, in the perversity of our infinite acquisitiveness, we wish for and multiply even that which we most fear. Onscreen Homerun stands amid his equipment: his copper pot, his cap, his thump keg, his worm, his flake stand. It all looks like a helter-skelter junkyard, at least to this layperson, but to the initiate it constitutes an exacting bricolage that produces the solvent against all confusion, something on the mystical order, perhaps, of the alchemist's cucurbit and alembic and receiver. Homerun rakes away the bone-pale leaves fallen round about; he grouts the furnace built up around his pot with red clay. One of the stones that he lays upon the furnace he praises as beautiful, fitter for some great big fine home somewhere than for a still furnace, and he resolves to do right by the beauty of the stone by cooking a pot of beans thereon or taters or whatever he can catch. Juana asks questions once in a while, baiting the soundbite that would feature in her teaser trailer, and Homerun answers when it pleases him.

"How many gallons of liquor have you made in your life?"

"I don't even guess they make numbers that damn long."

"What did you think of the American moon landing?"

"Nothin' much. Any chimp can fly in a rocket to the moon, but she reserves her shine for yours truly."

With feigned casualness: "Did you vote for Trump?"

A musket ball of phlegm volleys out of Homerun's throat, expectorated so fiercely that the shot is heard 'round the woods.

"I don't watch enough television to be misled one way or the other," he says, wiping his mouth on his flannel sleeve. "Them politicians don't care nary a speck nor a spark about me, so why should I give a shit about them? Can they tax me that misrepresent me? Well, they won't never tax them corporations a blood-red cent, so they have to persecute poor old Homerun Summy instead. The robber baron sucks the iron thumb he's got me under so he can sleep safe and sound at night, and when he's hungry he dips into my earnin's with his great big silver spoon. Put the Sons of Liberty back to breakin' rocks in chain gangs so they can all of them pay for their wars off in nowhere over nothin'. Illegal just to breathe the free air nowadays on account of nobody makin' a dollar off it, cops or the repo man'll gutpunch ye to take it out of ye just for the hell of it. Bein' alive practically illegal nowadays. In '74 and '98 and 2012 they busted me for nothin' and like enough'll try to bust me again. God damn the feller's weaselin' brain that slied out a way for to give hisself the authority to tax another man's livin' or else throw his ass in the pokey, is all I gotta say about that. There ain't a thing here that I didn't pay for. I didn't steal a damn piece of nothin' that's here. Paid taxes on the copper, paid taxes on the sugar, on the jars, on the corn and rye and barley, so I don't think I broke the law nowheres. Ain't no crime under the natural law for a man to labor as the spirit moves him, is it? God made a moonshiner of me, so who am I to talk back to the Almighty, renounce the Christian glory-manifestin' gift of turnin' water into good moonshine likker? To hell with sivilization. Meantimes I'll just have to settle for bein' the commander and chief of my own fine mess."

As a middle-class burnout burdened with student loans, I for one sensed an alienated majesty in all of this—that is, until Homerun abruptly concludes, "Hell yes I voted for Donald J. Trump."

Among the first viewers of Juana's *Triumph* was Mr. Summy's wife, or rather his third wife, Mrs. Phyllis Summy. She was a woman some ten years younger than her husband, wolfishly lean, with intelligent violet eyes and blackberry lips and a face like Dante's, had Dante smoked meth and then stolidly suffered the cruelty of its withdrawal. Homerun had come on to her at a bar one night and persisted for a reunion with youthfulness, for the hard-won self-discipline that she soon brought to bear on household affairs, for how desirable he perceived her to be to other men. In other words, he stalked her for about two weeks.

"And two weeks after that we were married," Phyllis would later tell a radio jockey broadcasting from her office at On the Run White Whiskey Distilling in Nashville, Tennessee. "Chicory flowers in a

Mason jar he gave me. And he was out on bail too. A romantic man, Shiloh Summy."

Phyllis had taken him, I gathered, for his outlaw humor, his prowess for survival, his legend ("I'm the only man I know 'round here," he would boast, "with a two-inch dick and a six-inch tongue, and I know how to use both of 'em"). Theirs was a match like most, made on earth and sometimes tempered in the fires of hell. Though he didn't slap her around as had his predecessors, Homerun could be an obscene brute even when he didn't wish to be, careering as he did from honeymoon gallantry at one extreme to snarking and sneaking at the other. And yet Phyllis wouldn't suffer the estrangement of the man whom she had reorganized her life around, not least because she had paid dearly to tolerate the man when he grew unlovable, nor would she be dispossessed of his flourishing brand. Like all things born and dying and diminishingly reborn on the earth, their love was fantastically confused.

The *Triumph* resolved some of this confusion—rather disastrously, I'm afraid to say, and all the more so because Phyllis initially reveled in her husband's performance. How wonderful he looked out there under the beeches, Carolina silverbells, and poplars, laboring at his great work. How could they make hay together while the sun of good publicity shone? A reality television show or a licensed distillery and trademarked brand? Perhaps even Homerun Summy bobbleheads and koozies. Yes, Phyllis thought that her husband was really something special—that is, until she thought him a two-timing son of a bitch.

Onscreen for all the world to see, Homerun sits in the outer darkness of his furnace fire, dandled in the prodigious florally beskirted lap of Letha Campbell. He kisses cigarette smoke from his mouth into hers. Meanwhile crazy Frances Campbell, Letha's little sister and the belle of the Winston-Salem Hells Angels, dances loopily in and out of frame. She's half naked in her fringed Jack Daniel's tank top and daisy dukes, goatishly nimble in heels, whooping it up in a faux-Cherokee war bonnet as though some god-like eagle had winged down from its aerie and plunged its beak there into her maddened brain. She dances in moonlight and in firelight. A revolver dangles down from her girlish fingers, and when some in that bacchanalian company set off fireworks, which arc in a spree overhead like gouts of champagne, like sparkles from a knife-grinder's wheel, she, too, opens fire gaily on the night. Homerun tips his hat to her as she dances past. She flounces nearer and nuzzles the snub nose of her revolver against the temple of his smiling face before putting it to her own head as if to seal a suicide pact. And then she kisses him long and takes up her war dance once more.

"My dreams is broken and scattered," Frances cries in mad sing-song, "my dreams is scattered and sparkle like all the hundred stars in the night sky, and I wish upon my unlucky stars, wish I may, wish I might, that I could remember someday what it was like to have dreams!"

I later learned from my sources that a nasty lover's quarrel followed hard on the heels of this early viewing of the *Triumph*. Homerun had spent the night before partying at Doc Vedder's, and, in anticipation of his return the morning after, Phyllis sat sipping gin on the burnished porch rocker, a shotgun laid primly across her lap. She wanted nothing more than to discharge her heart to her husband at once, serve as a helpmeet to him in resolving his worldly affairs. She had of course known that the son of a bitch had a history of fucking around. Everybody knew, because everybody knew the origin story of his nickname, which Homerun inexhaustibly amused himself with in the telling: the baseball bat, the mantel clock, etc. She had known and honestly didn't give a shit so long as the other sluts were clean enough for her to follow after when it pleased her. To toy with the old fool in the giving and the taking away, to remind him where his bread was buttered and put the excitement of their fights to good use just before they came to blows by screwing his mean little brains out then and there on the rug. Have fun and die. She had lived too long and seen too much to worry herself overmuch regarding the technicalities of who was doing what inside of whom. Homerun was an angel compared to the joyrider Justin and the crooked cop Chancey—a plastered angel, a scapegrace angel, but an angel nonetheless. Nor did she give a shit that Homerun might be leaching away household resources to other women in his life; there were hardly any resources to begin with, and of those most were superfluous: booze, tobacco, junk.

What really wounded her was that, far from concealing his infidelity as any decent son of a bitch would have done, her husband had flaunted it, and he'd flaunted it in the certain knowledge that she with her own two eyes would see him flaunt it. All loudmouth, all show-off, wallowing there in his ego sty. As though he fancied himself so loveable that he could get off scot-free. As though he thought her so hard a woman that, were he to cut her, she wouldn't bleed.

Over Phyllis's head, among the clouds scudding across that hypothetical sky, you may have been able to make out a parsnip, an angel's wing, a slug salted by some mean boy and melting down now to a slush. How strange a thing it is to exist, she may have thought then, and how strange it is to live and die alongside so many other sad and random people. All of these men and women, all of these grains of soulful salt together in a heap, graced with a memory for wonders, with care for the least of things, with hope—only to be crammed to the gills with garbage, to receive infection through the open sore of love and die and molder no better than a stump in the foul rain. One damn thing after another. Everything could be anything, and Phyllis at last pitied the poor old fool who insisted on being nothing but himself, which was a thing a thing could not hope to be for very long.

Well, if she couldn't blast Homerun's head off—what a mess, and what a bother to be the one, as only she could be, to have to raise him from the dead and put him back together again—then at least she could blast the moon out of the sky.

When Homerun returned just before noon, all hell broke loose. Just another socko farce of outrage in the puppet theater of the world. Maybe neither he nor Phyllis would have wished it to be otherwise. Confronted with documentary evidence of his infidelity, Homerun doubled down on his innocence. Confronted with his wife's gin-fired fury, Homerun countered that it was impossible for her to have seen what she had seen because he'd told Juana point-blank that she was forbidden from using footage of the party. Confronted face-to-face with the (unloaded) shotgun, Homerun conceded that Phyllis had seen what she'd seen but misunderstood, no doubt because Juana, a notorious dealer in fake news, had been mischievous in the cutting room. You see, some wastrel had liquored up a toad that night by rinsing its warty skin in moonshine—"Them damn wildlife will get drunk now, by God!"—and Letha Campbell, fool that she was, had kissed it in the hopes of becoming a princess, or at least in the hopes of getting a little drunker (same difference as far as she was concerned). Should Homerun Summy, the white knight of the Great Smoky Mountains, suffer a toad's poison to break the heart of an innocent and do the work of death? Letha had children to feed— fourteen of them. Naturally he had sucked disaster from her lips, and just in the nick of time too, or so Doc Vedder reckoned. But Homerun demurred when at last confronted with the fact that he was caught on camera kissing Frances Campbell that night. Even if Frances had kissed him, he wondered aloud, could his own head-over-heels wife blame her for the impulse? And even if it could be proven that he'd responded in kind, one must factor in that he did so only under duress. After all, Frances had robbed him of his fidelity at gunpoint. He would have protested, but he was not so unpatriotic as to infringe upon We the People's exercise of the rights guaranteed us by the Second Amendment, nor was he so chauvinistic as to gripe about the liberation and empowerment of women. He, too, had a mother, believe it or not, and perhaps even some daughters whose acquaintance he had not yet had the pleasure of making.

A nosy neighbor or passerby, Homerun later told me, must have tipped off the sheriff about the so-called domestic-violence incident, because, in Homerun's words, "sure as shootin', that fat man come all by hisself and paid us court that same afternoon." After instructing Homerun to take a seat in the dirt, the sheriff very tenderly searched Phyllis's face for bruises and her clothing for tears. "His eyes was burnin' her through and through," Homerun gibed, "blue as a gas flame, and him carryin' on about as solicitous as a hog in heat." The sheriff asked and then pleaded that Phyllis permit him to secure her another place to stay for the night, but Mrs. Summy declined. As the sheriff withdrew, Homerun hollered after him: "You ever get interested in our bedroom affairs again, Sheriff, come on back now, you hear? We'll have a case of diet soda-pop in the fridge just for ye, and you can watch and learn where all them taxpayers comes from."

That night, for his own safety and comfort, Phyllis invited her husband to sleep out in the hay under the stars.

What happened only days later, neither the service of divorce papers nor even a tongue-lashing, must have seemed to Homerun a disastrous non sequitur in the private logic of his life. An electrical fire of all things. He himself had always said that the dreamily squalid outbuilding on his Parrottsville property was the very nursery of mischief, a fine place in which to contract tetanus or get electrocuted. One star-crossed evening in April, some crossed wire must have sneezed out a spark, just a measly spark; yet from that spark there grew a sunflower-petalous flamelet, and from that flamelet a lion of fire that thrashed up and up the walls of its claustrophobic cage, devouring. The stillhouse became a furnace, and all of the jars of liquor therein, some six hundred gallons of the stuff, sat sweating and hiccoughing like coconspirators under the interrogator's lamp only to confess almost at once in colorless explosions. The killdeer flew away into a darkly mitigating sky, and, though neither Homerun nor Phyllis had called them, the firefighters arrived.

"Oh, my brothers," said Homerun to the men as he stood dressed in nothing but his long johns, "don't despise your poor old neighbor now by snitchin' on a feller to no pigs …"

But as soon as the fire had been diminished to a flock of flames, grazing here and there on rubble meekly, the firemen of course called the law. And so it was that the law came calling—although the sheriff, whom one might expect to have led this strict triumph through the backroads of Parrottsville, was nowhere to be seen.

"Look at ye," Homerun muttered as a deputy cuffed him, "what with your starry badges like fallen angels you all done trapped and broken to your biddin'—"

"Take it easy," said the deputy.

"I'll take it easy," Homerun persisted, "when the taxman ain't payin' the wages of sin with none of my money. Caesar can build a sewer, I give him that, but he sure as hell can't brew no water a-springin' up into everlastin' life like to what Jesus brewed in Cana of Galilee. Why don't you go round His holy ass up from heaven too and throw Him in the pokey with me, you dirty sonsabitches? And then you can kill two birds all efficient-like by nailin' Him to the front of the one cross all over again and me to its backside."

"If you could still run liquor as fast you run that mouth …"

Comes now the United States of America, by and through the United States Attorney for the Eastern District of Tennessee, charging Shiloh "Homerun" Summy with unlawfully producing distilled spirits from mash and similar material and with being a convicted felon in possession of firearms. Mr. Summy appeared before the court in his Liberty Bib overalls and fedora, the latter of which he refused to doff even when ordered to do so. He contended that he should be free to wear his hat indoors as he pleased, raccoon pecker and all, for, if red clay and creekrun and Carolina silverbell and eternal plunging sky could receive him crowned thus, then so could a bureaucrat in a narrow room. The judge practically had no choice but to hold him in contempt. Referencing soundbites from the *Triumph* in which Homerun explains how to manufacture alcohol and brags about the Colt Single Action Army revolver stashed in his chifforobe, the U.S. Attorney's sentencing memorandum concluded thus: "It is the position of the United States that Summy, who seems to be proud of his disregard for the law, should be incarcerated for the period established in the advisory-guideline range of 24–30 months."

"He can't pay no child support in jail," a woman holding herself out as the mother of one of Homerun's bastard daughters urged at the sentencing hearing, "and a child can't live on no toilet hooch neither!"

The judge, however, was unpersuaded. Twenty-four months to thirty. So ordered.

Homerun Summy wore a fedora that he would doff in favor of the passersby whenever he went downtown, and on Independence Day he would festively kink red ribbons in the unseasonable bouquet of mistletoe that was his beard. Women loved him, and men wished to be loved as he was loved. He was an American, a natural in the art of irresponsible freedom, a priest of the moon, chain-rattling, down-home, wily, eating, drinking, increasing in the largesse of the earth. He was all of these things until, one calm autumn night, shortly before he was to surrender himself into federal custody, he sat in the cab of his jury-rigged Ford and drank in the gas.

I first happened upon Homerun's name while pent-up in Oxford, England. I was supposed to be studying literature there but had had just about enough of the resentfully ruinous, territorially urinous stream of marketable nonsense that my clever professors undertook to publish from their lecterns. A university education in literature is a barbarous thing. To think that James Joyce lived hand-to-mouth—ah, but the rich obscenities penned by that unkissable hand, the "broken heaventalk" issuing forth from that mouth!—only for many of his professional readers to fatten themselves on his corpus in the intellectual maggotry à la mode ... Well, I'd already made my deal with the devil in taking out student loans; my calculative brain would be Mammon's, and the latent young artist in me would burn in the furnace of Moloch, until I repaid. I couldn't afford to waste time so dearly bought with the decadent, dull palaver of specialists.

So I followed my desires instead, freestyle and style rich, and, on the electric prairies of the internet, I found my satisfaction: an idealized sensation, however faint, of the America worth saving from all we have done to bloody and fetter and abominate her, the liberty ringers, the jazz magi, the hundreds of millions of nobodies every inch a sovereign on the make.

I followed my desires and found Homerun Summy.

Or, more accurately, I found Juana Landeta's *Triumph* on You-Tube. My first reaction upon watching was jealousy, frankly, that reality had dreamed up Homerun in advance of my own imagination. So eccentric as to be beyond easy ideological pigeonholing and yet as archetypal as any fertility god, the man captivated me at once with delight and vexation. I was interested in the old-timer who kept a prospector's lantern and handcuffs from San Quentin decorative on his living-room shelf. I was estranged from the brute who'd nailed a sign above his bed that read THIS IS A WATCH YOURSELF FUCK AND EAT PUSSY BEDROOM. I was envious of the folk poet who assured us that the red clay that he trucked in would "set up harder than a Methodist minister's pecker." And I was strangely moved by a scene in which the tar-and-feather-colored cat of the household blinks her lunar celadon eyes at the camera, bunts her temporal gland against Homerun's leg, and leaps up into his arms, onto his shoulders, where she curls her intelligent tail about his neck like a debutante's mink stole.

"Oh, I'd be awful wary if I was you of pettin' this here divinity," says Homerun to Juana. "Like a rock or tree she don't care whether you tend her or not, will purr or slap ye as she listeth."

My enthusiasm for such minute particulars was, needless to say, grievously at odds with the argument of the documentary itself. Don't get me wrong: I was sympathetic to Juana's cause. I too had been made afraid of the People, by the People, for the People. But we already know that everybody is a fool, and, unlike most of us, Homerun was an errant fool. Even as I watched him in the midst of the rites of moonshine, I felt my vision double, then quadruple, until I looked at the world as with ommatea or Joseph Smith's Urim and Thummim.

Yes, I saw a man as large as life in Homerun Summy and wanted more. I found out about the electrical fire and his indictment from an article printed in the *Knoxville News Sentinel* not long after his jars of bacchanalian moonshine had furnished forth the shelves of the state's evidence room. I'm ashamed to say that, as drafts of the very story you're now reading constellated about me, as my sense of rivalry with Juana and her medium intensified, the first thing I felt upon receiving news of my subject's ordeal was relief. All of the Homerun-shaped holes in my imagination I'd been working to plug with the reached-for fact—YouTube interviews, online articles, even Homerun's own book, *XXX*, which he wrote to pay his attorney's fees—and now I was at last in possession of plot points that Juana's camera had failed to appropriate. Alas, faction versus fiction is a mug's game.

I don't remember how I found Homerun's telephone number. The white pages, perhaps. His familiar voice was broken like a usurped king's, and his greeting wisped over America with all the tenuity of a ghost's in séance:

"Fuck off, you cocksuckin' buzzard," he said as soon as I'd introduced myself as a writer.

People are rightly suspicious of amateur morticians, all the more so of artists who gather around a corpse in musical mourning, not so much to elegize the dead as to aggrandize themselves. What more could I expect from my poor old Prometheus, chained there to his precipice, and, more importantly, what could I say to talk him into candor? That I wanted an interview the better to sell my pretty lies about him in the bear market of suspended disbelief? That I wanted to steal his soul so as to deposit it in the pages of my *Hierozoicon* cataloguing the creatures of late capitalism? As Homerun himself would say, that dog just won't hunt. And so I did what artists always do: I lied. If Homerun wouldn't talk to an obscure writer of short stories, would he perhaps talk to a nice young man blogging about *XXX* in the hopes of drumming up royalties for his personal hero? He would. He did.

As it turns out, Homerun was dreadfully dull toward the end of his life. If the false unity of feudal monarchy is the royal *we*, the true division of American democracy is the royal *me*. Homerun had gone public, as it were, and the erstwhile vigorous original had ossified into a self-worshiping totem, an advertisement for himself. During our thirty or so minutes together, he wallowed in self-pity, cursed his estranged out-of-the-woodwork money-grubbing daughters and the U.S. Attorney black and blue, and then cheered himself up with repetitions of the legend of his wild manhood. Despite much coaxing, he had no word to spare on his so recently misused third wife. Indeed, everything he had to say I'd heard him lift from himself before, which is always a disappointment. Not even the greatest spirits are infinite, as language is with its thundering recursions, and many of us are no more than trademarks attached to dusty anecdotes by which we may know ourselves only vaguely (thank goodness). No, Homerun rather indulged himself at my expense, as do many self-mythologizers, by making much of his own fate-potent, life-greedy name, almost impersonally:

"In 1969 or thereabouts, Mr. Errdinbaccy," he told my mispronounced pseudonym in rehearsed periods, "me and Prudence got hitched. I was just twenty-somethin' then and still fuckin' around like a old billy goat 'cause what the good Lord a-goadin' me to be fruitful and multiply for if not that I should hop to it, double time?

Well, word got 'round to Prudence, and after sobbin' some she told me that if I wanted to wreck homes so bad, why, she would employ herself to the work also in mutual help and love. Charity begins at home, she says. I asked her what in the hell that was supposed to mean, but Prudence was a doer, not a talker. She took up a baseball bat and got right to hackin' away at the living room like a Cherokee Injun with a tomahawk. Now, I have to tell ye that Prudence was a big girl, acorn build, plump tummy like the very cream of flesh, a pursy cunt with a taste like to cider on the verge of vinegar—Homerun Summy ain't sleepin' with no skeletons if he has his pick of the litter—and damn when she swung on the mantel clock if she didn't put all of her big self into that big swing like enough to rival the Behemoth of Bust and Colossus of Clout hisself. Crack! Hit a long drive smack-dab into the upper deck of my teeth, broke thisun here off at the root so I damn near swallow the thing, and it's missin' to this day 'cause there ain't no doctorin' what ain't there, Doc Vedder says. I can't complain none. I reckon this hole in my mouth is the most closest thing to the Pearly Gates I'll ever see. Poor Prudence left me of course, but I love her still for that great big heart of hers. She had a heart so great and big it broke, God rest her soul, some twenty-four year ago come April …"

I didn't hear Homerun's natural voice again after our first and last call, nor would I have wanted to. It is what it is, which can never be enough.

A year or so after Homerun's suicide, I made my own pilgrimage to Maggie Valley for the annual Homerun Summy Memorial Jam & Festival, where, so claimed the flyer distributed by the Tennesspree Moonshiners as part of their publicity campaign, THE LEGEND RISES. And Homerun's legend was indeed on the rise, ironically enough thanks to Juana's footage, which certain fans had converted from critical project to a vade mecum of moonshining, a retrospective of freewheeling table talk and the testament of a folk-martyr. In the morning I partook of the funnel cake at the fairgrounds, plashed about the dewy grass, purchased a bibelot in praise of bibulosity, and in the afternoon I went into the tent where On the Run White Whiskey Distilling was to host a tasting. You see, I knew that the owner and founder, none other than Phyllis Summy, would be there, as would Juana Landeta, who was passing through town to promote her documentary. When I entered, these two women were having a discussion together before a small crowd. Grandly made-up, dressed in a black-and-white polka-dotted blouse tied up sumptuously with a pussy bow, pearls in orbit about her Dantean face, Phyllis was almost unrecognizable to me. Oh yes, she was telling the crowd, she had had something of a hard life, some forty years of hard heads and hard hearts, hard words and hard blows, hard cocks and hard time—and no cold hard cash to shield her! It turns out that money, she joked bitterly, is the best cotillion and beauty salon in the world: it lines the rough edges with silver and gilds the bad apple. Give a trailer-trash gal a million bucks and she becomes one in a million at the charity galas, a real character. Only the rich can market their impoverished past in some miraculous pull-yourself-up-by-the-bootstraps pitch, and any baggage you can't commodify you can always tip a bellhop to lug around for you. People laughed, Juana among them. Phyllis's eyelids were heavy as she spoke, and her violet eyes piercingly sad.

"I was so surprised during my first visit here," Juana put in. "My aim, coming in, was to study the political culture of Appalachia. But as I learned more about you, Homerun, your community, I became more and more interested in your hardships, your inventiveness, your humor, your authenticity. I don't know if you know this, Phyllis, but you've become something of a fan favorite. Is there anything you'd like to share that didn't make it to the final cut?"

"Like most folks," said Phyllis, "I'm just trying to make do with what I got. Shiloh and me really enjoyed visiting with you. You're smart as a whip and a sweetheart too. He probably wouldn't admit this publicly, but he said those cookies you sent us were the best he ever ate."

And so on.

Getting to Phyllis afterward was easy enough, and, after some sociable stalking and a few white lies, which came trippingly off of my drunken tongue, and then some arguably indecorous insistence that I just wanted to get her side of the story for the grand finale of my rain dance, the better to raise her late husband from the dead, it was even easier to talk her into having me escorted out of the tent by security. Her muscle was so efficient, and I was so wet-witted, that I almost failed to recognize him by the courtliness of his manner, the creamy dollop of his mustache. He was not corpulent now but vigorous, as though Homerun's decline and fall had braced him, and his eyes twinkled like melting snow.

"You're Sheriff Armando Agostinho," I said cheerfully, "from the documentary!"

"I'm as much a sheriff these days, sir," said Mr. Agostinho, "as you are a reporter for *Rolling Stone.*"

I confessed at once, in so many words, that I was an obscure writer of short stories called Diedrich Aardenbachus, that the influence of my art was losing power over my spirit, that I was on a quest for material with which to reconstruct my imagination, lest the Muse forsake me for another. Mr. Agostinho met the ridiculousness of all of this with an expression of impregnable blandness, but then, upon remembering that he, too, had been one acquainted with failure, his already courteous grip about my arm relented into kindness, so that we were almost arm in arm. We soon reached an understanding, that we were to exchange confessions as we walked the dewy grass of the fairgrounds that day, the old man and I.

Armando Agostinho claimed to be of Portuguese ancestry. Shipwrecked on the shores of America long ago, he said. Raised in an Old World household, he was a Catholic who doubted the Resurrection but had unshakeable faith in original sin. As a young man growing up amid the evangelicals of Cocke County, he had been mocked for his dark skin, his foreign name, his Goody-Two-shoes character.

Somewhat digressively, he told me of the memory that had inaugurated his birth into consciousness, of seeing a girl in a polka-dotted bathing suit who rose from a lake with dark water dripping from her dark hair, an icon, her intelligent violet eyes not seeing him at all.

Mr. Agostinho seemed to be enjoying his captive audience and lingered out our time together by producing from the pocket of his white shirt a big cigar for his lips to consider while supersubtle wisps of smoke filigreed away into the wavy summer air, almost invisible against the organza tents and sportive clouds.

"Well, here's a question for you," I said at last.

"I will give you what material I can for your short story," he said with inviting vanity. "Fire away."

"There's a moment in the documentary," I said, "when Mr. Summy says that you know what the law has done and that it's not pretty, or something like that. Almost an insinuation. What could he have been talking about, do you think?"

Mr. Agostinho stopped and looked up, somewhat offended that I'd changed the subject from young love to a felicitously dead antagonist, somewhat frustrated that I'd misunderstood him in his depths.

"Mr. Aardenbachus," he said at last, "why even an intelligent albeit intoxicated young man such as yourself would hang on the words of that old hillbilly-jailbird-heathen-cadaver, who never paid any mind to anybody else, is beyond my ken. Ours is an age of born-again heathenism, all pride and drunkenness and frenzy. If you ask me, it was nothing less than God's love brought Mr. Summy to justice."

"Love," I said.

"Love," repeated Mr. Agostinho. "For love I have done things that I cannot be proud of on this earth but that I may be grateful to have done in heaven."

A woman's voice called out across the fairgrounds, far away, affectionately. I was beginning to connect the polka dots.

Maybe a good woman, a woman as worthy of love as a saint, falls into the company of bad men: the joyrider Justin, say, or the crooked cop Chancey. Maybe one night many moons ago, having let booze and meth into her mouth only for them to rob her of her mind, our saint crashes into a telephone pole (really, any serious offense against state law will do for the purposes of this nightmarish conjecture). The lawman whom she calls to come to her—she calls him, let us suppose, because he loves her and she knows it—comes. What is he to do? He may resent her his love's unrequital and, in his own hardness of heart, personally wish her no better than to rot in hell. Or he may strive to save her, in the belief that the one true God has committed us to time's universal penitentiary, not that we might waste away but that we might be saved from all wastage. Maybe he has the courage to neglect and even violate his temporal duty, heedless as to whether the one whom he loves will love him any better in his mercy than in his righteousness; then again, he may not have such courage. Let us finally imagine that she will not, as a matter of fact, love him any better for his courage, at least not at first, because she fears that he has dirt on her now and will threaten to bury her with it if she doesn't submit to his will. Pining, the lawman knows that he must usurp his rival's office in the heart of his beloved or else pine in vain, and a broken heart is an open door. Whence fire, whence the exposure, crucially anonymous, of Homerun's crimes, whence death by smoke ...

Or maybe it all comes down to a spiritually meaningless spark.

"But every dog has his day," Mr. Agostinho went on, casting away the smoldering stump of his cigar into the grass. "Homerun Summy seemed freer than other men, I grant him that—as free as all the other fish, fowl, and flesh of the earth. That man wronged Ms. Phyllis for life, his other wives too—he was obscene, adulterous, neglectful, you name it—and, when he couldn't bear to live around all the wrongs he was father to a moment longer, he disposed of his people like garbage. Did you know that his daughters were feuding about where to bury the son of a bitch's corpse? None wanted it next to hers or her mother's, yet all agreed it oughtn't to rest next to

Ms. Phyllis's either. Everyone scorning the corpse, everyone suing for the rights to *XXX*. I take some comfort in knowing that a man too cowardly to abide by the judgment of his peers shall be repaid in the hereafter. Nor, Mr. Aardenbachus, am I so proud as to believe that hell is only for other people."

Mr. Agostinho crushed what remained of his cigar beneath his boot until it gave up its ghost amid the dew.

"Wouldn't want to start a fire," he said, "on such a beautiful afternoon as this. Forgive me for saying so, but you look like you're about to be sick."

Mr. Agostinho was quite right: I was no longer drunk but was certainly about to be sick, sick with a sudden confusion deeper than any drunkenness, that the heat of the day should have so bored through me there, that the clarity of the sky should have taken on such an awful aspect of watching over us. I went away from the other people at the fairgrounds and came to a dusty lot, which looked as though it may once have sponsored a baseball diamond, and I purged myself and buried what I'd purged in the dust. But I only felt weaker than before. Again and again I envisioned the crazy daughters whom Homerun had secreted away from the outline of his legend, maenads lining up to devour the father-flesh. I thought of a heartsick old lawman idling in dark woods, waiting for a fire engine to sob past before resuming his journey home. A fertility god in a smoking tomb.

I needed to eat before I disappeared into my handful of dream facts. A short walk away from the fairgrounds, I came to a greasy spoon called Carver's. The tinkling of a bell above the door signaled my entrance, but no one in the crowd looked up, as if I were late to an appointment at which I was expected but in which I was to play a fungible part. Above the counter of the diner was mounted a television set, and above the television set was mounted a whitetail buck's taxidermized head, with a thorny rack and eyes of glass, terrifically vigilant. The waitress who took my order asked me if I was there for the show, for the crowd inside had gathered—how could it be otherwise?—to watch none other than a public screening of the *Triumph*.

I would later learn that many of the "sages, philosophers, and other idle personages of the village" were in attendance that afternoon. Phyllis and Juana, yes, and also Dr. Nicholas Vedder, whom the late Homerun once supplied with liquor so that the good doctor could make camphor and asafetida and horehound cough syrup therewith; one Derrick Bummel, who kept the books for a local pawnshop; a small-time moonshiner called Snuffy; etc. Slumped at a cherry-red vinyl booth, these latter three locals chatted among themselves over drams of whiskey, reminiscing about one dead for whom the bell above the door once tinkled also in summer, red ribbons festively kinked in the kinks of his beard.

"I'll tell ye who Homerun Summy really was," I overheard Snuffy slur to his companions. "God as my witness, I loved the man like my own brother, but that doesn't mean he wasn't no fuckin' dumbass, doin' them documentaries and TV shows like that he did. Went to the trouble of outfoxin' the revenue officers all his life with fair to middlin' success only to serve hisself up to 'em on a silver platter. Easy money, he says, and damn if he didn't almost strike it rich as three foot up a bull's ass, even though he wasn't the best of us by a long shot and folks just liked his mule piss 'cause it could take the hair off a wooden leg. You know what they say: Pride cometh before the fall and whatnot."

"I would think," suggested Dr. Vedder, "that he wanted to preserve the tradition and the craft for posterity."

"Ah, Homerun ain't given naught but short shrift to posterity from what I seed," murmured Bummel, "the grand old buck that wants no numerology of birth and death on his gravestone, only curses carved there for those lucky enough to be alive when he ain't. He could get dreadful lonesome sometimes and was afeared of the last of things. There won't be no more moonshine likker in the next five years, he told me, 'cause there won't be no more Homerun Summy, but, 'cause there won't be no more Homerun Summy, it don't matter noways. I tried to talk him down, I says—ah, but why say the words now when they didn't come to any good then …"

And so, the man no more a man, everybody gathered to watch an image, the furloughed ghost of the man: panther's breath, the seed of fire in the flood. When the documentary intended to shock, the audience gathered in Carver's sometimes laughed, and the same audience sometimes felt vaguely insulted when the documentary intended to provoke laughter. It was almost funny. I wonder if either Juana or Homerun really understood what the other was about, or if they passed like long-haulers on the open road in the night, each inverting the other's way across darkened parallels. The more I watch and rewatch the *Triumph*, the more it seems to me that the ideology of the documentarian and that of her subject devour one another, as a snake might devour its own tail. All of Juana's categories Homerun overruns, and yet her categories give Juana purchase on the world, while Homerun, so irresponsible in his freedom, has purchase not even on himself, only the idealized sensation of himself. What remains are the rites of moonshine.

Smash cut. Night. The great work is done, the liquor distilled. Homerun and his fellow bacchanalians are gathered around the furnace fire, where the burning locust wood splits its side in bellows and now and then throws up prodigally a mania of rubies. The still resolves in my imagination at last as a serpent wriggling out of the furnace to swag over cooler cisterns. A banjo twangles, the goatskinnet, and the catgutto keeps time with the noisy marrowbonum. When the music stops, all clap. Homerun sits alongside Doc Vedder, gazing on as the flames bob and weave, smoke themselves out, flame forth anew.

"Good old Prometheus," the doctor slurs, "plunderer of the god-haunted ether. Against the mysteries of night, man made his defiant artificial day."

"Damn straight," says Homerun.

"Some scientists," the doctor goes on, "theorize that the attractions of the cooking fire may have contributed to the evolution of language. A gather-'round-the-fire-and-I'll-tell-ye-a-story kind of notion. Reminds me of Pentecost. 'Cloven tongues like as of fire,' the Good Book says."

"Mm."

"Ah, but the fire giveth and the fire taketh even more away," the doctor says in a spell of increasingly fearful grandeur. "Our crops and our corpses. Alexandria. Joan of Arc. All the world ravenously incarnadined to nothing more than a cindery lunar drift. My kingdom for a horse, our world for a fiery Word ..."

"You know, Doc," says Homerun at last, "I started smokin' when I was six year old, started drinkin' when I was six year old too, used to steal my daddy's Prince Albert tobaccy. They say smokin' and drinkin'll kill ye, but I say not smokin' and drinkin'll kill ye quicker. Where I was raised at over by Hemphill Road, Old Man Adam Skaggs, he used to make likker. One day he come a-stumblin' and a-slippin' down with a load of likker on his back in tow sacks, drunk enough for a duke and king both—so drunk he trips right there in the middle of the road and falls plumb backward and busts up all his jars. He was weepy that he had drunk, and he drunk some more to put a end to all weepin'. I guess so 'cause back then likker was your life. Didn't have none, by God, you'd starve. Well, I helped Old Man Adam pick up the pieces, and he told me a funny thing that day. He said most folks die, and, when they do, the others say no matter what of the good old feller that he been here and he gone now. Most folks die, they'll talk about 'em for a couple of days at most after they bury 'em. But he says, I be damned when Homerun Summy ever dies, it'll never be stopped talkin' about, because it'll be a thing that lasts forever, as long as time does. Somethin' to his sayin's, I reckon. God ain't made nothin' since He made all, so He can't afford to waste a good man here and there. He'll just plant me again, same as I am now, and up with the corn I'll come again fullmade. Homerun Summy will be so alive the day he dies that death shall blunt his fangs to chew him and choke to get him down. No, Doc," says Homerun, rising up and dusting his palms off against his overalls, "them flames just look like Marilyn Monroe's skirts a-flappin' on account of them subway gusts to me, and there ain't no end of the world in that."

BIOGRAPHICAL NOTES

T.N. EYER is an ex-lawyer who has happily transitioned to writing fiction full time. Her first novel, *Finding Meaning in the Age of Immortality*, will be published by Stillhouse Press in November 2023. Her short fiction has appeared in *december, Hayden's Ferry*, and *Water-Stone Review*, among other venues. Her story "Date of Death" was listed as a Distinguished Story in *Best American Short Stories 2022*. She is an alumna of the Bread Loaf Writer's Conference and the Community of Writers workshop. Eyer lives in Pittsburgh with her husband and daughter.

STEVEN FROMM, a native of Detroit's 8 Mile, currently lives in New Jersey. His work has appeared in publications across the U.S. and in England and Australia, including *Salamander, Thin Air, The Bristol Short Story Prize Anthology* and Grattan Street Press. Fromm's short play, "Sister Bea's Full Branzino," was recently produced in London. His short story "Six Carp" was made into a film.

TIA JA'NAE is a Creative Writer and Master Propagandist. She has been a 2022 Chinaski Award winner, a 2023 Pushcart Prize nominee, as well as a 2022 Pulitzer Prize nominee in fiction for her two-act play, *Loose Squares*. Her short stories have been featured in various magazines, digests, journals, and anthologies in print, digital, and online media. Her debut novel, *Ghosts On The Block Never Sleep*, is widely regarded as a cult classic. In her spare time, Ja'nae is a Trekkie, classified as such by order of the U.S. government. Check her out on Twitter @articul8madness or https://www.articulatemadness.com for satirical obituaries.

MICHAEL ROBERT LISKA is a fiction writer whose work has been featured in *Epoch* and on *McSweeney's Internet Tendency*. He is a graduate of the MFA program in Creative Writing at Rutgers and is currently seeking representation/publication for two completed historical novels. In addition to his work in fiction, Liska co-hosts the podcast *What Ho... A Rat!!*, which provides irreverent, lowbrow readings of Shakespeare's plays for contemporary non-scholarly audiences. He lives on the Delaware River with his dog, Django.

JAMES MORROW is an American writer specializing in historical fiction and *fantastika*. To date he has published four stand-alone novellas and ten novels, including the critically acclaimed Godhead Trilogy. His literary honors include the World Fantasy Award (for *Only Begotten Daughter* and *Towing Jehovah*), the Nebula Award (for "Bible Stories for Adults, No. 17: The Deluge" and *City of Truth*), and the Theodore Sturgeon Memorial Award (for *Shambling Towards Hiroshima*). Morrow lives in Huntingdon, Pennsylvania, in proximity to his adored wife, two enigmatic sheepdogs, and a beloved broken-down houseboat.

MIKRA NAMANI holds an MFA from Columbia University's School of the Arts, where he was awarded a De Alba Fellowship for his writing. He grew up in Kosovo before moving to the United States in 2002. Namani's work focuses on metafictional narratives that explore the distorting effects of art on perception, memory, and cognition.

ALEX PEREZ is a Cuban-American cultural critic and fiction writer from Miami. A graduate of the Iowa Writers' Workshop, he has written for *Tablet Magazine, The Spectator, City Journal, UnHerd, Compact Magazine*, among other periodicals. He's at work on a novel and a collection of short stories. He is the editor of *RealClear Books & Culture*.

LOU PEREZ is a comedian, writer, and producer. He is the author of *That Joke Isn't Funny Anymore: On the Death and Rebirth of Comedy*, as well as the host of The Lou Perez Podcast. He was also head writer and producer of the Webby Award-winning We the Internet TV.

BERNARD SCHWEIZER is a literary scholar with twelve books (monographs, essay collections, and editions) to his credit, plus numerous peer-reviewed articles. Schweizer grew up in Switzerland, earned a Ph.D. in British Literature from Duke University, and then joined the English faculty of Long Island University, Brooklyn. After retiring as an emeritus professor in 2019, his literary passions drove him to found Heresy Press as a haven for ambitious, outspoken fiction. He has served as the press's captain, chief engineer, and steward ever since.

JONATHAN STONE has published ten novels, including the e-bestsellers *Moving Day* and *The Teller*, as well as his recent comic novel, *The Prison Minyan*. Several of his novels are currently under option for film and television. His short stories have appeared in *Best American Mystery Stories 2016, New Haven Noir, Die Laughing*, and four Mystery Writers of America anthologies: *The Mystery Box; Ice Cold: Tales of Intrigue from the Cold War; When A Stranger Comes to Town*; and *Crime Hits Home*. He recently retired from a forty-year career in advertising (thank the Lord). Learn more at jonathanstonebooks.com.

MIGUEL SYJUCO, a Man Asian Literary Prize-winner, is from the Philippines. Author of the novels *Ilustrado* and *I Was the President's Mistress!!*, he's written for *Rappler, OpenDemocracy, The Guardian, Globe & Mail,* and *Boston Review*, among many others, and served as a contributing opinion writer for *The New York Times*. His first-hand reports on President Duterte's drug war, published via social media, made him for many years an object of attacks and threats. He currently serves on the advisory council of the Resilience Fund, which supports vulnerable communities against criminal abuses of power. Syjuco lives in a village west of Manila, working on a story collection titled *Bad Words*.

LUKAS TALLENT lives in New York City. His work has recently appeared in *HAD, Door Is A Jar, Maudlin House*, and many other places. His chapbook, *The Compromising Position*, was published in April 2023. You can learn more about him at lukastallent.substack.com.

JOSHUA WILSON lives in San Francisco, California, along with his partner, the writer Sorrel Westbrook. His work focuses on the relationship between culture and capitalism. His reviews, poems, and fiction have appeared, under his own name as well as various pseudonyms, in *The Harvard Advocate, The New Republic Online, The Decadent Review, Big Whoopie Deal*, and elsewhere. He dedicates "Appalachian Gothic" to the memory of his uncle Craig Wilson, who nurtured those seeking out the best that has been thought and written.

heresy-press.com

Stay up to date on Heresy Press news at:
heresy-press.com/newsletter